A WOMAN OF CONTRADICTIONS

By Ina Taylor

A Woman of Contradictions:
The Life of George Eliot

Victorian Sisters

The Edwardian Lady:
The Story of Edith Holden

A WOMAN OF CONTRADICTIONS

THE LIFE OF GEORGE ELIOT

INA TAYLOR

William Morrow and Company, Inc.
New York

Library of Congress Cataloging-in-Publication Data

Taylor, Ina.
A woman of contradictions: the life of George Eliot
p.   cm.
Includes bibliographical references.
ISBN 0-688-09405-8
1. Eliot, George, 1819–1880—Biography. 2. Novelists,
English—19th century—Biography. I. Title.
PR4681.T37   1990
823'.8—dc20

[B]   89-38405
CIP

Printed in the United States of America

First U.S. Edition

1 2 3 4 5 6 7 8 9 10

For Dad, Mum and Evelyn

Contents

Acknowledgments

I am especially grateful to the following people for their generous help in various ways: Mrs Kathleen Adams, Mr and Mrs Percival Allen, Mrs Jo Balmer, Mrs Janet Bishop, Mr John Wallis Chapman, Mr Norman Chapman, Mrs Joy Cook, the late Mr Charles Evans, Mr Robin Evans, the Reverend Tenniel Evans, Miss U. K. Everest, Mrs Bettina Gojnic, Mrs Dorothy Goldsack, Mr Hector Goldsack, Mrs Elizabeth Grissinger, Mrs Florence Harvey, Canon Michael and Mrs Peggy Hennell, the Dowager Duchess of Iddesleigh, Mr Jeremy Maas, Mrs Susan Lowndes Marques, Mrs Mary Milne, Mr and Mrs Robert Nuttall, Mrs Joan Osiakovski, Mr Jonathan Ouvry, Mr Romilly S. Ouvry, Mr A. A. Phillips, Lady Reigate, Miss Ann Robson, Mr Ron Spillman, Mr Colin Thornton, Reverend Philip Tidmarsh, Mrs Peta Tracey, Mrs Valerie Traill, Mrs Susan Womersley, Mr Gabriel Wolf.

On a personal level I am grateful for the continual support and encouragement of my husband Colin and daughter Heidi, who have cheerfully assisted with the research and never complained about the inconvenience of living with George Eliot for the last few years.

The following institutions kindly helped me in my search for George Eliot: Beinecke Rare Books & Manuscripts Library, Yale; Bodleian Library, Oxford; British Library, Department of Manuscripts; British Museum, Department of Prints and Drawings; Castle Howard Archives, York; Coventry City Libraries; George Eliot Fellowship; Girton College Archives, Cambridge; Lichfield Joint Record Office; New York Public Library; Nuneaton Library; Nuneaton Museum & Art Gallery; Public Record Office; Warwick Record Office; Wellcome Institute for the History of Medicine.

Illustrations

What's New About George Eliot?

I think that is a fair question considering the shelves upon shelves of literature about the novelist. Most of these books have been concerned with a critical assessment of her literary works but in the hundred years since her death there have been several biographies. All have fed from the three-volume account of George Eliot's life written by her husband of seven months, John Cross, and published soon after her death. As one close to her and with access to private papers, his account of her life might be regarded as authentic. In fact it was a most effective smoke-screen which has hidden the real woman for over a century. Even the late Professor Gordon Haight, accepted as the authority on George Eliot after more than thirty years' study, compiling and editing nine volumes of letters and writing the standard biography of the novelist, fell into the same trap. He too readily accepted the idealized portrait Cross painted of his wife.

John Cross had a great many facts he wanted to hide, not least being that he had found marriage to the greatest novelist of the day so unbearable that he had tried to commit suicide on their honeymoon. With divorce almost impossible in Victorian times the forty-year-old Cross faced the prospect of being tied to an elderly woman for the rest of his life, or hers. It was something of a surprise when George Eliot, who appeared in good health when the couple returned from their honeymoon, sickened suddenly, and died after a few months of married life.

Cross's memorial to his dead wife took the form of a biography which described a woman so noble and great that he could erase the nightmare and worship the idol he had created. It would be unfair to criticize Cross for misleading his readers, for he did exactly what all Victorian biographers attempted. They followed after the undertaker entrusted with the task of writing a suitably laudatory epitaph which would not only provide inspiration for future generations but give an extra sheen to the halo. To this end the biographer was expected to be very discreet and suppress any actions or events which would detract from the embalming process. Not until Edwardian times did anyone dare to write a life-story which implied any criticism.

At this point in the twentieth century, we look for different priorities in a biography. We find little inspiration in somebody who is perfect. We want the truth, the living, breathing sinful character who does make mistakes, does have foibles, does find life difficult, but is able ultimately to triumph. Only that sort of person is believable or identifiable in our world.

The woman behind George Eliot has successfully eluded biographers for so long it is hard to discover the reality. Was she Mary Ann (with or without an 'e') Evans, Marian Evans, Pollian Evans, Marian Evans Lewes, Mary Ann Cross or George Eliot? In addition to these names, she used various nicknames for herself drawn from the language of flowers or literature. If the names are not confusing enough, consider what she actually looked like. Whenever the famous George Eliot was asked for a photograph of herself, she repeatedly said she had never had her likeness taken. The three photographs reproduced in this book certainly prove the truth of the matter, but they all look so different it is tempting to agree with her. Although the camera does not lie, the photographer might. All three photographs show signs of 'artwork' to the face and other parts of the body, which were probably more the result of remedial work on these extremely early photographs than a deliberate attempt to alter the subject's looks. The end result is three photographs of George Eliot with different noses and chins.

Artists' impressions of George Eliot are an even more unreliable guide to her appearance as each painter did his best to produce a picture which would please the sitter and improve upon nature. Unlike the photographers, the professional artists had the sense to avoid her profile and most studies of George Eliot are full face, but there the similarities end. Her appearance continues to be as elusive as her name.

There are also contradictory accounts of the woman in memoirs of her contemporaries, accounts which not surprisingly conflict with Cross's *George Eliot's Life as Related in her Letters and Journals, Arranged and Edited by Her Husband*, but also sometimes with each other. There is the woman who found herself the object of lesbian affection, yet loved men and experienced several love affairs before she finally married; the woman whose 'immoral' behaviour meant she was cast out of society, yet was fêted by intellectuals, aristocrats and even royalty; the woman who flouted the rules, yet was desperately concerned to be respectable; the woman who claimed her writing as an art form, yet approached it from a mercenary angle; the woman who was the best advertisement the Women's Movement had ever had, yet refused to help them. The life of George Eliot raises so many questions and as many contradictions.

I set out to consider the novelist as a product of her time. Too often literary biographies muddle information extracted from the works of their subjects with historical evidence, and perpetuate the hagiography rather than reveal the real person. I was determined to use only primary sources, to examine all the available evidence myself, to take nothing on trust and to form my own conclusions unhindered by the opinions of previous biographers.

This approach yielded a welter of new information and exploded many myths. Close examination of the first thirty years of George Eliot's life, spent with her family in the provinces, provided the key to understanding the personality of this extraordinary woman, whilst a reappraisal of the second half of her life, unhindered by the plots of her novels, revealed a woman with a keen appetite for sex and money, who steadily worked her way to the top of her profession.

When Cross's smoke has been cleared away, what emerges is not a stuffy Victorian novelist but a woman whose life was far more dramatic than anything she permitted her heroines. The old adage that truth is stranger than fiction most certainly applied to George Eliot.

CHAPTER 1

A Proud Race

Victorian readers were captivated by *Adam Bede* with its sensuous descriptions of cool dairies and burgeoning hedgerows. Suddenly it was no longer *passé* to have such rural origins, and the celebrated novelist George Eliot basked in the image of her own idyllic country childhood. She admitted the honest hard-working hero of *Adam Bede* was modelled on her own father and that cheese and butter were made in abundance on his farm. Observant admirers who clustered round the literary luminary believed her right hand to be larger than her left and deduced that the years of squeezing curds and shaping butter pats had left their mark. She did not disillusion them.

When such stories reached the ears of her brother Isaac Evans, he dismissed them curtly as nostalgic rubbish. 'She could never be persuaded to touch a cheese and never made a pound of butter in her life,' he muttered contemptuously.[1] He was disgusted with his sister and preferred not to be associated with the novelist but he was concerned that such stories might damage his family's reputation. No daughter of the Evans household had ever been obliged to undertake menial tasks. Theirs was a middle-class family well able to afford to employ local labour in the dairy and in the fields. The novelist herself became irritated when apocryphal stories about her origins described her as 'a self-educated farmer's daughter', an insult no Evans would tolerate. She dashed off a furious retort to the person she suspected had perpetrated such falsification.

The Evanses were a proud race, their men clever and ambitious with an extraordinary capacity for work which virtually guaranteed success in their chosen field. Mary Ann Evans, the novelist George Eliot, possessed exactly the same characteristics but with one difference: she was a woman. Robert Evans and his daughter Mary Ann rose in wealth and public esteem as a result of their own efforts. Both felt an intense pride in their personal achievements and expected others to pay due regard to them.

Robert Evans's children grew up with the belief that they came from good stock, with a pedigree equal to many of the gentry. So concerned was Robert Evans to establish his lineage that he had searches made in parish registers and paid the College of Arms to trace his genealogy and coat of arms. Predictably a Welsh origin was revealed. In the early seventeenth century, it was said their forebear Sir Thomas Evans had resided at Northop Hall near Chester in the county of Flintshire, now Clwyd (recent genealogists doubt the accuracy of this descent). This was the high point in the family's history they were all keen to remember and was to provide inspiration for some of Mary Ann Evans's earliest literary efforts.[2] After the Civil War one branch of the knight's family settled in Staffordshire, minus wealth and title, and for the next hundred years Evanses lived either side of the River Dove on the boundary of Derbyshire and Staffordshire.

Robert Evans was born in 1773 at Roston Common, a hamlet on the Derbyshire side of the river, barely three miles from Rocester. As a freeholder and tradesman his father was considered a man of means in the area.

Little detail has survived about the paternal grandfather of the novelist, but it is evident that George Evans was a man of exceptional ability who imparted to four of his sons the necessary talent and ambition to develop impressive careers. Only his eldest son, named in time-honoured fashion after his father, disappointed him, and George Evans junior's career is shrouded in secrecy. He refused to toe the line, rejected involvement in the family carpentry business and went off in pursuit of his own ideas. As happened a generation later when his niece Mary Ann chose an independent line, the family were disgusted with his way of life and cast him off. No mention of this black sheep was ever made, no visits were paid, and when he died young, no assistance was given to the seven children he left. Charity was all very well in its place, but the Evanses' good name mattered more.

The next son, William, established himself as a 'Gothic' builder of repute in the Midlands working on lucrative commissions with the renowned architect James Wyatt and ending up the wealthiest member of the Evans family. Another son, Thomas, rose to become county surveyor for Dorset, whilst the youngest pursued a more spiritual path. As an early convert to Methodism, he spent much of his youth travelling the countryside as a preacher, but after his marriage to one of the rare female Methodist preachers, Samuel Evans worked in a ribbon-manufacturing firm and eventually became owner of the Derbyshire mill. Robert, the fourth of George Evans's five sons, earned wealth and respect managing the estates of the gentry.

From the start Robert and his brothers were made to understand the importance of education. No craftsman was any use if he could not read, write and calculate, so all the Evans boys were sent to the day school in the front room of Mr Bartle Massey's cottage at Roston Common. Robert never regarded his elementary education as adequate for his purposes and continued attending Massey's school for evening classes two or three times a week. For sixpence a week, Evans was taught accounting, 'mechanics' (which appears to have been a combination of elementary science and technical drawing) and 'to write a plain hand'. From Bartle Massey, Robert Evans also gained a love of music, particularly singing, a trait which he passed on to his daughter Mary Ann.

After serving an apprenticeship in his father's workshop, Evans went to work for a carpenter in the neighbouring village of Ellastone who specialized in cabinet making. Whilst working on an assignment for him, Evans met Francis Parker junior, son of the tenant at nearby Wootton Hall. A friendship grew up between these two men of similar age, but vastly different rank, which was to transform Evans's prospects. Impressed by the carpenter's abilities, Francis Parker junior persuaded his father to offer Evans permanent employment on the estate. Although Evans's upbringing had instilled in him pride in being a free man bound to no person, he foresaw nevertheless the advantage of linking his future to the young squire's, especially since Francis Parker junior expected to come into his own estate soon.

Now with good prospects, Robert Evans looked around for a suitable wife. In this he was as careful and calculating as in everything else and did not allow himself to be swept away by a pretty young thing of no means. Instead he chose a woman who would advance his career. A proposal of marriage was made to Harriet Poynton, who at thirty-one was three years his senior. Harriet was locally born and had been lady's maid to the second Mrs Francis Parker senior ever since her teenage years. The two women were the same age and over the years a bond of affection grew up between mistress and maid which was as strong as their relative positions permitted. For Robert Evans, marriage to someone on such intimate terms with his employer's family was a distinct advantage.

In 1802, the year following their marriage, Robert Evans was offered the management of a small estate bequeathed to Francis Parker junior at Kirk Hallam, over towards Nottingham. This was a reward for Evans's four years of excellent management of the woodland at Wootton Hall as well as for his friendship with the Parker heir. Robert, his wife and new-born son Robert moved on to this new estate, where he planned to experiment with the agricultural innovations he had been studying in books.

Never at any time did Robert Evans consider turning to farming for his livelihood. He was merely gaining first-hand knowledge of a subject which would be useful in his future as a land agent. Thereafter, Robert Evans always lived on and worked a farm of his own, but it never provided the bulk of his income, merely buttered his bread. When his daughter Mary Ann leaped to his posthumous defence in the face of suggestions that he was 'a mere farmer', her motivation was a strong sense of injustice rather than simple snobbery. 'My father did not raise himself from being an artizan to be a farmer,' she wrote in high dudgeon.

> He raised himself from being an artizan to be a man whose extensive knowledge in very varied practical departments made his services valued through several counties. He had a large knowledge of building, of mines, of plantation, of various branches of valuation and measurement – of all that is essential to the management of large estates. He was held by those competent to judge as *unique* amongst land-agents for his manifold knowledge and experience which enabled him to save the special fees usually paid by landowners for special opinions on the different questions incident to the proprietorship of land.[3]

That was no more than the truth.

Harriet Evans, who never had any aspirations to be a farmer's wife after the genteel life she had led with the Parkers, produced a second child. With an eye to the future, family tradition was set aside and the

4

baby girl christened Frances Lucy, in honour of Mrs Parker senior; in the family the girl was always known as Fanny.

News of the death of Sir Roger Newdigate of Arbury Hall in 1806 was received with jubilation in Derbyshire. Good as his word, Francis Parker junior invited Robert Evans to move down to Warwickshire with him and take charge of the two thousand acres he now inherited from his cousin, with Astley Castle. Mrs Evans was pleased with the move not just because it brought promotion to her husband but because it reunited her with her beloved mistress. The Parker family senior were also moving to Warwickshire to take up residence in the splendid mansion of Arbury Hall, and Harriet had been invited to resume her duties as lady's maid even though she was married. As a further incentive, if one were needed, the Evanses were offered the tenancy of a much larger farm on the Arbury estate.

When Robert departed from Kirk Hallam, he asked to retain the lease on his farm so that it could be sub-let, and to continue administering the Kirk Hallam estate on behalf of the Parkers. This was the beginning of Robert Evans's little empire.

At Arbury the family were comfortably accommodated in a moderately sized farm house, flanked by tall trees and enjoying splendid views across open fields at the front. It was a mile walk through an avenue of elms to the breathtaking façade of Arbury Hall, recently renovated in the fashionable High Gothic style, which made it second only to Horace Walpole's house at Strawberry Hill, Twickenham.

The will which gave Francis Parker senior Arbury Hall and its estate for his lifetime also stipulated that the incumbent had to take the Newdigate surname, so from then on he was known as Francis Parker Newdigate. His son, installed at Astley Castle, similarly took the Newdigate surname, prefaced in his case by a military rank, for he had a commission in the army. Sir Roger Newdigate's will ruled out any possibility that Colonel Newdigate could ever inherit the large Arbury estate, which was to pass to another branch of the Newdigate family on the death of his father. The ramifications of this complex will, which gave some members of the family the use of the estate for their lifetime within certain limitations, occupied the lawyers for nearly half a century. The case of Newdigate *vs* Newdigate plodded on in the Court of Chancery and House of Lords throughout Mary Ann Evans's time in Warwickshire. Being involved with some aspects of the estate, Robert Evans was regularly drawn into these disputes over repairs to properties or sale of timber off the estate, and he loathed it. His attitude towards this debilitating legal exercise can be seen in his daughter's portrayal of lawyers in her writings, especially in the novel *Felix Holt, The Radical*. According to George Eliot, all lawyers were evil parasites who dragged out legal battles as long as they could simply to feather their own corrupt nests.

Two years after the Evanses' arrival at South Farm, Mrs Parker Newdigate contracted a fatal illness. Her faithful maid Harriet, then heavily pregnant, fell victim to the same illness, gave birth prematurely and died a few days before Christmas 1809. The baby girl was hastily christened Harriet but died in the New Year and was buried with her mother. So intense had been the love between mistress and servant that the Newdigate family took the exceptional step of honouring Harriet on the same memorial stone as her mistress. In Astley Church the Newdigate family tablet, in the form of an open book, is affixed to the wall near the altar. On the left-hand page is recorded the demise of Francis Parker Newdigate in 1835 and on the right-hand that of his wife Frances Lucy. Below her entry in smaller letters is the inscription 'In Memory of Harriet, wife of Robert Evans, for many years faithful friend and servant of the family at Arbury', an accolade few domestic servants have received.

Robert Evans was devastated by the double loss of wife and child. Not only was it a personal tragedy, but it left him with two children aged seven and four, a farm to run and the Astley and Kirk Hallam estates to administer. The latter took him away from home regularly. A second wife was essential. In choosing her, Robert Evans exercised as much consideration as before. Although he was approaching forty, he required a younger wife who would be able to provide him with more children. Child mortality in the early years of the nineteenth century was so horrific that Robert Evans needed more than one son to ensure the succession of his name. In selecting a second wife it was equally important to him to choose a woman whose family would either enhance his social standing or at least cement it. His eye fell on Christiana Pearson, the daughter of a respected yeoman farmer on the edge of the Astley estate. The Pearsons were regarded as a pillar of the community in Astley and neighbouring Fillongley, where they had farmed their own land for generations and served as churchwardens and parish constables. A marriage alliance with such a family would establish Robert Evans's position in the locality more effectively than anything he might do on the Newdigate estates.

At twenty-eight years of age, Christiana Pearson came with the added attractions of a well-stocked marriage chest and a substantial dowry. She did not possess the social graces which the first Mrs Evans had acquired from contact with the gentry, but Christiana had valuable experience in running a large farmhouse and dairy and was known to be an excellent housekeeper. Despite her comparative youth, she had a brusque, no-nonsense approach to life and could turn her hand to anything if the circumstances demanded. Christiana might not have received the same education as her husband but she was no fool. What she lacked in learning she made up for in common sense laced with a liberal dash of folklore. She preferred the traditional methods to any new-fangled ideas which might be in vogue. There was a proper day for boiling the washing or making the cheese; a season for setting the broody hen or hiring the servants. To go against this hallowed pattern would, in her eyes, be flying in the face of God and nature. Under new management, life at South Farm ran like clockwork, not only in the house but in the poultry yard and the dairy. Robert Evans found his efficiency in business matched by his new wife's skill in the domestic sphere.

In 1814, the year following her marriage, Christiana produced a daughter, naturally called after herself but always known in the family as Chrissey. Two years later she gave birth to the desired son, who received both names of his maternal grandfather and of previous generations of that family, Isaac Pearson. In 1819 on 22 November (St Cecilia's Day, appropriately enough for one who enjoyed music all her life), another daughter was born to the Evanses. Her birth caused little stir in the Evans household, as she was the fifth of Robert Evans's children and he would have preferred another son. She received christian names in common use on both sides of the family – Mary Ann. The only difference in her case was that the christian names were always used together, except when she was called by the more homely Warwickshire nickname for Mary: Polly.

Equally unheralded had been the birth of another girl six months earlier in Kensington Palace. No one suspected the significant role that Princess Alexandrina Victoria, daughter of the Duke of Kent and fifth in line to the throne, would play in the nation's life. It was far more likely that another of George III's sons would soon produce the necessary heir to secure the succession. What the country needed, it was believed, was a strong king not prone to the insane exploits of George III or the immoral ones of his son the Prince Regent.

There was an uneasy atmosphere in the country following the Napoleonic Wars. Although the French Revolution had erupted thirty years before Mary Ann's birth, there was still a fear that revolution could break out at any time in England. Men returning from the Wars in search of work joined others who had lost their livelihood to the machines of the Industrial Revolution; all were hungry and discontented, and since hunger had ignited the French Revolution, the Tory government under Lord Liverpool intended taking no chances in England. The merest hint of trouble was suppressed harshly. Panic measures were rushed through Parliament in 1819 enabling local constables to disband any gathering they considered threatening. One result of this legislation was the Peterloo Massacre when crowds gathering in St Peter's Fields near Manchester to listen to speakers pressing for representation in Parliament found themselves confronted by four troops of hussars, who dispersed them so viciously that six people were killed and seventy injured.

Although the confrontation in Manchester was the most violent incident in the country, it was by no means the only one. In the silk-weaving town of Nuneaton, only two miles from the Evans home, trouble flared up days after Peterloo. A cut in the rate paid to silk weavers brought an angry crowd on to the streets; bricks were hurled and windows broken. One man accused of accepting less than the list price for his goods was 'donkeyed'. The unfortunate victim was dragged on to a donkey, tied down facing the animal's tail and led through the streets to the jeers and missiles of the crowd. When fighting broke out the Nuneaton magistrates called in the yeomanry cavalry. A potentially lethal situation was defused when the cavalry were halted outside the town. Terrified of a repeat of Peterloo, the Nuneaton crowd melted away. Although the ringleaders were arrested, the magistrates bravely granted them bail in an effort to maintain calm. A bloody encounter was avoided on this occasion, but the threat was never far away.[4]

The unrest, though only a short distance from South Farm, might as well have taken place on another planet. On the Arbury estate all was calm; everybody knew their place. Any who did not faced instant dismissal. Mary Ann writing many years later recalled:

To my father's mind the noisy teachers of revolutionary doctrine were, to speak mildly, a variable mixture of the fool and the scoundrel; the welfare of the nation lay in a strong Government which could maintain order; and I was accustomed to hear him utter the word 'Government' in a tone that charged it with awe, and made it part of my effective religion, in contrast with the word 'rebel', which seemed to carry the stamp of evil in its syllables, lit by the fact that Satan was the first rebel.[5]

When Mary Ann was only a few months old, the family took the lease of another farm on the edge of the Arbury estate closer to Nuneaton. Griff House was an impressive building which had started life as a farmhouse in the middle of the seventeenth century and was famed locally as the birthplace of Henry Beighton, an engineer and maker of some of the earliest scale maps. A hundred years later the house was extended. The previous timber-framed house became the service area at the back and a much larger, L-shaped Georgian wing was added, hiding the earlier structure. When the Evanses moved to Griff House on Lady Day 1820, there were eight bedrooms, three attics above and four reception rooms on the ground floor. At the back, the old part looked out on to a cobbled courtyard surrounded by various farm buildings, including a dairy, dovecote and labourer's cottage. Little of the house could be seen from the turnpike road because a number of tall trees screened it. Apart from the kitchen garden, most of the four-acre garden comprised neat lawns bounded by gravel walks under long-established trees. Dotted around the garden were little arbours with stone seats hidden under rustic arches. Griff House was an idyllic place for a child to grow up in and Mary Ann, who spent twenty-one years there, adored the house and grounds.

The gracious Georgian style of the Evans house, the largest and most prestigious in the village, was in marked contrast to the rest of the locality, essentially an industrial community 'dingy with coal-dust and noisy with the shaking of looms'.[6] Whoever lived in Griff House and farmed its 280 acres was looked up to by the rest of the village. Two public houses and numerous unofficial drinking houses, a blacksmith's and a number of squalid cottages were strung along the coach route between Stamford and Coventry. Few villagers earned their living from agriculture, the majority being employed in the local coalpits. Griff's name comes from the Anglo-Saxon word 'graefan'

9

meaning 'to dig' and mining has been carried out there from prehistoric times. The Newdigates' fortune derived from the coal deposits on their estate, which made Robert Evans's job as manager of the Griff colliery of equal importance to his management of the Astley estate. No one at Griff House could forget the close proximity of the colliery because the Newcomen steam engine, used to pump the water out, could be heard chugging away day and night. One of the canals dug across the estate to facilitate the transport of coal sliced Robert Evans's farmland in two and was a perpetual worry to Mrs Evans, whose young children wandered freely over the fields. On some parts of the farm the coal was so near to the surface it made the land of little use beyond rough grazing, and field names like Coalpit Field and Engine Close abounded.

For a child, Griff was more fun than the pastoral tranquillity of South Farm because there were always things to watch. Some of Mary Ann's earliest memories were of rushing down to the large gates at the end of the drive to watch the stage-coaches pass: 'Royal Accommodation', 'True Blue' and 'The Greyhound' went by twice a day. Life during her first three years was much like any other country child's. She played with her brother Isaac, two years older than herself, messed about with a string and pin fishing in the canals and ponds on her father's land, and made pets of the animals, especially the farm dogs. As an old man looking back, Isaac recalled there was nothing exceptionally clever about his sister, indeed he said she much preferred digging pits in the garden to learning her letters.[7] Mary Ann always looked back on her early years with her brother with nostalgia. In her writings she was keen to portray the relationship between a brother and sister as being very close, yet she herself enjoyed that intimacy only for a short time.

One of the legacies of childhood which also comes out in her writings was a fear of drowning. Surrounded as they were by hazardous deep ponds and canals which had claimed other young lives, Mrs Evans made a point of instilling an appreciation of the dangers of water in her children. In Mary Ann it became a deep-seated terror which emerged in some guise in most of her novels.

Isaac, Chrissey and Mary Ann enjoyed life at Griff with their mother, but not so the older children, who regularly found themselves in dispute with their stepmother. The second Mrs Evans had exacting standards and brooked no compromise, which caused friction with eighteen-year-old Robert junior and fourteen-year-old Fanny. Since Robert junior was being trained in estate management by his father, it was decided to send him to Kirk Hallam as soon as practical. With his sister Fanny to act as his housekeeper, the younger Robert moved to the farm and ran the estate under the eye of his father. It was a solution which met with everyone's approval.

Mary Ann was so young when this happened that she hardly noticed that her half-brother and sister had vanished from the scene and she did not get to know them until much later. Life for her centred on the two males in her family, her brother Isaac and her father. Robert Evans was forty-six when she was born, old enough to be her grandfather, and he always seemed an impressive patriarchal figure to her: 'A parent so much to my honour, that the mention of my relationship to him was likely to secure me regard among those to whom I was otherwise a stranger', was how she described him.[8] Mary Ann adored him and though her father was often away from home on business he had more time for his youngest child than for the others. He took her to see things on the farm or told her stories of his past exploits, which she was to recall years later and weave into her novels. Mary Ann never cherished the same affection for her sharp-tongued mother, and the birth of twin brothers in 1821 only confirmed in Mary Ann's mind that she was of no significance to her mother. The infants, christened William and Thomas, lived only ten days and Mary Ann thus continued to enjoy her position as her father's youngest child.

CHAPTER 2

The Long Sad Years
of Youth,
1819–1836

Mary Ann's childhood taught her that there were three vital things requiring attention and respect if you were to succeed in life: politics, religion and education. All were equally important, and those who ignored them did so at their peril. As a child she accepted her father's views on these matters but as she came to know her own mind she found herself at variance with his stance on all three subjects.

Her youth was spent at a time of political ferment. The affairs of the nation were as popular a topic of discussion in the drawing room of Astley Castle as in the tap room of the Griffin Inn, just yards from the Evans home. News from London reached the area quickly, borne by the daily stage-coaches. Royal births, deaths, marriages or coronations became the meat of gossip in Griff within twenty-four hours of their announcement in the capital, and the fortunes of the monarchy were followed closely, since life depended on them. Any royal death plunged the silk weavers into despair because the six weeks of deep mourning which followed, during which no fancy ribbon was worn, were long enough to send a weaver's family to the workhouse.

The French Wars had been extremely popular in Nuneaton and Griff by keeping out imports of French and Swiss ribbon. With peace came the resumption of foreign imports; trade slumped and the weavers went hungry. So bad was the situation by the winter of 1829 that soup kitchens opened in the streets of Nuneaton, ladling out seven hundred gallons of broth a week. With more than half the looms in the area idle, there was terrible hardship. Hunger brought unrest and for most of the 1820s and 1830s there were sporadic outbreaks of violence in the town. Workers on the Newdigate estates at Astley and Arbury were just as interested in politics but, unlike the starving townsfolk, they wanted the Corn Laws, which banned the import of cheap foreign grain, maintained.

Most people in Mary Ann's part of Warwickshire held strong political opinions even if these were derived from limited facts. Her father had a better than average knowledge of what was going on politically and was actively involved in advancing the Tory party. He had long ago come to the conclusion that his fortunes were bound up with those of the gentry and it was therefore in his own interest to ensure their survival. Neither Francis Parker Newdigate of Arbury Hall nor his son Colonel Newdigate of Astley Castle stood for Parliament but they gave moral and financial support to the Tory Member of Parliament for the Northern Division of Warwickshire. It pleased Colonel Newdigate to hear his land agent, Robert Evans, request permission to attend the meetings of the Nuneaton and Coleshill Conservative Club as a representative of the Newdigate family, and Evans's political activities were encouraged.

With a father so heavily involved in politics, it was not surprising that Mary Ann Evans grew up with a strong political awareness. There was no sympathy for the radical in the Evans household and as a child Mary Ann formed a mental picture of a radical as some evil subversive creature who resembled the Devil. Although her allegiance changed over the years, her interest in the subject never wavered, as her novels show. She gained an excellent knowledge of election procedures and abuses from her father's conversation at home. The description of the election campaign in *Felix Holt, The Radical* is a precise account of the bully-boy tactics employed in the 1832 election in Coventry, with only the names of people and streets being changed. At the time of that election, Mary Ann was at school in the town and watched one particularly bloody encounter between drunken thugs, employed by the Tories, and supporters of the Radical cause take place on the green in front of the school windows. It was this she related in her novel.

For Robert Evans politics was closely bound up with religion. Everyone was assigned their God-given place in the social order and in his view any attempt to change this structure would lead to anarchy and the end of the civilized world. Fearful of such consequences, his young daughter Mary Ann understood the necessity of dropping a

13

curtsey at the approach of a Newdigate carriage or any important-looking visitor to Griff House. Although she personally found it irksome to have to genuflect when she was in the middle of a game, she understood that it was essential for everyone's well-being. Even her father bowed in a suitably deferential manner to old Mr Francis Parker Newdigate, about whom he said many uncomplimentary things in private.

Religious observance was important in the Evans family life because, in religion as in politics, Robert Evans liked to play a prominent part. He had been a regular churchgoer since his boyhood days in the church choir. There had been a brief dalliance with Methodism in his teens when an itinerant preacher fired Robert and his brother Samuel with enthusiasm for Wesley's ideas. Robert never felt completely at home with Methodist doctrines and returned to the mainstream of the Church; his brief encounter with nonconformity, however, made a lasting impression. Robert Evans was always more in sympathy with the Evangelical wing of the Church than with the High Church favoured by many of the gentry he served.

Once settled as a family man in Warwickshire, Evans began to serve the church as a warden in the parish of Astley. 'I find it is every churchman's duty to do all they can to support that church which I hope will never fail,' he told Colonel Newdigate.[1] If his church-warden's accounts are to be believed, most of his time at Astley was actually spent ridding the parish of hedgehogs. As an old man he talked to Mary Ann of his days with the Reverend Bernard Ebdell shortly before she was born. A version of Robert Evans's reminiscences is the basis of George Eliot's second story 'Mr Gilfil's Love Story' in *Scenes of Clerical Life*. With only minor adjustments to the name, the Reverend Bernard Gilpin Ebdell emerged as the hero, the Reverend Maynard Gilfil, possessing the same characteristics and past history as the former curate at Astley.

The move to Griff House took the Evanses into the larger parish of Chilvers Coton, where Robert Evans rapidly became a pillar of the establishment. From an early age the young Mary Ann was aware that her family were important both in the community and in the church. Ritual Sunday church attendance was something which could not be missed for any reason. Even her father, whose weekday business sometimes took him into Kent, made a special point of arriving home by Saturday evening to be certain of attending church the next day. At a quarter to two on Sunday afternoon all the Evans family, including the servants, would process up the lane to church, acknowledging the obeisance of the villagers of Griff along the way, to take their place in the Evanses' pew, prominently positioned a few seats back from the squire's. Although strict Sabbath-day observance is associated with the middle years of Queen Victoria's reign, in the Evans household there were rules which had to be obeyed. Farm work was forbidden on Sunday no matter how favourable the weather. This was based more on the country superstition that money earned on the Sabbath never prospered than on any profound theological doctrine; similarly great emphasis was placed on the propriety of attending church, but no mention was made of any spiritual benefit which might be derived. As far as Mary Ann understood, it was essential to go to church in your best clothes because there were visits to be paid afterwards. Sunday was the one day in the week when the Evanses set work aside in favour of socializing with their family and neighbours, either to exchange business information or to mull over local births, deaths and marriages.

The clergy were regular visitors to Griff House. They came on weekdays to consult Mr Evans about administrative matters in the area and sometimes to borrow money. It was known that the prosperous land agent would advance cash to certain professional people like doctors and curates, who might find themselves tempo-rarily 'embarrassed'. Evans was always discreet and set the matter on a proper business footing by requiring a promissory note for the amount and charging his client interest. He regarded it as part of his Christian duty to assist those in need in the parish. As churchwarden at Chilvers Coton and representative of the Newdigates, he was involved in the collection and distribution of parish relief; he drew up the church accounts; he helped administer the workhouse (euphemis-tically entitled the Chilvers Coton College of Industry), Lord Lifford's Clothing Charity, the Bedworth Hospital Trust, the Sunday School, several day schools and a dispensary which was endowed by the Newdigates. The endless list was thanks to the recognition Evans received as a first-rate manager. He thus received many requests to undertake such duties either on behalf of the Newdigates or in his own right. He rarely turned work down; he just took on another assistant. Not only did he believe he was using his particular skill to the glory of God, but he found it paid well. There were fees for drawing up accounts, for designing a new Sunday School building or administer-ing a charitable trust. At the same time the name of Robert Evans was publicized and further work came his way. Not everybody approved of Evans's efficiency though: complaints were made that he ran the Sunday School more like a business than a charity.[2]

From her mother, Mary Ann learned there was a clear difference between the sort of good works expected from men and those expected from women. Despite having no truck with scroungers, Mrs Evans would render assistance to those she thought were in real need. Her charitable works involved sitting up with the dying or those in a difficult child birth and distributing old clothing and food to the poor in Griff and outlying hamlets. Mrs Evans liked to take her two daughters with her on such errands so that both girls would grow up understanding that they had a responsibility for the less fortunate. With the appointment of an Evangelical curate to Chilvers Coton in 1831, Mrs Evans's private acts of charity were incorporated into more organized philanthropy in the parish.

Robert Evans's religion held no comfort; it was a grim Old Testament view of life which demanded endurance rather than enjoyment. Fortune or failure were handed down by the Almighty and had to be accepted. Writing to Colonel Newdigate to offer condolences on the death of his son, Evans reminded him: 'We must be always prepared for those losses as long as we remain here.'[3] Even when faced with bereavement himself he was just as fatalistic: 'I have gone through a great deal of pain and Greif [sic] but it is the will of God therefore I submit to it as cheerfully as far as Human Nature will *permit*,' he wrote barely a week after his wife's death.[4] This grim sense of fatalism was always present in his daughter Mary Ann. At the height of her success as a novelist, when she had long before abandoned her faith, she was essentially pessimistic. Her next book was likely to be a failure, while she herself might not live through another year.

Mary Ann's religious views were shaped not only by her parents but by the people she met at school. In contrast to the prevalent view, Mr and Mrs Evans wanted their daughters educated at school. The motives behind this, however, were not as enlightened as they might appear. Robert Evans viewed his daughters like his farm stock: time and money invested in preparation and grooming would pay off handsomely in the long term because they would fetch a better price on the marriage market. While he was the first to agree that no man wanted a 'clever' wife, he knew that many middle-class men liked to ape their betters and did look for some education and accomplishments in a spouse.

Mary Ann's first experience of schooling was at a dame school which she attended several mornings a week with her brother Isaac when she was four. The word 'school' is misleading, for in the decrepit two-up-two-down cottage opposite the main gate of Griff House, the elderly Mrs Moore operated a crèche for local mothers. Despite the impressive claims of such establishments to teach the children their letters, numbers and catechism, most did no more than keep their charges out of mischief. Mary Ann and Isaac, like most of the village children, learned nothing.

The family's attention focused on Isaac's education because he was the boy and destined to take over his father's agency work in Warwickshire. When Isaac left Mrs Moore's, so did Mary Ann, and at five she was thought old enough to join her sister at Miss Lathom's Seminary for Young Ladies in Attleborough. It sounds very harsh for a five-year-old to be sent away from home and boarded out in an institution, but the reality was slightly gentler. Attleborough was a weaving village two or three miles from Griff, where Mary Ann's Aunt Everard lived. Miss Lathom was not especially intelligent and had little knowledge of teaching. Such 'schools' were usually run on a shoe-string with as many pupils and as few expenses as possible. It is not surprising that Mary Ann's abiding memory of her time at Miss Lathom's was of huddling round a fire with some older girls trying to keep warm.

In 1827 the future of Mary Ann's education was once more decided by the needs of another member of the family. Chrissey was rising fourteen and Mrs Evans decided that her elder daughter could read, write and reckon up household accounts sufficiently well and had received an adequate veneer of culture, in the form of drawing, singing and embroidery, for her to leave. It was time for Chrissey to learn the housewifely arts at home before a suitable husband was found for her. Since Chrissey was leaving Miss Lathom's the time seemed opportune to move Mary Ann to a school in Nuneaton which had been strongly recommended to Mrs Evans by the local solicitor's wife.

Mrs Wallington's Ladies' Boarding School in Church Lane had much to recommend it, not least that the proprietor was selective about her intake. Mrs Wallington preferred to have girls whose fathers were in professions and not 'in trade'. Although this school in Nuneaton charged more than the Attleborough one, Robert Evans felt his money was being well spent in the case of Mary Ann. He admitted to his wife that this youngest daughter, of whom he was very fond, was extremely ugly. She had a large head, very prominent chin and a bulbous nose. In the future it might well be that Mary Ann's 'learning' would have to provide her with a livelihood, if her dowry was not a sufficient incentive to a prospective husband.

It had pleased Mrs Evans to hear that Mrs Wallington did not place too much emphasis on academic subjects. Both women were agreed that a young girl had as much need of drawing-room accomplishments and instruction in the catechism and scriptures as she had of book-learning. Nevertheless the curriculum included English, elementary calculation and 'some little French'. The foreign language was regarded more as an accomplishment than as an academic subject and was Mrs Wallington's excuse for pitching her fees higher than the other schools in the neighbourhood. Most emphasis went on English, which included reading, handwriting and recitation. Any knowledge of history or geography which a pupil might acquire was merely incidental and not considered of any consequence. By the time Mary Ann went to the school at The Elms, Mrs Wallington, a widow in her sixties, delegated most of the teaching to a fellow Irish woman, Miss Maria Lewis from Tipperary, and only put in a guest appearance herself on a Saturday morning.

Mary Ann was nine when she started at the school and found no difficulty in mastering the work Miss Lewis set her class of mixed age and ability. With a good brain and excellent memory, Mary Ann was soon known as 'the clever girl of the school', as one of her contemporaries recalled.[5] But she drew no admiration as a result. Most of the girls thought she was a swot because she would always be found reading and never wanted to take part in any of their games or pranks. Mary Ann Evans was not only an odd-looking little girl, she was a loner who never wanted a bosom friend like the other girls. The only talent she had which they did admire was piano-playing. Mary Ann was a far better pianist than any of the other girls, with or without music. It was in fact one of the few attainments she had brought from Miss Lathom's, and since Mary Ann adored music she had practised assiduously to become proficient.

The strong religious tone of the school impressed Mrs Evans. She had not only met Mrs Wallington and Miss Lewis at The Elms, but also received them to tea at Griff House, and on both occasions had been assured that they were virtuous and genteel ladies whom it would profit Mary Ann to emulate. Both women might be Irish, but they made a great show of being staunchly Protestant and every Sunday the girls in their charge were paraded into Nuneaton parish church, opposite the school. The elderly curate was a frequent visitor and girls were expected to prepare for confirmation at the school. If there were any special services or lectures held in the parish church, Mrs Wallington made sure her girls attended for what she claimed would be 'a high intellectual treat'. One of these treats was to be listening to the evening lectures given by a new curate from one of the neighbouring villages.

The Reverend John Edmund Jones was a pale consumptive cleric in his early thirties in 1829. So controversial was his preaching that he had already received bricks through the windows of his own church in Stockingford. There had been outrage among the normally sleepy congregation there when Jones publicly held up a copy of Foxe's *Book of Martyrs* from the pulpit. Half the congregation walked out. Not all recognized that this was a very defiant Protestant gesture on Jones's part, but they felt his evangelistic hellfire sermons smacked of puritanism. The granting of a licence for Jones to give evening lectures in Nuneaton church raised enormous interest in the town among Anglicans and Dissenters alike. When Mrs Wallington realized that Nuneaton was dividing into two camps, for and against Jones, she decided it would be more sensible for the future of her school if she found the girls something else to do on Sunday evenings.

Mary Ann never attended Jones's lectures, although her father did, and so did Miss Lewis, who taught her. Since Mary Ann worshipped both, she began to mould her ideas along the lines they favoured. The twenty-one-year-old Maria Lewis had the most effect on Mary Ann because she was in daily contact with her at school. The teacher's kindly interest in her young charge was rooted in the similarity she saw between herself and the lonely, unfortunate-looking little girl. Miss Lewis was cursed with a severe squint in one eye which made her the butt of schoolgirl jokes and ensured she remained husbandless. Responding to Miss Lewis's special attention, Mary Ann took extra care to learn her lessons well and engaged in the sort of good works her teacher would admire. This included teaching at the Nuneaton Sunday School which her father had recently designed and built. When she was home at Griff House on the brief school holidays – six weeks at Harvest, two at Christmas and two at Whitsuntide – Mary Ann also pleased her parents by her willingness to take part in distributing clothing to the poor.

By Whitsun 1832, Mary Ann had learned all that Mrs Wallington's school could offer, so she returned to Griff. It was an unhappy period for the twelve-and-a-half-year-old girl; she found she did not fit into life at home. Isaac was sixteen and no longer wanted to be bothered with a younger sister. In the intervening years he had been away, tutored by various clergy, and when he was home he liked to be out with his father riding round the estates or fox-hunting. Chrissey at eighteen was a young woman who identified better with her mother than with her little sister. Even Mary Ann's father, who had always found time for her as a child, was increasingly busy. In addition to the management of the Astley Castle estate, he had taken on the much larger estate of Lord Aylesford at neighbouring Packington, and his lordship's lands in Kent. This involved Evans staying away from home for a few days every week, often at the cottage his lordship had leased him on the estate. Despite his frequent absences, Robert Evans was sensitive to his youngest daughter's loneliness and sent one of his men over to Griff House with a fawn from the Packington estate, as a present for Mary Ann.[6]

That summer, a bored Mary Ann had plenty of time to absorb local gossip and speculation. The real facts of an incident concerning a prolonged visit of a lady to the vicarage at Chilvers Coton have been lost in the mists of time. But George Eliot's story 'The Sad Fortunes of the Reverend Amos Barton' was sufficiently close to the truth for the Reverend John Gwyther to recognize himself twenty-four years later.

After the harvest in 1832, Mary Ann collected her belongings and departed for a new school in Coventry. This school in Warwick Row run by the two Miss Franklin sisters was the most academic and expensive of those she attended. The teachers, Miss Rebecca and Miss Mary Franklin, were themselves better educated than most women, having attended school and extended their knowledge by reading. Miss Rebecca could also boast of a year spent at school in Paris, and boast she did. No parent was left in ignorance of her special accomplishment, nor any pupil of the extraordinary privilege they were accorded in being taught French with the correct Parisian accent. Mr George Franklin, brother of the two ladies, was imported to teach the girls the art of drawing twice a week. Arithmetic, however, being a more minor subject on the curriculum, was the province of Miss Mary Franklin, who did not possess the same superior intelligence as her sister.

Once again Mary Ann was the model pupil and to her delight was always chosen to be paraded in front of visitors and asked to perform on the piano or recite Bible passages. It did, however, present her with an agonizing dilemma. While she adored being the centre of attention and praise, she also believed it was wrong. One of her fellow pupils remembered her rushing away from such a performance in floods of tears and throwing herself on the floor in a dramatic gesture of penance.[7] Under the Franklins' strong Baptist influence, Mary Ann's religious creed grew more austere. She knew that the glory for any personal achievement was due to God and not to herself but she could not subdue her longing for praise. Everything in her upbringing had shown her the importance of ambition and achievement. It grieved her that in her own family she was the least significant member because she was the youngest, the ugliest and female. Her only hope of gaining their approbation was by excelling at school. No matter how much Mary Ann told herself that worldly praise was of no consequence, she could not prevent herself from seeking it. The constant battle between personal ambition and humility was to occupy her for the next eight years and ensured that these were the unhappiest years of her life. Her solution to the problem in her mid-teens was to become ever stricter in her religious observances. This not only appeased her conscience, but brought the much-needed approval of the Misses Franklin. They might have been pleased by the model of piety that they had created, but one mother in Coventry was horrified. She objected to sending her daughter to their school because she said sarcastically, 'it was where that saint Mary Ann Evans had been'.[8]

The sixteen-year-old Mary Ann who came home for Christmas in 1835 was not a person the Evans family found easy to live with. This was another problem for all concerned in a year which had dramatically altered the family's life. Fanny, Mary Ann's half-sister, had ceased governessing and at the age of thirty found herself a husband who was a bailiff on one of the Newdigate estates in Derbyshire. Chrissey's fiancé, Dr Edward Clarke, the medical officer at one of the workhouses administered by Robert Evans, pleased the Evanses much more, because he actually came from the gentry, even though only as a younger son. At last the Evanses had achieved social recognition. Mary Ann's father had expanded his land-agency work enormously, acting for five different estates by 1835. His most recent and most prestigious acquisition had been in February that year when management of the five-thousand-acre Arbury estate was offered him on the death of the much-hated Francis Parker Newdigate (Nuneaton celebrated his demise with delight: 'He was a despicable character – a bad unfeeling landlord – a notorious violator of his word and promise, particularly with his Tenantry who he ejected from his farms without mercy. Universally hated as a tyrant ought to be and detested by the honest who knew him of all parts,' one diarist wrote.[9]) Just as the Evans star seemed to be in the ascendant, Mrs Evans developed cancer of the breast. Although various medical opinions were sought the outlook was bleak. Mr Hodgson 'advises her not to have it taken out as he believes it would grow again and much quicker than it has done,' Robert Evans confided in Colonel Newdigate, 'and he tells me it will be dangerous, her condition is so bad I am now afraid she will not have much more comfort.'[10] When Mary Ann came home at Christmas, she learned her mother was dying. Her own schooldays had come to an abrupt end.

CHAPTER 3

Neither Use Nor Ornament, 1836–1841

Mary Ann was present during the final agonizing months of her mother's illness. By then the cancer had spread through the whole of Mrs Evans's body, giving intense pain for which no relief could be found. Finally in the early hours of 3 February 1836 she slipped into a coma and died with her husband and children round her bed. Even the stepchildren, with whom she had had a stormy relationship in the past, were summoned to witness the final moments. So terrible had Mrs Evans's sufferings been that her husband could write honestly: 'I was happy to see her go off.'[1]

At the age of sixteen, Mary Ann was deeply affected by what she had witnessed and looked to religion for consolation. She spent hours in private prayer in a struggle to accept that it was the will of God her mother should undergo such torture. Although all the family were upset by the death of the forty-nine-year-old Mrs Evans, Mary Ann's depression was deeper and longer than anyone else's. The death of her mother symbolized the end of childhood and the orderly world of school. Gone was the possibility that she might be able to do something else with her life besides get married. Mary Ann secretly cherished a dream that after the Misses Franklin's school she might be permitted to move to another educational establishment in Manchester, where in the past one or two of Miss Rebecca's ablest pupils had gone. But when her mother became ill she was told firmly her place was at home. This destruction of her ambition was the hardest cross to bear.

From school, where she basked in praise for her academic prowess,

23

Mary Ann came home to find her particular talents were considered useless. The household ran smoothly under the eye of her sister Chrissey. At the suggestion of Colonel Newdigate, Isaac had been made an official business partner of his father and was frequently away from home conducting rent days on far-flung estates. Mary Ann could not see where she was going to fit in because she had a strong disinclination for anything practical: 'My mind is nauseated by feeding on material trifles,' she confided to a friend, but no one in the Evans family had any time for her delicate stomach.[2] With Chrissey's marriage planned for the end of the year when the period of deep mourning was over, Mary Ann had twelve months to acquaint herself with housekeeping duties at Griff.

Although in her family's eyes she was more of an encumbrance than an asset, Mary Ann did receive encouragement from an unexpected quarter. The new residents at Arbury Hall following Francis Parker Newdigate's death in 1835 were Charles Newdigate and his widowed mother Mrs Maria Newdigate. Since the heir was a minor, a trust was set up to run the estate until he came of age. As merely the mother of the heir, Mrs Newdigate had no real status herself. However, she determined to wield as much power as she could during her short reign.

Robert Evans could not abide her. Within two months of his taking over the management of the Arbury estate, he handed in his notice, saying he was unable to work with Mrs Newdigate.[3] Mindful of Evans's exceptional abilities, however, the members of the trust managed to placate him and he resumed his duties. Evans was not the only person to object to Mrs Newdigate's interference. Her decree that all tenants must attend church and pay their servants and labourers full wages to attend services on Christmas Day and Easter Sunday was received with most unchristian comments on the estate. Nevertheless, Robert Evans noted in his diary that the church was filled to capacity for the first time that Christmas.

Mrs Newdigate was strongly Evangelical in her faith and used her influence as lady of the manor to inaugurate many philanthropic ventures in the neighbourhood. Soon after her arrival at Arbury, she commissioned a list of the poor in the surrounding villages, with details of their particular circumstances and needs. This Charity Book survives to the present day and gives not only a fascinating insight into social conditions but also an indication of the source of George Eliot's inspiration for some of the characters in her novels. The pauper John

Onell living in Griff is entered there as 'a poor silly man' who went round telling everyone that Arbury Hall and Hawkes Wood should be his because his mother was really Lady Hawk. Well known to Mary Ann, this person can easily be identified with Tommy Trounsem, the bill-sticker in *Felix Holt, The Radical* who believed he came from a great family and was heir to Transome Hall. Even the character of Mrs Transome herself, a clever but tragic figure, who ran the estate for her feeble-minded husband, was modelled on Mrs Maria Newdigate. Although Robert Evans denigrated Mrs Newdigate for meddling in men's affairs, in later years Mary Ann came to realize that the woman had been enjoying a rare opportunity to exercise the power normally denied her sex.

Arbury Hall's lady expected the wives of the more important tenants on the estate to take charge of their own list of deserving poor to whom they would give bundles of flannel, shifts or blankets which she supplied. After Mrs Evans's death, Mrs Newdigate asked that one of the Evans daughters should take her mother's place in the Clothing Club. With Chrissey's departure imminent, Mary Ann was the obvious candidate. Eager for praise, she volunteered to administer the Griff and the Astley lists, giving herself forty-two families to visit, ranging from 'a poor woman with eighteen children shortly to be confined again' to another family where the breadwinner had been killed in the coalpit when a chisel smashed through his skull. Mary Ann also engaged in other worthy causes which the great lady espoused, like serving at the bazaars, teaching in the Newdigates' Sunday School, taking tracts to the workhouse and assisting with the Circulating Library of religious books. It pleased Robert Evans to see Mary Ann involved in such philanthropic ventures, for he was mindful that Mrs Newdigate's good opinion of his daughter might make life easier for him.

For the next five years, until Mary Ann left Griff, her social life centred on the church. This girl in her late teens joined other earnest spinsters – who according to George Eliot's description in 'Janet's Repentance' (the final story in her *Scenes of Clerical Life*) were inspired to good works by a secret passion for the curate – in stitching covers for library books, discussing the merits of Sunday's sermon and participating in all prayer and study groups. Ritual church attendance with her family continued as before, though Mary Ann became critical of the socializing which took place before and after the service, claiming this was most people's sole reason for church-going. At home she rose early and spent several hours alone in prayer and meditation.

The change from school to home depressed her despite Chrissey's attempts to explain to her younger sister that it was a milestone in growing up. Far from offering new opportunities, Mary Ann thought it only limited her horizons. She had no control over her future because her everyday life was dictated by her father and, in his absence, by her brother. They ruled that she had to keep house for them. They never told her how long this had to continue nor did they say what would happen to her when her sixty-four-year-old father died.

Mary Ann was in one of her regular bouts of self-pity when Maria Lewis arrived to stay. The former teacher from Mrs Wallington's school had been forced back into governessing when the school changed hands following the proprietor's death, and it had become customary for her to take her annual holiday at Griff House. Maria's appearance at Griff in 1838 was timely because she was able to help the girl take a more positive attitude towards the situation she found herself in. Things could be far worse for Mary Ann, Maria pointed out. At least she had a warm, comfortable home provided for her and did not have to teach pupils who despised her and were intent on making her life a misery. When Mary Ann protested that she had no purpose to her existence, Maria showed her that in reality she had received a God-given opportunity to humble herself in the service of others. Mary Ann should try to 'emulate the character of a Christian who professes to do *all* even the most trifling duty as to the Lord demands', then she would find a purpose in life.[4]

Maria's advice, added to Mrs Newdigate's steady pressure on Mary Ann to lead a more God-fearing existence and Miss Rebecca Franklin's letters, which urged her not to neglect her spiritual life, all directed Mary Ann towards intense religious observance. 'God is best served by diligence in occupations became Mary Ann's text and enabled her to settle to the intricacies of engaging servants and setting jam with a better heart.[5] With Chrissey married and living a few miles away at Meriden, Mary Ann's position was better defined and she believed herself to be 'an important personage at home'.[6] To have some status, no matter how minor, always mattered to her. If she carried out the household chores efficiently she knew she would gain her father's admiration, and by paying especial attention to his personal comfort she hoped to be reinstated in that particular place in his affections she had enjoyed as a child. Then at least there would be one person to whom she mattered.

Robert Evans was pleased with the way his daughter took up her domestic duties and enjoyed hearing her good works praised around the parish. Knowing that Mary Ann missed school, he subscribed to *Chambers's Journal* to entertain her and suggested she order whatever books she required from Short the bookseller in Nuneaton where he would gladly meet the bill. Among the packages delivered to Griff House by the bookseller were titles like *Night Thoughts* and *Jacob; or Patriarchal Piety* and commentaries on the gospels, theology being the subject Mary Ann intended to excel in. She resumed the strict Baptist practices she had learned from the Franklins and looked for more ostentatious ways of demonstrating her piety: 'I need rigid discipline, which I have never yet had,' she told Maria Lewis as she rejected all signs of pleasure in her life.[7] Turning to the writings of Calvinists in her search for austerity, Mary Ann indulged in fasting and incorporated predestination and fundamentalism into her personal creed. By the time she was twenty, Mary Ann Evans had become a formidable Puritan.

Her father and brother found it most uncomfortable to live with an ascetic who frowned on their everyday activities. Isaac's gentlemanly pastimes of hunting, shooting and fishing were condemned as sinful pleasure-seeking; the musical evenings at Griff were transformed into sombre recitals of hymns and dirges, and Mary Ann's insistence on humble fare and minimal alcohol tried everyone's patience to the limit. Believing his daughter was getting too introspective for her own good and their comfort, Robert Evans arranged to take her to London with Isaac and himself on their next business trip. Isaac was told to entertain his sister, while Robert Evans went to Blackheath to discuss a client's annual accounts. Suggestions that Mary Ann might like to go to a theatre with Isaac were fiercely rebuffed as a devilish attempt to lead her into temptation. He could indulge in the fleshpots of the world if he must, but she would stay in her room studying the scriptures until her father called to take her home. They returned to Griff with the differences between them exacerbated: Isaac carried a pair of fox-hunting scenes he had purchased, Mary Ann a copy of Josephus' *History of the Jews* she had bought to study. The only thing they agreed on was that the London visit had been a disaster.[8]

Mary Ann's fanaticism reached its peak at the beginning of 1839 when she managed to alienate even her Methodist Aunt and Uncle Samuel Evans during their stay at Griff House. So dogmatic and

27

intolerant did Mary Ann appear that Robert Evans obliged her to write and apologize afterwards. Even then she managed to turn the letter into a grovelling form of self-abnegation in which she scourged herself for her lack of humility. However in a moment of rare insight Mary Ann admitted: 'I feel that my besetting sin is the one of all others most destroying, as it is the fruitful parent of them all, Ambition, a desire insatiable for the esteem of my fellow creatures. This seems the centre whence all my actions proceed.'[9] That was only the truth, and once Mary Ann recognized it her deliverance was at hand.

The concentrated diet of theology failed to satisfy her intellectual appetite and in March 1839 she confessed to Maria that she was ready to sit down and weep at the impossibility of understanding even a fraction of the knowledge that existed in books and in life.[10] Eager to make up for the years of 'girlish miseducation and girlish idleness',[11] Mary Ann began reading avidly for academic as well as spiritual enlightenment. When it came to novels, her Puritan aversion lingered; she said it was because there was so much to learn that was true, that she did not intend wasting her time on fiction.[12]

The discovery of subjects other than theology opened a whole panorama to Mary Ann. She consumed biographies, histories and travel books with equal voracity. Despite her remarks about fiction, by the end of 1839, Mary Ann was familiar with the works of Wordsworth, Southey, Shakespeare and even Byron. With reading came the desire to write. Her early efforts in verse owed more to the sanctimonious doggerel she had copied as handwriting exercises with Miss Rebecca Franklin than to the literature she was reading. Her poetry was technically accurate but inspirationally dead. Nevertheless one such piece of poetry found favour with the Evangelical periodical, the *Christian Observer*, and was published in January 1840.

Mary Ann was proud to see her poem in print. That was public recognition of her talent, she considered, and led her to contemplate writing as an occupation. It had the advantage of being the sort of intellectual exercise she enjoyed, of bringing the fame she hankered after and was about the only thing she could do, incarcerated as housekeeper at Griff. Other women had succeeded: Mary Ann knew of the Evangelical Mrs Hannah More, whose tracts and book *Practical Piety* she had studied. Also there was Mrs Anna Jameson, who had written a book on Canada which had enthralled Mary Ann. In letters she exchanged with a former school friend, she confided her intentions and learned that Martha Jackson had also been thinking along similar lines and was working on a treatise on metaphysics which she planned to publish. Rivalry spurred Mary Ann on. At school it had been recognized that Mary Ann Evans was cleverer than Martha Jackson and Mary Ann had no intention of relinquishing her position of superiority. Encouraged by Mrs Newdigate, who placed the comprehensive Arbury Hall library at her disposal, Mary Ann began to compile a chart which traced the history of the Church from earliest times to the present. She intended that the finished object should be printed and sold in aid of Mrs Newdigate's latest project, the building of a church at Attleborough. In the end the chart was stillborn because a similar ecclesiastical table appeared on the market first.

Mary Ann was undeterred. If she could not publish that, she would publish something else. Then and throughout her life she was always a woman who thrived on challenges. As Mary Ann continued her personal devotions and regular church attendance, she cast her mind round for a new project. For a while she seemed almost to be leading a dual existence. One part of her perpetuated the outward signs of Puritanism while the other reached towards an understanding of history, astronomy and poetry. Study became a sheer pleasure and an end in itself. Armed with her newly garnered knowledge Mary Ann could not resist a little one-upmanship on her old teacher, then wallowing in servitude in a rectory near Kettering. Mary Ann's letters to Maria Lewis became littered with recommended reading, scholarly references and Biblical quotations as the younger woman sought to establish the upper hand in their friendship. Maria knew she could not compete and responded with peevish complaints which signalled the end of the friendship. Though letters and visits trickled on for another year or two, the pupil had outgrown her teacher.

Mary Ann turned increasingly to Martha Jackson as a kindred spirit. When Martha wrote about the classical studies she had begun, Mary Ann immediately ordered a Latin Primer from the bookshop and settled down to work on that. Her days became dominated by study and no time was wasted. After her early morning devotions, she would set herself chunks of Milton or Shakespeare to learn as she got dressed. Although she was obliged to devote herself to household chores in the morning, later in the day Mary Ann would turn to chemistry, Latin or whatever she had been able to get books on. There was subdued rejoicing in the house when it became clear that, rather than a saint, Mary Ann had opted to be a blue-stocking, which was a character the family felt more at home with. Robert Evans was even prepared to overlook the fact that his daughter had been so engrossed in her studies one night that she forgot to lock up and they were burgled.[13] Wishing to encourage Mary Ann, Evans suggested engaging a tutor to give her lessons. There was a gentleman newly arrived in Leamington, who came to Arbury Hall to give lessons in French, German and Italian and was reported to be very good. It might profit Mary Ann to take some instruction from him, for there might come a time in the future when she would be grateful for some language ability. Veiled hints that Mary Ann might have to look to governessing if she did not find herself a husband were ignored. That was not the alternative to marriage she envisaged. Nevertheless she was willing to accept her father's offer to pay for lessons with Signor Brezzi and decided to start German.

What Mary Ann was totally unprepared for in March 1840 was the effect that the self-styled Professor of Languages would have on her. Far from being the aged scholar she had imagined, Joseph Brezzi was a handsome Italian in his early thirties, who came from Piedmont but claimed descent from an aristocratic Swiss family. The twenty-year-old Mary Ann Evans, whose limited experience of eligible men had been restricted to clerics and her brother's hunting cronies, was bowled over by the suave European. The highlight of her week was that delicious moment when Brezzi's horse could be seen walking up the drive and she could anticipate a full hour in the company of her beloved. Not surprisingly with her affections engaged so strongly, Mary Ann's German progressed at an astounding rate. Lessons in Italian were also booked to give her more time in the presence of this attractive male. 'I am beguiled by the fascinations that the study of languages has for my capricious mind, and could e'en give myself up to making discoveries in the world of words,' was Mary Ann's explanation to Maria Lewis.[14] Her teacher, she mentioned in passing, was 'all external grace and mental power', but the manner in which he had thrown her into emotional turmoil and upset all her previous notions of keeping herself to be a bride of Christ was not revealed to the governess. In fact Mary Ann was extremely embarrassed about her reaction. She worked herself to such a pitch that, at a supper party given by old family friends, she had a fit of hysterics, which she had to try and explain away as being brought on by the loudness of the music.[15]

After that outburst, Mary Ann decided to stay at home more and concentrate her attention on German and Italian, which were bound to win the Signor's approval. Although she knew Signor Brezzi was unmarried, Mary Ann never really considered him as potential husband material. 'The noose of matrimony' was shunned after she saw what it had done to her lovely sister.[16] The former Chrissey Evans was barely recognizable as Mrs Edward Clarke, weighed down by one trouble after another. There were continual pregnancies, childbirths and miscarriages to contend with as well as the extravagance of a husband, who seemed destined to ruin them both. Chrissey's domestic life was one continual endurance, Mary Ann confided sadly to Maria Lewis,[17] and though the sensation of falling in love was exhilarating, Mary Ann reassured her old friend, 'Cease ye from Man' was definitely engraved on her amulet.[18]

Miss Evans was not the first young lady to fall in love with the language teacher and Signor Brezzi knew how to handle the situation without losing his job. He was not attracted by the unfortunate-looking young woman anyway, but did sympathize with her longing for education, particularly as it was obvious that Miss Evans had a good brain. In addition to giving her plenty of grammar to learn, Brezzi encouraged Mary Ann to read European literature to widen her general knowledge. Since the Nuneaton bookshop found it difficult enough to get Mrs Somerville's new publication *On the Connection of the Physical Sciences*, Mary Ann thought there was small likelihood they would manage Italian books. Signor Brezzi lent her some of his own copies and Maria Lewis was prevailed upon to collect titles from London bookshops when she travelled to the capital with her charges.

Signor Brezzi had a greater influence on Mary Ann than she realized. She learned that the opposite sex could be far more attractive and cultured than Isaac's companions and was capable of more stimulating intellectual discussion than she had found in any woman. From then on Mary Ann was always drawn more towards men than women. It also meant she would fall in love with several more intellectual men who crossed her path before she found her life's partner. German, the first subject she studied with Brezzi, remained her favourite language and culture throughout her life, and the study of that country's philosophy and theology played a significant part in shaping the embryonic George Eliot. Brezzi, with the fascinating aura of a world outside Warwickshire, even outside England, made Mary

Ann more determined to escape the mould into which her family were trying to fit her.

While it was quite in order for Isaac to travel to Paris in 1840 on a humbler version of the Grand Tour which the Newdigate heir had recently undertaken, it was not for his sister. The farthest Mary Ann went that year was Derbyshire, when her father insisted she travel with him and pay her respects to the Evans aunts and uncles. Though she was not given the opportunity at that time to see the places Brezzi spoke of, Mary Ann laid plans for the future when she would be free of her family, and she patiently continued her self-education as a preparation. Just as she settled into a routine of study and lessons alongside housekeeping and religion, the wishes of someone else in the family once again upset her world.

On his twenty-fourth birthday in May 1840, Isaac announced his marriage to Sarah Rawlins, sister of the Reverend Richard Rawlins, a former curate in Coventry and one-time tutor to Isaac Evans. Although Miss Rawlins was six years her fiancé's senior, being already thirty at the time of the engagement, the match met with Robert Evans's approval because the Rawlins family were wealthy leather-merchants in Birmingham. The wedding was to take place that summer and Isaac would then return with his bride to Griff House. At sixty-seven, Robert Evans was reluctant to be uprooted and so it was decided he would remain at Griff and be looked after by his daughter-in-law. That left the problem of what to do with Mary Ann.

She was horrified by this unexpected turn of events, which highlighted the precariousness of her existence. Mary Ann had grown used to taking charge of household matters at Griff but realized the new Mrs Evans would not tolerate that. Equally Mary Ann was adamant that she was not going to take orders from Isaac's wife as well as from her brother and her father. Understanding the difficulty, Chrissey offered her a home at Meriden where Mary Ann could take charge of the ever increasing brood of Clarkes. There was a certain attraction in that proposal for Mary Ann, who adored little children and willingly assisted with them when she stayed at Meriden. But the thought of spending the rest of her life as a maiden aunt totally dependent on her brother-in-law's charity appalled her – the more so since Dr Clarke teetered on the edge of bankruptcy.

The problem seemed to resolve itself when Isaac got cold feet and called the engagement off. Then to everyone's annoyance he prevaricated. For twelve months Mary Ann was in doubt about her future. It seemed to her that she was like an unwanted bundle to be passed round the family in the hope that someone could make use of the contents, or at the very least give them a home. The uncertainty made her ill with worry. Eventually in July 1841, Isaac decided the marriage was definitely going ahead. To encourage him, Robert Evans agreed to transfer the lease of Griff House and farm to Isaac, as well as make over a substantial part of the business. Mr Evans senior then planned to retire to his cottage at Packington alone. Mary Ann protested so vehemently that she did not want to live with Chrissey that her father agreed to rent a house in Coventry. There he could spend his final years in comfort and his daughter could try to find herself a husband. Although Mary Ann did not concur with all her father's plans she gratefully accepted the offer of a home where she would have some independence. Leaving Griff, which had been her home for most of her twenty-one years, was deeply painful. 'It is like dying to one stage of existence,' she tried to explain to Martha.[19] It did indeed signal the end of one phase of Mary Ann Evans's life, but Coventry symbolized the kind of rebirth she could never have foreseen.

CHAPTER 4

You Excommunicate Me
1841–1843

Had Robert Evans received any hint of the turmoil in his youngest daughter's mind in March 1841, he might well have looked somewhere less risky than Coventry to move to. As it was, he was too preoccupied with arranging the transfer of some of his business assets to his son to concern himself with the trivial problems of a young lady. He knew her to be better off than most women of her age, with her material needs well catered for and as much leisure to indulge her whims as the gentry. At twenty-one she ought to be married and settled.

At sixty-eight Mr Evans believed the painful spasms he suffered in the kidney region might prove fatal at any time. If Mary Ann were unmarried when he died, it would be Isaac's duty to support her. None of the family harboured any illusions about the likely success of that arrangement. Brother and sister were noted for their intransigence, so the chance of Mary Ann adjusting peacefully to life at Griff as the maiden aunt, assisting the new Mrs Evans with her children and undertaking the family's sewing to justify her existence was remote.

Robert Evans made the decision to take a house in Coventry because he was aware that Mary Ann had not been given much opportunity for meeting eligible young men. Being less sociable than Chrissey, she hardly went anywhere apart from church, and Robert Evans was quite sure there were no suitable husbands for his daughter among the impoverished curates. Coventry, six miles from Griff, was a large town with a population of thirty thousand which, Evans thought, would offer a broad enough spectrum of society to interest even his studious daughter. It made Nuneaton, barely a quarter the size, look parochial by comparison, especially as the railway had arrived at Coventry three years previously and London could be reached in six hours for the cost of a sovereign.

Coventry was more forward-looking in other ways. Steam power was already widely used to drive the weaving looms which had taken ribbon manufacture out of the cottages and into the factories. This had created a wealthy factory-owning middle class who sought to destroy the traditional power of the gentry and govern the town themselves. When the Evanses arrived in Coventry in 1841, the council was dominated by radicals and nonconformists and the town was entering a period of social reform aimed at providing schools, medical facilities and improved water supplies and sewage disposal.

The home Robert Evans arranged to lease was on the northern perimeter of the town, at the side of the Coventry-to-Leicester turnpike road. Though within walking distance of the town centre, the substantial Georgian mansion was set back from the road in its own grounds down a wooded drive. All around were fields and streams, but no sign of the teeming slums where most of Coventry's population lived. Robert Evans thought Mary Ann would be pleased to discover that the house at Foleshill had strong links with the parish church, for the property had actually been leased from the vicar of Holy Trinity. Furthermore, their next-door neighbour, Mr Abijah Pears, was a prominent churchman. As churchwarden and Director of the Poor for the parish, Pears was only too pleased to involve the newcomers fully in ecclesiastical activities. The highly respected Mr Evans was instantly offered a post as sidesman and his pious daughter welcomed into the Bible-study class. Knowing that the Vicar of Holy Trinity was an uncompromising Evangelical who regularly jousted with the heathens in Coventry, Evans was sure Mary Ann would settle into the community easily.

The ecclesiastical advantages of Foleshill were of minor importance to Evans compared with the social ones. Having handed much of his authority on the Arbury estate over to his son, Evans looked forward to giving Coventry the advantage of his wisdom. Lord Aylesford had laughed when he heard of Evans's move to the town and said it would not surprise him to hear his land agent had been elected mayor. In fact Evans made no headway in the town, mainly because he was the wrong colour politically, but Abijah Pears became mayor shortly after their arrival. This Evans thought most fortuitous as it could provide his daughter with a vital entrée into the upper reaches of Coventry society where potential husbands might be found.

Friendship between the Pears family and Mary Ann Evans developed naturally out of a mutual acquaintance with the Misses Franklin, her former schoolteachers, whom she still visited. Abijah Pears was in partnership with the ladies' brother as the ribbon manufacturing firm of Pears and Franklin. His marriage to Elizabeth Bray forged links with the Bray silk firm, and through her family with the Hennell ribbon factory as well. Friendship with the Pears therefore opened many doors to Mary Ann, but usually into more radical households than her father would have chosen.

Mary Ann did not have the same social aspirations as her father and continually bemoaned the need for them to have to move at all. She was a country girl, she maintained, and town life held no interest for her; more likely she would get a 'mindful of accumulated scum from continued intercourse with the herd'.[1] All she asked was to be left alone with her books. The family were not pleased. Isaac complained that too much money was being wasted on the Coventry house which, though far bigger than Griff House, was going to accommodate only two people. Its sole purpose was to give Mary Ann a chance to find a husband. She in defiance went around determinedly ignoring her appearance and placing absurd emphasis on being scholarly, which he knew would deter any man from proposing to her. She would be better in a convent than Coventry, he muttered, well aware that money spent on this house detracted from his future inheritance.

While others were busy inveigling Mary Ann into position and pointing her in the right direction of eligible bachelors, no one bothered to ask the lady herself about her hopes for the future. She might be twenty-one and legally an adult, but in the family's eyes she was merely the youngest daughter under the care and control of her father until transferred to the custody of a husband. All assumed she wanted to marry, but her own thoughts on the subject were confused. On the one hand she craved affection, but on the other she had observed that most marriages failed to live up to the woman's expectations. The perpetual tragedy of Mrs Edward Clarke's married life cast a shadow over Mary Ann and made her reluctant to contemplate wedlock herself.

Once settled in the Foleshill house she found life far better than she had anticipated. Now that she was no longer mistress of a farmhouse, there were fewer chores but ample opportunities and money to do what she liked. Her father willingly met the bills for her books and clothing, so Signor Brezzi continued to visit her in Coventry and give lessons in Italian and German. With time no object Mary Ann contemplated lessons in Greek and Latin as well.

The classics appealed to her as subjects which required serious study and were not usually offered to young ladies as a social refinement. There was no danger of her falling in love with the classics tutor, for the Reverend Thomas Sheepshanks, headmaster of the boys grammar school, was a scholarly eccentric in his mid-forties, with unkempt appearance and a rapid shrill voice which the pupils mimicked mercilessly.[2] When teaching Greek Sheepshanks used the New Testament as material for translation, and for the first time Mary Ann realized how subtle theological nuances had grown up simply from the choice of one particular English word in the translation. This had given rise to interpretations which had not been present in the Greek Gospels.

The new subjects were demanding and therefore intensely satisfying for one who sought constant intellectual stimulation. At the same time Mary Ann gained unexpected pleasure from her next-door neighbour. Despite Miss Rebecca Franklin's enthusiastic recommendation of her friend Elizabeth Pears, Mary Ann thought it most unlikely she would have anything in common with the thirty-four-year-old wife of a factory owner with a young family and a social position to keep up. Mrs Pears, however, came of a liberal-minded family and had been encouraged to develop her intellect. Marriage had not curtailed her educational progress as Abijah Pears was a founder member of the Mechanics Institute and was pleased to escort his wife to their lectures. When it came to religion, Elizabeth Pears had travelled along a similar path to Mary Ann and had a far better understanding of her young neighbour's gloomy creed than was appreciated. She had been brought up in the established Church, then with her brother become a Calvinist for a short time, going to even greater lengths than Mary Ann to withdraw from the contaminating influence of the world. Her brother Charles Bray had then reacted against all that and become agnostic, while she had settled for what she termed 'liberal-spirited nonconformity'.[3] Though Mr Pears was an

Anglican, he was tolerant of his wife's occasional attendance at the Unitarian chapel.

Mrs Pears was not put off by Mary Ann's reserve, seeing only a poignant reminder of herself in her unhappy neighbour. Instead she gently worked towards breaking down the barriers the younger woman put up and offered her friendship. Mary Ann was surprised and pathetically grateful that anyone should take an interest in her: 'I am not one of those people with whom others seem to get fat and ruddy; rather I fear their catching the infection of my *pallid* mind,' Mary Ann confessed.[4] It did not take long for the warmth of Elizabeth Pears's personality to win through and Mary Ann to be calling her neighbour 'the more precious character of a friend'.[5] With amity came invitations to join with the Pears socially, which Robert Evans was only too pleased for his daughter to accept. Soirées at the Pears establishment were often musical and thus Mary Ann was able to make good use of her skill on the piano.

Shepherded by Elizabeth Pears, Mary Ann found herself moving in the circles of the Coventry intelligentsia, which were far more radical and nonconformist than she had experienced before; but, with the conversation being more concerned with scientific and literary subjects than religious ones, she experienced no disquiet. To her surprise she felt the opposite. Among these new acquaintances, she was not regarded as an embarrassing oddity; rather her learning was appreciated and her opinions often sought. Those she met did not condemn her strict religious beliefs since they argued for the freedom of the individual to hold what views he or she liked, Anglican, Dissenting, even agnostic.

Here was a concept totally new to Mary Ann, and closer acquaintance with these people who held widely differing beliefs from her own demonstrated they were not necessarily 'infidels', as she had once thought. She noticed a more sincere commitment to improving the plight of the poor among those who called themselves radicals and Dissenters than among those who prayed for the poor on a Sunday at Holy Trinity church while being quite capable of evicting a sick tenant from their slum tenement on a Monday. She was led to ponder what really mattered, the creed a person professed or the morality they practised.

The doubts which began to appear in Mary Ann's mind were increased by the disputes which raged over education in Coventry.

Elizabeth Pears was intent on raising money to build another elementary school in the town, and Mary Ann, whose slum visits had shown her how widespread illiteracy was among the poor, wanted to do something positive. After a visit to the school which Elizabeth's brother had built and continued to maintain in one of the poorest areas of the city, Mary Ann began assisting with various of Mrs Pears's fund-raising events.

Some time later Mary Ann was confounded to hear Mr Bray and his infant school condemned as evil from the pulpit. From Elizabeth Pears she learned that Bray's well-meaning efforts to teach the poor at his own expense had met with opposition and provoked a religious dispute of unprecedented proportions. While many nominally supported the concept of universal education, they refused to accept Bray's belief that schools should be non-sectarian and therefore open to all children, no matter what their faith. The vicar of Holy Trinity insisted that schools were traditionally places where children were drilled in the Apostles' Creed, Lord's Prayer and Ten Commandments by teachers who were communicants of the Church of England. It would be heresy to change this. That view effectively barred half of Coventry from school, for nonconformity was strong in this industrial town.

Mr Bray's war-cry, 'all schools supported by a public rate ought to be secular', was interpreted as an attack on the church, but when he went on to add, 'all secular knowledge is religious knowledge', there was public outcry.[6] The vicar of Holy Trinity marshalled his troops, Bray paraded his, and battle commenced. Infant schooling was only part of the dispute. Adult education caused an even bigger rumpus, the Anglicans claiming that the Mechanics Institute, set up in 1828 for the self-improvement of the working man, had been infiltrated by radicals and Dissenters. Their response was to set up 'the Society for Religious and Useful Knowledge' with a bishop as President, an archdeacon as Vice-President and every clergyman in the town on the committee. It was not long before middle-class Coventry was in a state of civil war. The vicar of Holy Trinity claimed he was regularly abused in the radicals' newspaper and Bray claimed he had received physical abuse from members of Holy Trinity's congregation. Meanwhile membership of the Mechanics Institute shot up from sixty to two hundred.

Mary Ann was sickened by the whole affair: 'Doctrines infinitely important to man are buried in a charnel heap of bones over which nothing is heard but the barks and growls of contention.'[7] The battle was everything, the cause forgotten. For the first time she felt no empathy with this Church which had lost sight of its true purpose in a childish squabble to score points off the Dissenters. The opposition were no better when they continually held public meetings which merely prolonged the fight.

Mary Ann's disillusionment with the Church coincided with her increased interest in secular subjects. The widening of her intellectual horizons, which had begun at Griff, continued apace. Scientific subjects particularly intrigued her, though the Church's disapproval of some aspects had made her suppress this interest. But in the summer of 1841, when 'the eternal dragons of Church and dissent' were at each other's throats, Mary Ann ventured into astronomy and geology, both subjects likely to shake her fundamentalist beliefs.[8] The geological treatise by Charles Lyell arrived at the conclusion that the earth was far older than the date given in Genesis. From Lyell she moved on to a far more heretical work entitled *An Inquiry into the Origins of Christianity*, the second edition of which appeared in September 1841.

The author, Charles Christian Hennell, was a Unitarian who had undertaken an examination of the Bible to prove the authenticity of the life of Christ. To his horror, after two years' research he arrived at the opposite conclusion and felt he must publish his findings for the enlightenment of others. Though he had started from the premise that the Bible was a divinely inspired piece of writing, he discovered so many discrepancies in accounts of Christ's life in the Gospels that he was forced to the conclusion that the Bible was no more than an historical document, subject to the same mixture of facts, errors and legends as other writings of that age. Hennell rejected the miraculous elements in the Gospels as pure myth, with no more truth in them than in the legendary exploits of other heroes. The central implication of his argument was momentous: Christ, whose life was a miracle from start to finish, could no longer be regarded as divine.

Mary Ann found Hennell's scholarly book absorbing, and though she read it over several times and examined every piece of his evidence in detail, she could not fault his logic or his conclusion. By the end of 1841 she had become a 'free-thinker' (the Victorian term for an agnostic), though not yet ready to proclaim her changed views publicly. Elizabeth Pears was entrusted with Mary Ann's confidence. To Mary Ann's amazement she learned that Charles Christian Hennell was related to Mrs Pears by marriage. The book came to be written because Charles Bray had demanded that his new bride should abandon her Unitarian beliefs and become a free-thinker like himself. In confusion Mrs Bray turned to her brother Charles Hennell to supply the ammunition necessary for her to counter her husband's arguments. Hennell's unexpected conclusions delighted Bray but brought deep unhappiness to Caroline Bray and to Charles Hennell, who suffered recurrent bouts of illness and depression as the full import of his researches sank in.

Mary Ann requested Elizabeth to introduce her to the main actors in the drama. Charles Hennell she had just missed, as he had returned to London after a stay with his sister at Rosehill House, but a meeting with Mrs Bray could easily be arranged since she lived but a short walk over the fields from Foleshill. Mary Ann had already met Charles Bray at one of Elizabeth Pears's soirées where the conversation had been restricted to innocuous pleasantries after Elizabeth had privately warned her brother about Miss Evans's narrow views. Their second meeting took place one morning in November 1841.

Mary Ann was exhilarated to find herself able to pour out the thoughts and doubts which had been gathering inside her and to discover she was not alone. Though she disliked what she had heard about Bray battling with the Anglicans over education, she found herself liking the intelligent man who sat down to discuss philosophy and theology with her as an equal.

The excision of her religion left her surprisingly exuberant, but this was shortlived. As was so typical of Mary Ann, she plummeted from the heights into an abyss when she considered what lay ahead of her. As in Hennell's case, enlightenment was followed by deep depression and illness. Though there was always Elizabeth to confide in, Mary Ann felt lonely and vulnerable without the comfortable certainty of religion.

With the Christian festival of Christmas looming, Mary Ann wondered what to do. Given her new convictions, could she in all sincerity celebrate the miraculous birth of one she no longer believed was the son of God? There was the added problem of her family. Plans had been made for them to dine together. Christmas Day in the early 1840s was nothing like the traditional Victorian Christmas portrayed in *A Christmas Carol*; indeed the book which did so much to create our modern 'tradition' had not yet been published. There were no Christmas trees, turkey dinners, plum puddings or presents, but families usually met together. Mary Ann, feeling lonely, invited Maria Lewis to spend Christmas with her: 'I long to have a friend such as you are I think I may say alone to me, to unburthen every thought and difficulty,' she told her, shutting her eyes to the fact that their correspondence during the year had highlighted the divergence in their thoughts.[9] Grateful for any welcome at Christmas, Maria accepted.

The Christmas of 1841 was the worst Mary Ann had ever experienced. She felt tense and sick at the thought of what she must confess. Faced with the formidable presence of Isaac and Sarah Evans, Edward and Chrissey Clarke, Henry and Fanny Houghton and the patriarchal Robert Evans, Mary Ann kept her own counsel and attended church as expected. Maria Lewis was not told either: their conversations convinced Mary Ann that Maria would never be able to grasp the radical change that had taken place in her former pupil.

So, if not Christmas, then it had to be at New Year, for she could not stand the strain of living a lie much longer. On the first Sunday of the New Year Robert Evans was preparing to go to church to take communion alongside Mary Ann and Miss Lewis when his daughter made her declaration: 'I could not without vile hypocrisy . . . join in worship which I wholly disapprove,' and refused to go with him.[10]

Robert Evans lost his temper at such an open display of dis-obedience and wilfulness on her part. As the service was imminent, he did no more than express his anger in the strongest terms and leave her at home, but on his return he planned to have the matter out with her. That was not easy as he had always found Mary Ann the most stubborn of his daughters. Despite his marshalling all manner of argument, she refused to listen.

What made Mary Ann the more determined to stick to her beliefs was that her father seemed not to care about the reasons for her rejection of Christianity; he was more concerned about his own loss of face. How could he take his pew at church or hand round the collection plate when everybody could see he was unable to command his own daughter? What about the shame that would fall upon the family if ever it got out that they harboured a free-thinker?

Maria Lewis was made extremely uncomfortable to be caught in the middle of these acrimonious exchanges where each accused the other of the wildest things. She had not been as surprised as Mr Evans by Mary Ann's heresy for she had sensed her growing coolness for some time and laid the blame for her 'fall into infidelity' firmly at the feet of those Baptists, the Misses Franklin.[11] They had thrust their religion down her throat so much that Mary Ann was bound to rebel, she told Mr Evans, and, assuring him that she thought the phase would soon pass, she disappeared from the scene post-haste.

The phase did not pass and relations between father and daughter worsened. Both were strong characters and regarded any climbdown as a sign of weakness. When anger failed to move Mary Ann, Robert Evans lapsed into cold hostility. All the family were shocked by the youngest member's outrageous behaviour. Isaac shared his father's fury at the disgrace which would surely follow and lectured Mary Ann on the necessity of conforming; Fanny, who also admitted reading Hennell's book and arriving at similar conclusions, told Mary Ann that she ought to have had the sense to keep her opinions to herself rather than selfishly upsetting the family; Chrissey sympathized with her young sister's desire to be an individual but thought it futile to take on the combined might of father and brother.[12] When Mary Ann still would not 'listen to reason', her father told her to go elsewhere. Significantly it was, however, the warm embrace of Chrissey and not the cerebral company of Fanny that Mary Ann sought in the first instance.

In the weeks following her earth-shattering announcement, Mary Ann shuttled between brother and sisters, unsure what she should do next but determined she would not return to Foleshill unless she was permitted the freedom to choose her own faith. But Mary Ann was in no position to dictate the terms; she had been evicted and her father refused to have anything to do with her. What he intended to do in the future she could only guess at, but felt sure the Coventry house would be vacated. She wrote to him defiantly:

From what my Brother more than insinuated and from what you have yourself intimated I perceive that your establishment at Foleshill is regarded as an unnecessary expence [sic] having no other object than to give me a centre in society – that since you now consider me to have placed an insurmountable barrier to my prosperity in life this one object of an expenditure held by the rest of the family to be disadvantageous to them is frustrated – I am glad at any rate this is made clear to me, for I could not be happy to remain as an incubus or an unjust absorber of your hardly earned gains which might be better applied among my Brothers and Sisters with their children.[13]

The letter he received from her only hardened his resolve. The lease of the house was put in the hands of agents and orders given for his house on the Packington estate to be made ready for him. He washed his hands of his daughter; she could look elsewhere for support.

Mary Ann spent much of the time with Chrissey, but when her sister became ill the kindest thing Mary Ann could do was to leave and take the two eldest children with her to give Chrissey some respite. With nowhere else to go she returned to Foleshill, confident that her father would let her in since she had his two grandsons to look after. Mary Ann determined to brazen it out and believed the need to teach and entertain her two nephews would be sufficient distraction from 'the usual amount of *cooled* glances and exhortations to the suppression of self-conceit' which she received.[14] Whenever possible she disappeared to visit Mrs Pears or Mrs Bray in the sure knowledge of a warm and understanding reception.

To prevent her new friend sinking deeper into the Slough of Despond, Caroline Bray counselled her to plan for the future. She had no money now that her father had cut off her allowance and, if he went ahead with his intention of moving to Packington, she would have no home either. Mrs Bray suggested that Mary Ann should try to secure a governessing post to give herself a home and a little money. Mary Ann did not like that idea; doleful lodgings and scanty sustenance were her forecast, judging by Maria Lewis's experiences, but Mrs Bray pointed out there was nothing else a respectable woman could do.[15] It was becoming patently obvious to Mary Ann that she would also have to leave Coventry because everybody knew about her heresy and she found herself stared at and whispered about. Reluctantly she asked Mrs Bray to make enquiries among her friends in neighbouring Leamington Spa to see if a suitable post could be found.

When the Evans family realized that Mary Ann was not going to yield, and indeed planned to go her own way, they shifted their ground. It was not that they really wanted her back, but they believed it would cause more scandal if she left saying they had forced her out. Isaac appeared at Foleshill and suggested perhaps she was being too hasty in making arrangements to go to Leamington; great minds were never ashamed of owning that they had been at fault, he told her, believing that he was offering her an honourable way to back down.[16] Mary Ann could only stare back at him coldly.

At the request of Elizabeth Pears, Miss Rebecca Franklin went to try a little feminine charm on Robert Evans and achieved limited success. Evans said he was prepared to resume Mary Ann's allowance and give her a home provided she recant. Mary Ann was furious that her father so little understood her that he thought material inducements were sufficient to buy her orthodoxy.

Uncertainty about Mary Ann's future dragged on for well over twelve months, during which time the lease of the house in Coventry was taken off the market, a fact of which Mary Ann was not informed. Life began to return to something resembling normality at Foleshill, but conversation between the two inhabitants was strained. Mary Ann had no idea what the future held for her, but, as far as she knew, she was permitted to stay in the house until the new owners took over. Not wishing to be a governess, she left that plan in abeyance and carried on with her private studies.

Eventually, in the spring of 1843, a bargain was struck between Robert Evans and his daughter in order to make life tolerable. Mary Ann agreed to a token church attendance in exchange for a home with her father. Appearances were what mattered to the Evans family, so they were able to claim and proclaim a victory. Mary Ann despised herself for having to bow to their demands but really had little option. Her mind was still her own, and though she was to be seen by her father's side in the family pew, she remained as convinced in her agnosticism as ever.

Relations between Mary Ann and her family had been badly damaged by the experience. Both sides felt they had seen the other in their true colours, and mutual trust vanished for ever. Mary Ann had received the clearest indication yet that if she was to make her own path in life, it lay outside her family.

CHAPTER 5

Rosehill and the Inhabitants of that Paradise, 1842–1849

The appearance of the Brays on the scene was most opportune. The coldness and hostility of the Evans family weighed heavily on Mary Ann: 'I have no one who enters into my pleasures or my griefs, no one with whom I can pour out my soul, no one with the same yearnings the same temptations the same delights as myself,' she complained in the summer of 1841.[1] When the dashing Charles Bray offered himself as a friend and confidant, Mary Ann accepted with alacrity. This Don Juan of Coventry was an extrovert thirty-two-year-old, a dabbler in all manner of things who loudly broadcast his unorthodox views. After the sobriety of life with the Evans men, friendship with Bray was an eye-opener.

Her attachment to Charles Bray was the first of three love-affairs with larger-than-life characters, the sort of men who held a magnetic attraction for Mary Ann Evans. She was completely enamoured of Bray. Though she walked across the fields to Rosehill to pay a call on Mrs Bray, when she arrived, she only had eyes for Charles. She hung on his every word, laughed at all his jokes and immersed herself in his interests. Any friend of his was one of hers; age was no barrier. Writing of the proposed visit of an elderly Bray uncle, Mrs Bray confided to her sister that she had no doubt Mary Ann would fall desperately in love with him too. 'In spite of what some caustic people may say, I fall not in love with everyone,' the lady in question retorted angrily, but her behaviour suggested otherwise.[2]

One particularly embarrassing episode took place when she stayed with relatives of the Brays in Wiltshire. Her host was the elegant Dr

Robert Brabant, at sixty-three retired from his medical practice and his time devoted to theological investigations. His admiration for Charles Christian Hennell's *An Inquiry into the Origins of Christianity* had led to the two men meeting and Hennell eventually marrying Brabant's daughter Rufa. Immediately after this wedding in November 1843, Mary Ann was invited to go and stay with the Brabants in Devizes. Encouraged by Dr Brabant, who declared himself lost without his daughter to care for him, Mary Ann lavished great affection on the doctor, to the annoyance of his wife and sister-in-law. Learning that the scholarly gentleman was missing his female assistant now that Rufa had married, Mary Ann had no hesitation in offering to devote her life to him. Her rapt attention to the doctor's words to the exclusion of everyone else, the large amount of time spent alone with him in the study, the sight of the two walking arm-in-arm round the garden and exchanging quiet words in German proved more than the rest of the household could tolerate. The shameless Miss Evans was sent packing and Dr Brabant was told that, if ever that woman set foot in the house again, his wife would leave instantly. With Charles Bray, however, Mary Ann was on safer ground: he welcomed her adoration, and nobody at Rosehill objected to her behaviour.

Bray thrived on an audience, and the devotion of a clever young woman really boosted his ego. At the end of his life, he looked back to the nine years of 'intimate friendship' with Mary Ann Evans as one of the bright spots. He said she was a delightful companion because she seemed to know something about everything.[3] The fact that she had little self-assertion and tried to show off her friends to their best advantage made her a great asset for an extrovert. As Bray recalled, she was good at polishing up people's witticisms, but in such a way that they, and not herself, received the credit.

Although Bray had inherited a silk-ribbon-weaving factory from his father, it played a very minor part in his life. Most of his time was taken up in a plethora of activities, literary, scientific, educational, philanthropic and political, but all geared to the betterment of society. As a result of his highly developed social conscience, Bray's attitude towards business contrasted sharply with the commercially minded Evanses. Influenced by intensive study of the writings of Robert Owen, Bray showed far greater concern about the welfare of his employees than he did for company profits, which drew scorn from other Coventry industrialists. While the Lancashire cotton-mill owner, Robert Owen, had succeeded in caring for his employees and at the same time making a profit, the Coventry silk manufacturer failed. The profits of the Bray firm declined, and his operatives shunned the Working Men's Club with its reading room and temperance bar, preferring instead the delights of the public house. Never one to be downhearted, Bray went on to establish the Coventry Labourers and Artizans' Co-operative Society, which offered gardening as a healthy pastime for weavers after a week of being cooped up in the factories. That was a hobby which never fired their imagination either. As part of the enterprise he created a co-operative store in Coventry a year before Owen's famous Toad Lane one in Rochdale. The Lancashire store is remembered as a landmark in history, the pioneer of the modern co-operative movement; the Coventry one is forgotten as an ignominious failure. Bray's venture ran into trouble when the Coventry shopkeepers united in opposition because of the threat to their livelihood. A panic run on the co-operative's bank was engineered and the enterprise folded, with Bray picking up the bills.

The infant school he founded for children in a poor area of Coventry was far more successful, much to the chagrin of the Anglican clergy, whose public battles with Bray over secular education had provoked a state of Holy War in Coventry. Bray proclaimed himself an educational expert on the basis of a series of lectures he had given and two publications, *Address to the Working Classes on the Education of the Body* in 1837 and *The Education of the Feelings* in 1838. While some of the middle classes greeted these publications enthusiastically, the illiterate workers remained no wiser for Bray's advice.

The limited interest his writings aroused was sufficient to inspire Bray to venture into print more often, and in the autumn of 1841, shortly before Mary Ann met him, he published the awesomely titled work, *The Philosophy of Necessity; or, The Law of Consequences, as applicable to Mental, Moral, and Social Science.* The avowed aim of this treatise was 'to inquire into the nature of the constitution of man; to ascertain his place in creation, the object and aim of his existence and the boundaries of his mind' – Bray had decided that his real mission in life was to be a philosopher and over the next forty years he gave the public the benefit of his opinion on all manner of subjects from physiology to religion. Mary Ann was captivated; she had never met such a learned person, nor one who wrote books.

The earliest known photograph of Mary Ann Evans in her mid twenties taken when she lived in Coventry, at the instigation of Cara Bray. Years later the novelist pleaded with her friend to let the picture vanish. Instead, Cara employed someone to draw round the fading outline and in the process a little 'cosmetic surgery' was applied to Mary Ann's hooked nose.

Above left: Isaac Evans, Mary Ann's brother, photographed in later life. Isaac and Mary Ann were strong characters and intolerant of each other's views. So violently did they disagree that for most of their adult life they never communicated.

Above right: Mary Ann's adored sister, Chrissey, painted around the age of twenty when she became engaged. Marriage destroyed her health, her spirit and her fortune and set Mary Ann firmly against 'the noose of matrimony'.

Right: Emily Clarke, the only daughter of Chrissey's to survive into adulthood. After Chrissey's premature death, Mary Ann took over the welfare of her niece. Emily never married and despite severe deafness supported herself by teaching the piano.

Robert Evans, Mary Ann's father, aged sixty-nine and painted in 1842 by Carlisle. Evans was a highly successful land agent whose business acumen was inherited by his daughter.

Griff House, where Mary Ann spent the first twenty-one years of her life and for which she retained a deep affection. This farmhouse with its Georgian frontage was the most impressive residence in the village.

The farmyard behind Griff House with its byres and dovecote visible.

Broadgate, one of the main streets in Coventry, in the mid-nineteenth century. Although Mary Ann only lived in the town for eight years, the people and ideas she encountered there changed her life.

A pastel study of Dr Robert Brabant, the elderly, debonair physician and aspiring theologian, over whom the twenty-three-year-old Mary Ann Evans made a complete fool of herself.

Dr Brabant's daughter, Rufa, photographed in her fifties. Mary Ann and Rufa remained lifelong friends and Rufa was the first person brave enough to welcome Mary Ann and her lover after their elopement.

Rosehill House, Coventry, home of the Bray family where Mary Ann was a regular visitor throughout the 1840s.

An unfinished ivory miniature of Cara Bray aged twenty-seven, painted by Carlisle. This former Miss Hennell taught Mary Ann the manners and social graces of the London drawing room.

A daguerreotype of Sara Hennell taken in the 1840s. She was eight years older than Mary Ann and of similar intellectual calibre though she chose to devote her literary talents to theological discourses.

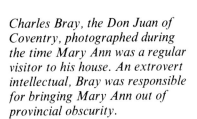

Charles Bray, the Don Juan of Coventry, photographed during the time Mary Ann was a regular visitor to his house. An extrovert intellectual, Bray was responsible for bringing Mary Ann out of provincial obscurity.

Charles Christian Hennell, brother of Cara and Sara, was author of the controversial Inquiry Into the Origins of Christianity *which rocked Victorian religious beliefs and profoundly influenced Mary Ann's thinking.*

A picture of Marian Evans (as she then called herself) by an unknown artist, painted soon after she went to London in the early 1850s.

Some people admired Mr Bray for his unusual ideas, which he liked to air on the town council. A 'florid Anglo-Saxon with an air of good-natured bonhomie sitting well on his handsome features, who carried on his work in life with a sanguine and easy freedom from care,' was one opinion of him.[4] But that opinion came from a relative and was definitely a minority one. Most Coventry people thought him a loud-mouth and took every opportunity to exploit his surname. Others went so far as to call him an enemy of society who sought to undermine its foundations with his crackpot ideas. 'A man of decided individuality,' was how his obituary tactfully described him. 'Wherever he went he made his own mark. One might agree with him or not but he was never accused of being commonplace . . . a man of intellectual capacity and conspicuous honesty, who often hit the nail on the head while more cautious people held their tongues.'[5] Not surprisingly, he was smartly manoeuvred off the town council.

What impressed Mary Ann about Charles Bray was his knowledge of all the latest discoveries. He kept himself up to date by subscribing to numerous publications. Invariably he would write to the author of an article putting forward his own opinion and, whenever possible, enter into prolonged correspondence. If he discovered that the writer lived in London, he was quite likely to make a point of visiting the unsuspecting author. This meant, moreover, that Bray could always reel off a most impressive list of 'acquaintances'.

At the beginning of the 1840s Bray was expounding the virtues of mesmerism, which we would call hypnotism today. It was the Victorian belief that an invisible electrical fluid, which derived from the stars and powered the universe, could be collected by a 'trained operator' and made to flow into a subject by manipulation of the hand. The subject would then fall into a magnetic sleep from which they would gain restorative powers. Bray was not convinced of the medical properties of mesmerism but he perceived that it gave access to a person's subconscious: this he thought would aid his philo-sophical investigations.

He had already read a great deal about mesmerism but had not succeeded in mastering the necessary sleight of hand to create the sleeping condition by the time Mary Ann arrived at Rosehill. She was, however, quite prepared to trust Charles to experiment on her in the interests of scientific advancement. As one who found it difficult to relax, she was not a good subject, and it took the visit of an expert finally to impart the celestial power. As Caroline recalled, Mary Ann found the experience terrifying and piteously begged the operator to release her, for she could not open her eyes without permission.[6] Having been the subject once, she never volunteered again.

Her continuing interest in the subject took her to Birmingham with Bray to attend a series of lectures on the clairvoyant aspects of this pseudo-science. There she watched performances where the subject was mesmerized, then given a folded letter and asked to reveal the contents. More spectacularly the person in a trance often went on to give a physical description of the writer, his age and occupation. Though Mary Ann later dismissed much of the supernatural elements as fraudulent, ideas she gained on these expeditions were to form the basis of a macabre short story she wrote in 1859 called 'The Lifted Veil'.

Phrenology soon replaced mesmerism as Bray's pet hobby when he ordered a book on physiology by A. Combe but was mistakenly sent one on phrenology by G. Combe. The contents of the wrong volume proved so enthralling that Bray was an immediate convert, believing yet again that he had stumbled on the key to the universe. Originally he proposed to use phrenology to identify the characters of children in his school and adapt the education to their specific needs, but then he realized he could use it to authenticate his philosophy. In a fit of great excitement Bray went down to London, and had his head shaved and his own cast taken (he said he wanted to learn to read the skull by starting with the character he knew best). A little study was sufficient for him to become an expert and he arranged his own lecture tours. Armed with a selection of plaster casts of criminals, purchased from Deville's in the Strand, Bray rode round the Warwickshire country-side, his saddlebags filled with heads.

All visitors to Rosehill were requested to have their head felt for bumps. 'I never missed an opportunity of examining a head where the character was at all marked,' Bray explained.[7] The prospect of examining the cranial contours of the unusual Miss Evans was irresistible, and Mary Ann was naturally delighted to oblige him. Not only did she sit for him, but she went to classes in phrenology with him, conducted by the great organologist Mr Cornelius Donovan, who was touring the country, and she went so far as to have her own head cast. As Bray was eager to point out, Mr James Deville was now advertising a modern method of casting which did not render the subject bald:

PHRENOLOGICAL CHART.

TAKEN BY MRS. HAMILTON, PHRENOLOGIST, LONDON.

(LATE OF EDINBURGH) 294, REGENT STREET, LONDON.

	INCHES.		INCHES.
AVERAGE SIZE OF THE MALE HEAD	22	AVERAGE SIZE OF THE FEMALE HEAD	21
Circumference of the head		Anterior Lobe, or Intellectual Region	
From Occipital Bone to Individuality		Coronal, or Moral Region	
From Destructiveness to ditto		Posterior ditto	

THE DOME OF THOUGHT, THE PALACE OF THE SOUL.	MAN, KNOW THYSELF! THEN OTHERS LEARN TO KNOW.

" *It is heaven upon earth to have Man's mind to move in charity—rest in Providence—and turn upon the poles of truth.*"

Cerebral Development of

RELATIVE PROPORTION OF THE ORGANS:—Very Large, 20; Rather Large, 18; Moderate, 16; Small, 12; Very Small, 10.

NOTE.—The Organs that are large are those that are naturally most powerful, and which may be most easily cultivated, and in some instances need to be restrained.

DOMESTIC AFFECTIONS.

1. *Amativeness.*—Marriage; love. " A man shall leave his father and mother, and cleave to his wife."
2. *Philoprogenitiveness.*—Love of offspring and animals.
3. *Concentrativeness.*—Love of home; attachment to particular objects and places.
4. *Adhesiveness.*—Attachment, friendship, and social sympathy.

PROTECTING FACULTIES.

† The *Love of Life.*
† *Appetite for Food.*
5. *Combativeness.*—Courage to meet danger; inspired with boldness to overcome opposition.
6. *Destructiveness.*—Gives energy in overcoming difficulties, &c.
7. *Secretiveness.*—Prudence in not giving utterance to ideas until judgment has approved of them.
8. *Acquisitiveness.*—Industry; a desire to possess articles; provision for old age.
9. *Constructiveness.*—To construct houses, machinery, and furniture.

MORAL REGULATING FACULTIES.

10. *Self Esteem.*—Inspires the mind with confidence and independence; gives dignity to character; self respect.
11. *Love of Approbation.*—Respect for a good name; will inspire to the acquisition of honourable fame.
12. *Cautiousness.*—Circumspection before commencing any undertaking.
13. *Benevolence.*—Sympathy and charity. " I was hungry, and ye gave me meat."
14. *Veneration.*—Respect for the good and great, and revealed truth.
15. *Firmness.*—Decision of character.
16. *Conscientiousness.*—The sentiment of equity.

IMAGINATIVE POWERS.

17. *Hope.*—Keeps up the spirits under misfortunes; inspires the belief in a better state of human existence.
18. *Wonder.*—Desire of novelty; admiration of the grand.
19. *Ideality.*—Poetic taste; produces the sentiment of beauty.
20. *Wit.*—Quick perception of the meaning of others; presence of mind.

OBSERVING FACULTIES.

21. *Imitation.*—To imitate virtue; copies the manners of others; necessary to the artist.
22. *Individuality.*—Memory for names; produces a desire for the knowledge of objects.
23. *Form.*—Observes and recollects forms of persons and shapes; necessary to mechanics.
24. *Size.*—Gives the idea of space; is essential to the landscape painter and land surveyor.
25. *Weight.*—A knowledge of the law of gravitation; essential to genius for mechanics.
26. *Colour.*—Perception of colours, and the power of distinguishing shades.

KNOWING FACULTIES.

27. *Locality.*—The power of recognizing places; confers a talent for geography; a desire for travelling.
28. *Number.*—A talent for arithmetic and calculation.
29. *Order.*—Taste for arrangement; neatness in dress.
30. *Eventuality.*—A memory for passing events and occurences; facts of political and natural history.
31. *Time.*—The power of judging of the lapse of time; punctuality; essential to the musician.
32. *Tune.*—The power to perceive harmony, and relish music.
33. *Language.*—Power of acquiring languages, and a readiness in the use of words to express the thoughts of the mind.

REFLECTING FACULTIES.

34. *Comparison.*—A tendency to compare one thing with another; traces analogies.
35. *Causality.*—Traces the relation between cause and effect, and is not satisfied with analogies, but searches to a Great First Cause.

OBSERVATIONS.

1. Memory depends on the size and activity of any intellectual organ.
2. An organ may be enlarged by exercise.
3. All teachers of youth ought to study Phrenology, as it expands the charitable feelings.

TEMPERAMENT.—*Parts.*—Lymphatic, ; Sanguine, ; Nervous, ; Fibrous,

A phrenological reading of the head bumps of Mary Ann's friend, Bessie (Elizabeth Rayner Parkes). Under the influence of Charles Bray, Mary Ann became a convert to this pseudo-science and travelled down to London with Bray to have her skull read professionally. A cast of Miss Evans's unusually large cranium was made by James Deville in the Strand and treasured by Bray all his life.

51

Ladies or gentlemen desirous of having casts taken from their own heads, for phrenological studies, or as family memorials, are respectfully informed, that by a new simple, and easy process, occupying not more than five minutes, they may have perfect facsimiles of their own heads, and at a very small expense.[8]

Few people nowadays would accept phrenology as anything but misguided, yet Bray's 'diagnosis' of Mary Ann Evans's character has been the one scholars have accepted. In his favour it should be said that the phrenological reading always quoted was written down by Bray at the end of his life when he had her head cast in front of him and the events of the past in his mind. It would have required a superhuman integrity, which Bray never possessed, to have refrained from making the reading fit the known facts.

Bray's analysis of his friend's character was predictable. He concluded that the intellect was dominant and that the subject's animal (sexual) feelings were safely balanced by her moral feelings. As a person who maintained women were the weaker vessels and ought to be under man's special protection, Bray decided Mary Ann was 'not fitted to stand alone' and always required someone to lean on.[9] Unfortunately this remark, which owes more to the traditional attitudes and prejudices of a mid-Victorian male than to the actual personality of Mary Ann Evans, has coloured biographers' views of her ever since despite the subsequent events of her life actually showing she possessed a strong character. The only significant points in Bray's character analysis were his references to her being very affectionate and emotionally clinging.

Reminiscing about their friendship, Bray recalled the lightning changes of mood to which Mary Ann was subject. The charming companion of one day could on another occasion be very provoking, and he remembered that they had had some violent quarrels. But these were as quickly forgotten, and when they met the next day no allusion was made to them. Her swift transition from adorer to fighter made for some stormy encounters which characterized Mary Ann's private relationship with men throughout her life.

Other residents at Rosehill were initially less attractive to Mary Ann, though in the long term they proved good friends. There was Charles Bray's wife Caroline, known to close friends as Cara. Her attitude towards the young woman who doted on her husband was surprisingly generous. She raised no objection to Mary Ann being Charles's perpetual companion, nor to her staying in London with him unchaperoned. Rather, Cara displayed great warmth towards 'poor Miss Evans', four years her junior, and encouraged her to treat Rosehill as her second home. Mary Ann was pathetically grateful for the welcome she was afforded, particularly coming at a time when she was so out of favour with her family. To everyone's amusement, she was for ever thanking them. With the naivety of one who had led a sheltered life, it never crossed Mary Ann's mind to question why Cara was not jealous of her husband's clear preference for Miss Evans's company over his wife's.

Mrs Bray was a quiet, unassuming person. As a former Miss Hennell she had enjoyed a comfortable middle-class upbringing until the premature death of her father left the family with financial problems and forced most of the daughters into governessing. Since Cara was one of the youngest and most attractive of the sisters, unbeknown to her another scheme was hatched. She was despatched to Coventry from her home in London to spend a holiday with her aunt and uncle. There she was introduced to Charles Bray, a young, wealthy business associate of her uncle, who had just inherited his father's factory. Bray was captivated by the pretty little Miss Hennell and impulsively proposed marriage. To her horror the seventeen-year-old Cara found that everyone expected her to accept even though she hardly knew the man. Her uncle favoured a union between two established silk firms, and with four more daughters on the list, her mother wanted to tick the first name off. 'How terrible it must be to find oneself tied to a being whose limitations you could see, and must know were such as to prevent your ever being understood!' Mary Ann said when she heard Cara's story, but her sympathies really lay with Charles, who was disillusioned with the unintellectual wife he had lumbered himself with.[10] Having watched the Evanses' machinations at close hand, Mary Ann was cynical about the way marriages were contracted. She agreed with Cara that although arranged marriages did not officially exist in England, too often young people were deliberately brought together and received intimations that an engagement was desired and expected. As a result, people found themselves trapped in unsuitable relationships for the rest of their lives.

In Cara's case, only her brother Charles Christian Hennell had voiced any doubts about the Bray–Hennell match. He had warned his mother of 'some incompatibilities of modes of living and thinking' between the two young people which he feared would take a long time to harmonize.[11] He had also heard that Bray was too cavalier in his business dealings for his firm to survive for long.

Hennell's premonitions proved correct. The honeymoon was even more disastrous for Cara than for most nineteenth-century brides. She was shocked by mental as well as physical revelations, for her husband declared himself to be agnostic and demanded his wife follow suit. Thus the Bray marriage got off to a bad start with both partners unhappy and disillusioned, and there was intense anger among the Unitarian Hennell family that Bray had kept his heretical opinions a secret.

In the early years only the constant visits of Hennell brother and sisters kept Cara's spirits up. Of a more academic inclination than her younger sister, Mary Hennell became an especially frequent visitor and formed a close attachment to Charles Bray. She worked with him on three books, having had more literary experience through being a contributor to *Knight's Penny Cyclopedia*. It was Mary Hennell who researched and wrote the history of co-operative communities which appeared as an appendix to Bray's *Philosophy of Necessity*. Rumours circulated in Coventry that notions of co-operative living were taken a little too seriously at Rosehill and that relations between Bray and his sister-in-law were far more communal than necessary. One relative was indiscreet enough to whisper that 'Miss Mary Hennell used to live with the Brays, and she was the especial object of his affections and shared his literary interests when writing his book, and his wife who was reasoned into the marriage was a secondary person and far from happy.'[12] Mary Ann met the object of Bray's affections during her early visits to Rosehill but was unaware of the woman's status; soon afterwards the onset of consumption forced Mary back to London into the care of her mother, to meet a premature death.

Her absence produced a gap in Charles Bray's life which Mary Ann Evans conveniently filled; aware of her husband's wayward tendencies, Cara accepted the situation without comment. She was fond of the guileless Miss Evans and preferred her husband to attach his affections to someone like that rather than a person she did not care for. Cara also needed a friend and believed she and Mary Ann could share other interests besides Charles. Mary Ann, eager to please, willingly accepted all overtures of friendship and found herself accepted into the Hennell and Bray family as though she were a relative.

Sara, another older sister of Cara's, struck up a particularly close friendship with Mary Ann which lasted for much of Mary Ann's life. She was seven years older than Mary Ann, widely read and regularly referred to as 'Mrs Bray's gifted sister'. She had a completely different personality from Cara, being full of nervous energy and prone to deep depressions. In the beginning, Mary Ann looked up to the older woman as her mentor, but was encouraged by Sara to think of her more as a husband figure. The resultant letters which passed between them contained lavish expressions of endearment. 'My soul kisses thee dear Sara in gratitude for those dewy thoughts of thine in this morning's note,' Mary Ann wrote on one occasion.[13] Some letters were even terminated 'thine ever affectionate Husband'.[14] Language such as this not only lends weight to contemporary charges that she fell in love with all she met, but to more modern scholars' hints at a sexual ambivalence in George Eliot. Mary Ann had no interest in developing an intimate relationship with someone of her own sex. She always preferred the love of a man but was prepared to respond to Sara's overtures on paper. Sara had no interest in men and was both critical and jealous of her friend's overriding obsession with the opposite sex. The two women's friendship never developed beyond excessively affectionate written words because Sara was obliged to work as a governess in the south of England in order to support her mother.

A contemporary who knew all the women at this time said Mary Ann looked to Sara for intellectual sympathy and to Cara for affectionate companionship or sympathy when she was in pain or trouble.[15] Cara was the person Mary Ann had most daily contact with and, in return for the loving reception she was always accorded at Rosehill, longed to give a *quid pro quo*. All she could think of was to assist Mrs Bray with the infant school she visited regularly. Mary Ann's offer to teach required tactful handling because it was quite obvious to Cara and one of the assistants at the school that Miss Evans had no aptitude for this sort of work at all. Since she was so insistent that she help, the only thing they could find for her to do was to draw some illustrations for a natural history lesson. The well-meaning attempts at a squirrel drawing were, in the opinion of the pupil-teacher, proof that Miss Evans's talent lay elsewhere.[16]

The visits to Rosehill proved more of an education to Mary Ann than she had foreseen. Although the Hennells had fallen on hard times, there was still an air of gracious living about the family and they had the manners and polish appropriate to a London drawing room. All this was alien to Mary Ann, used only to the provincial ways of prosperous farmers, doctors and solicitors. Under Cara's tutelage, she developed her musical talents and lost some of the painful shyness that had always dogged her public performances. She was invited to participate regularly in the Brays' musical soirées, either by adding her alto voice to part-singing or more usually by performing as a pianist. Cara taught Mary Ann to appreciate art, and though she clearly never managed to improve her young friend's sketching ability she did transmit her own enthusiasm, so that later, when Mary Ann lived in London, she became a regular visitor to art studios and the galleries.

For Mary Ann, the highlight of an evening at Rosehill was always the conversation, which ranged over subjects she would never have dared discuss before. Literature and politics were naturally popular areas where she felt quite at home, but it was quite another matter when the debate moved on to population control. Charles Bray was a strong advocate of contraception, claiming that ignorance and disregard of the organic laws which governed paternity and maternity was resulting in not only bad, but insane, children. In line with Malthusian principles, he also maintained that the population must be kept within the means of subsistence.[17] Even the genteel Cara Bray included Alison's *Principles of Population and Their Connection with Human Happiness* on her reading list.[18] One visitor to Rosehill, present at the same time as Mary Ann, noted in his diary that they had passed the evening discussing 'the expediency of giving or withholding from girls, when they reached puberty, a knowledge of the nature and consequences of the sexual function and its uses and abuses; comprehending of course careful instruction and guidance in respect of their relation with the male sex'.[19] The consensus of opinion was that truth was of the essence.

Discussions like these would have been considered very risqué in most mid-nineteenth-century drawing rooms, especially when conducted in mixed company. Had the Evans family ever suspected that Mary Ann was joining in such conversations, they would have been shocked. As it was, Cara reported to Sara, tongue-in-cheek:

Brother Isaac with real fraternal kindness thinks that his sister has no chance of getting the one thing needful – i.e. a husband and a settlement, unless she mixes more in society, and [he] complains that since she has known us she has hardly been anywhere else; that Mr Bray, being only a leader of mobs, can only introduce her to Chartists and Radicals, and that such only will ever fall in love with her if she does not belong to the Church.[20]

What Isaac certainly did not know was that, in line with the beliefs and practices of Charles Bray, Mary Ann was already proclaiming 'the *truth of feeling* as the only universal bond of union', not marriage.[21]

Being a close friend of Charles Bray gave her an insight into marriage and other less formal arrangements. Since the Bray marriage did not suit either participant, Charles had persuaded Cara that they should each lead separate lives. It was everyone's duty to search for happiness, he argued, and, drawing on various philosophers for support, he proposed an open marriage as the sensible solution to the impasse. The partner he chose was Hannah Steane, the cook at Rosehill. She was two years younger than his wife and doubtless she was selected for her cranial contours rather than her bodily curves because Bray vigorously expounded the wisdom of using phrenology in the selection of a mate. Over a period of ten years Hannah bore Charles Bray six illegitimate children. For all his apparent openness Bray tried to keep this affair quiet and went to great lengths to arrange for his mistress's confinements to take place outside Coventry.[22]

Mary Ann knew about Charles's mistress because Bray could never resist the opportunity to reveal his daring liaison to close friends. Moreover by 1845 Rosehill contained living proof of the illicit union. Since Cara had failed to produce children of her own, Charles persuaded her to consent to a surrogate arrangement. He contrived to introduce his daughter Elinor Mary, born to Hannah in January 1844, into the Rosehill household as their adopted daughter. The baby's presence bolstered his paternal pride, but did not fulfil Cara's maternal longings because with the baby came her nursemaid, Hannah Steane. That was never the plan Cara had envisaged, but she felt obliged to accept the situation until late in 1846 when the nursemaid gave birth to a son. He was proudly named Charles after his father. This was more than Cara could stomach, and Hannah was dismissed from her service, though not from Charles's. He rented a house for her in another part of the town and set her up as Mrs Charles Gray, the wife of a traveller who was rarely at home.

The child Elinor, known familiarly as Nelly, was always closer to her father than to her foster mother. Though kind to her, Cara had no love for the child she had been tricked into taking in, and, when Sara Hennell came to live at Rosehill in the 1850s, it was she who concerned herself with Nelly's welfare and education.

Encouraged by Charles's rejection of her, Cara began to make use of the freedom Charles permitted her. A family gossip reported that 'Mrs Bray is and has been for years decidedly in love with Mr Noel, and that Mr Bray promotes her wish that Mr Noel should visit Rosehill as much as possible, and that she in return trys [sic] to promote his happiness in any way that his wishes tend'.[23] The said Edward Henry Noel was a romantic figure – an illegitimate relation of Byron and in possession of an estate on a Greek island; he spent his time travelling round Europe, writing poetry and translating German novels. When his consumptive young wife died, Cara was more than willing to assist with his three children, and his visits to Rosehill, which began in 1843, increased in frequency and duration in proportion to Mr Bray's declining interest in his wife.

Although these relationships were a revelation to Mary Ann, she so admired the people involved and so completely understood the reasons for their unconventional arrangements that all seemed quite acceptable to her. 'The great lesson of life is tolerance,' Mary Ann told a young neighbour, but she admitted that that was easier said than done.[24] The stringency of the marriage laws caused the most unhappiness, she insisted, and it would be far better if the continental idea was adopted where separations did not necessarily discredit either party.

These were exceptionally advanced views, which would have been abhorrent to the rest of the Evans family. With his free thinking and loving, Charles Bray came to exert an enormous influence over Mary Ann.

CHAPTER 6

His Inspiration Has So Quickened My Faculties, 1842–1849

Friendship with Charles Bray proved anything but mundane; what he lacked in wisdom he made up in courage. After the conservatism of the Evanses, there could hardly have been a better person to lead the diffident Mary Ann Evans out of obscurity. 'I may claim to have laid down the base of that philosophy which she afterwards retained,' he stated with his usual abundant self-confidence, but with some justification in this case.[1] The novelist-to-be owed her development as a person more to this man than to any other. He introduced her to a wide spectrum of subjects, concepts and people and gave her the inspiration to approach life boldly. It has to be said that this rates as the only success story of his life.

It is no coincidence that the only letters to survive from the correspondence between Mary Ann and Charles Bray are the ones dated after 1848 – Cara made sure of that. The intensity of their affection was something she wanted hidden from public view. Even towards the end of her life, when the two participants had long been dead, one of Cara's relatives noticed that it was 'ever a pious and trusted point of honour with this kind old lady to run no risk, even with trusted kinsmen, of enlarging upon the "George Eliot" chapter of her life'.[2] Enquirers were always referred to the 'official' biography of George Eliot by John Cross as containing all the world needed to know.

A century and a half later, it is impossible to uncover the full story of Mary Ann's relationship with Charles. Hints abound that it was more than mere goodneighbourliness. Even late in Mary Ann's life rumours persisted about 'a passionate affair' she had had before she came to London with a 'very attractive man, I think a Doctor Something with whom and with whose wife she was intimate as a girl', as one of her friends whispered.[3] Passionate the affair undoubtedly would have been, given the two participants, but it was unlikely to have been sexual. Mary Ann was intrigued by theories of communal living and free love but not ready herself to put them into practice. She was also too fond of Cara Bray to do anything which might hurt her. Another strong piece of evidence which argues against the suggestion that they ever became lovers is that, in 1851, Charles Bray confessed. The recipient of his confidences was George Combe, author of the book on phrenology which had had such a profound influence on Bray, who might well have thought Bray was doing a little sensational boasting rather than advancing the course of scientific studies. To assist in the interpretation of his skull, Bray told Combe about his sex life which, he claimed, began at the age of twelve when he was seduced by one of the servants. From then on he indulged himself extensively. He did try a period of abstinence, he admitted, but found his health suffered, so he was obliged to carry on as before. Significantly Bray also confessed that, though married, he kept a mistress who had borne his children. Had he enjoyed a sexual affair with Miss Evans, it is likely he would have mentioned it, unable to keep a secret as he was. Combe was well aware that the information he had been given was explosive and took the precaution of entering it in his notebook in a private shorthand, whose meaning eluded scholars until 1977.[4]

Early in their friendship, Charles Bray introduced Mary Ann to the philosophies of Robert Owen, whom he admired greatly; he thought Mary Ann would too. Aside from interest in the way the philosopher ran his factory, Bray was taken with his experiments in communal living. An Owenite commune was set up in Hampshire in 1842 with Bray a regular visitor, so he was able to keep Mary Ann informed of the group's progress. When he told her proudly that the first child born to the group had been given the names Primo Communis (with the surname Flitcroft to boot!), she could only laugh. His dream of this group changing the world gradually faded and in 1846 Bray admitted that the Hampshire experiment had failed like previous attempts at pure communism.

He remained a loyal supporter of Owen's principles all his life, but Mary Ann was never converted. This daughter of Robert Evans had her feet firmly on the ground and thought Owen's notion of changing the world by removing small groups from it was too simplistic. If society was to change, she said, it needed far more ruthless measures. Evenings at Rosehill resounded to the arguments between Mary Ann and Bray over this issue. Hoping to win her over, Bray arranged for her to meet the seventy-two-year-old philosopher. This proved counter-productive. 'If his system prosper it will be *in spite* of its founder, and not because of his advocacy,' was her cynical opinion after dining with Mr Owen at Rosehill in 1843.[5] Though she was to meet him several times over the next ten years, she saw nothing to change her mind; indeed during the 1850s she penned some criticism of the elderly idealist in anonymous articles for the *Westminster Review*. The only portions of his philosophy that ever earned her support were those attacking marriage and supporting divorce and birth control.

The practical message of the Anti-Corn Law League, however, did win her support, and knowing her father and brother to be firmly on the opposing side only added zest to Mary Ann's commitment. Charles Bray was naturally to be found at the helm as chairman of the local branch of the League. Committee meetings, League bazaars and tea parties designed to rally the faithful and relieve them of their money were all held at Rosehill. Mary Ann willingly entered into the activities, assisting Charles in a clerical capacity and Cara on the domestic front.

Most of the visiting speakers at League meetings stayed with the chairman; as Bray once remarked wryly: 'Everyone who came to Coventry with a queer mission, or a crochet, or was supposed to be a "little cracked", was sent up to Rosehill.'[6] In those days before mass communication, anyone with a cause was obliged to hawk it personally the length and breadth of the kingdom, so at Rosehill Mary Ann found herself in the company of Cobden and Bright, the leaders of the Anti-Corn Law League, Robert Moore, the Irish political economist, and Ralph Waldo Emerson, the American philosopher – and all within a stone's throw of her own home. Conversations with these notables could not fail to widen her general knowledge, sharpen her political awareness and exacerbate the differences with her family.

At Bray's instigation but without her father's knowledge, Mary Ann attended the more inflammatory meetings of the Irish Home Rule group. Charles stood with the men in the main body of the hall, while she and Cara were seated with a small group of women up in the gallery. At one meeting in 1844 addressed by the fiery Irish leader Daniel O'Connell, there was such uproar for two hours that the police had to be called to disperse the crowd.[7]

Mary Ann was in a different sort of danger at the next meeting she attended with Bray. This time the cause was total abstinence from alcohol. Bray, though not teetotal himself, was a leading light in the Temperance Movement and permitted the group to hold its annual tea party in the grounds of Rosehill. So persuasive did Mary Ann find the Reverend Thomas Spencer (uncle of Herbert Spencer, a recipient of her affections ten years later) that at the end of the lecture she was out of her seat and heading towards the front to sign the undertaking. Only with the greatest difficulty did Bray make her stop and weigh the matter up before committing herself to a lifetime of abstinence. Suffice it to say that Mary Ann Evans, who always enjoyed her food and drink, never took the pledge.[8]

Charles Bray's radical politics naturally swayed Mary Ann but were only partially responsible for shaping her views. Her own family with their comfortable smugness and refusal to countenance change also played a part. The same fervour she had once applied to Evangelicalism was channelled into the cause of social reform. Middle-class philanthropy solved nothing, she said. The meagre handouts of food and clothing were cleverly designed to undermine the self-respect of the poor and perpetuate the chasm between the 'haves' and the 'have-nots'. By contrast with Bray's desire for a gentle Owenite transformation, Mary Ann wanted social upheaval.

When violence broke out in Europe in 1848, she was ecstatic – at last the revolution was at hand.[9] Details of the Paris uprising in the papers caused her to be wildly excited: 'I thought we had fallen on such evil days that we were to see no really great movement. . . . I would consent however to have a year clipt off my life for the sake of witnessing such a scene as that of the men of the barricade bowing to the image of Christ "who first taught fraternity to men", ' she enthused to a friend. Although delighted with the way revolution was spreading round Europe like a bush fire, Mary Ann remained pessimistic of it taking hold in England. 'Our working classes are eminently inferior to the mass of the French people. In France, the *mind* of the people is highly electrified – they are full of ideas on social subjects – they really desire social *reform*,' she continued, though she had no first-hand knowledge of the subject and was merely reiterating what she had read and heard others say.

She had, however, arrived at her own plan to dispose of European monarchs humanely after the revolution, proposing that they be lumped together in a zoological garden. 'It is but justice that we should keep them, since we have spoiled them for any honest trade,' she conceded.

Her delight in the European insurrections was shared by two men of similar age to her, both living in London. Karl Marx and Friedrich Engels published their *Communist Manifesto* in March 1848. Its message of class struggle and revolution would have appealed to Mary Ann, but at the time the work went largely unnoticed.

Coming from a family where politics was treated very seriously, Mary Ann could not help but hold strong opinions, but she had no wish to take to the platform herself. By 1848 her sights were firmly set on a career in another male-dominated world – literature. From the time she had seen her poem printed in the Evangelical newspaper, she had contemplated becoming a writer but had been unsure how to progress. As a first step, the possibility of working on translations arose unexpectedly in 1842.

Appalled by the mental aberration which had caused an Evans to utter heresies, the family had requested a cleric to try to make Mary Ann see sense. The Reverend Francis Watts never succeeded in shaking Mary Ann's agnostic convictions, but he tried to keep the line of communication open by talking to her about literature. He was widely travelled and had assembled much European writing which he was more than happy to lend to Miss Evans. She was full of admiration for Vinet's *Liberté des Cultes* and thought it a pity that so clever a book should be accessible only to those with a knowledge of French. Urged on by Signor Brezzi, who realized Mary Ann needed some intellectual occupation to pass the time at home, she proposed to become its translator.

It was hard work – four hundred pages of philosophical argument in French – but Mary Ann enjoyed the challenge and took heart from the odd scrap of encouragement handed out by Watts. When the task was completed, she triumphantly handed the manuscript over to him, trusting he would arrange for its publication. 'I beg you to understand that I consider myself *your* translator and the publication yours,' she told him, thinking it might spur him on.[10] Despite her repeated enquiries about the progress of her work, he did nothing. Gradually the truth dawned: Watts had only regarded the Vinet translation as therapy for a disturbed mind and made no attempt to find a publisher.

She was angry that the work had been in vain and without any knowledge of the publishing world despaired of ever getting back into print. But in the company of Charles Bray, Mary Ann found it impossible to be out of sorts for long, for he always had some incredible new scheme he needed assistance with. In 1842 he wanted help in the preparation of his lecture on sanitary reform and wondered also whether Mary Ann could assemble some material for his next series of lectures on 'The Means in the Power of the Working Classes to Improve Their Character and Condition'.

Mary Ann was involved in this research when Bray heard of some translation work and put her name forward as the ideal candidate. What was required on this occasion was an English version of the controversial *Das Leben Jesu*, written by the German theologian Friedrich Strauss. The task had been started by Rufa Brabant, then passed to Sara Hennell after Rufa's marriage. When Sara saw the length and complexity of the task she declined: it was not that she lacked the linguistic skill, but being obliged to work as a governess she knew she would never have enough free time to devote to the task. Charles suggested Mary Ann, and Sara agreed, with the proviso that she supervise the task and edit the final version to ensure that Mr Parkes, the radical MP for Birmingham, who was paying, received good-quality prose.

When Mary Ann received the German book, she understood why Sara had backed out: there were fifteen hundred pages of involved religious dispute. It was a formidable undertaking and required continual encouragement from Charles, Cara and Sara to prevent her losing heart. Despite setting herself a rigorous schedule to complete six pages a day, the work still required an interminable two years. There were times when she loathed it, doubted her own ability and was ready to tear the whole thing up, but what really kept her working was the will to succeed. She had been provided with an opportunity to prove to herself that she was capable of more than housekeeping. It was a matter of personal pride that she should not fail, though she wrote feelingly to Sara, 'I am only inclined to vow that I will never translate again if I live to correct the sheets for Strauss.'[11]

She did come through, and along the way gained valuable experience in manipulating language. It was hardly surprising that Robert Evans's daughter should have been professional in her approach to the work. The Calvinist regime she had followed a few years earlier stood her in good stead when it came to disciplining herself to produce the necessary six pages, no matter how long into the night she laboured. Sara Hennell proved an excellent editor: no inaccuracies, accidental omissions or untidy handwriting escaped her eagle eye.

Eventually, in June 1846, the results of Mary Ann's exertions appeared in three volumes as *The Life of Jesus, Critically Examined by Friedrich Strauss*, published by Chapman Brothers of London. The translator was never mentioned and the two years' work earned her only twenty pounds, but what mattered most to her was that she had succeeded. Thereafter her future was to be in writing in some form, for in a perverse way she had enjoyed the intellectual stimulus. What also mattered to Mary Ann was that writing was a job which could be undertaken from home; duty demanded she remain there and care for her father for the rest of his days. This was a sacred obligation she never considered shirking.

As a diversion during the endless Strauss translation, the Brays took Mary Ann to dine with one of their relatives. Harriet Martineau, famed as a journalist and novelist on both sides of the Atlantic, was distantly related to Cara through the marriage of Harriet's brother to Cara's cousin. Miss Martineau, herself unmarried, was in her early forties in the spring of 1845 when she was introduced to the twenty-five-year-old Mary Ann Evans. The meeting was quickly forgotten by the older woman, but made a lasting impression on the junior. Mary Ann was already well acquainted with Miss Martineau's magazine writing, which frequently dealt with controversial subjects like working-class education, trade unionism and population control. Miss Martineau also deplored the way any woman who had taken the trouble to educate herself was labelled a 'blue-stocking' and singled out as a freak of nature. She argued instead that girls should be given a wide education so that those who did not marry could support themselves instead of being a burden on their relatives, a sentiment which earned Mary Ann's whole-hearted support.

From Cara Mary Ann heard that the eminent novelist came from a similar provincial background to her own. Born in Norwich, she had educated herself and determined to make her own way in the world by writing. Miss Martineau, however, had the complication of severe deafness which necessitated her carrying round an ungainly ear-trumpet. Those meeting her for the first time were often disconcerted to find a huge ivory cup thrust into their faces whenever Miss Martineau wanted them to make conversation. It was all too reminiscent of 'a churchwarden stepping with his collecting plate in front of one at church, where one would like to be generous in the face of the congregation but cannot find one's purse', a visitor recalled.[12] Mary Ann suffered no such inhibitions when she met the woman and indeed pronounced her charming. By contrast with the Robert Owen encounter, Mary Ann thought Harriet Martineau 'one of those great people whom one does not venerate the less for having seen'.[13]

Throughout the dinner party all the great lady could talk about was her 'wonder cure'. After years of being crippled by a painful gynaecological ailment, Harriet Martineau had been mesmerized and her problems had vanished. As an expert on the subject, Charles Bray was in his element, holding forth all evening about his own experiences of mesmerism and clairvoyance, so that Cara and Mary Ann found themselves relegated to the ranks of interested bystanders. Before they left, Charles begged the honour of examining Miss Martineau phrenologically, but what interpretation he gave the novelist is not known. Privately he confided to Cara and Mary Ann that he had been disappointed with Miss Martineau's small ordinary-looking head and wondered how such a poor specimen could have achieved so much.[14]

Though Mary Ann wanted to hear about Harriet Martineau's spectacular cure, she also hoped to learn how the novelist had started writing articles for the *Monthly Repository* magazine and been able to progress to the prestigious *Westminster Review*. In the event, all she could glean was that the move to London had been crucial to Miss Martineau's career. If she had stayed in Norwich, she was heard to say, she would never have made any headway as a writer. That was depressing to Mary Ann, committed to staying in Coventry with her father. It did however sow a seed in her mind. When she was eventually released from her filial duties, there was never any doubt in Mary Ann's mind but that she should go to London.

A year after that meeting, Mary Ann was unexpectedly offered an opening in journalism by Charles Bray. While she was engaged in checking the final proofs of her Strauss translation, he was buying the local newspaper. The Coventry *Herald* was a weekly paper established at the beginning of the century as a radical counterweight to the Tory Coventry *Standard*. Lured by the prospect of being able to broadcast his views to an even wider audience, Bray began an additional career as a newspaper proprietor in June 1846. Mary Ann was the obvious choice for Bray's assistant because she had already proved her worth in compiling lecture notes and, with her first book behind her, was naturally looking for another outlet.

Initially Bray asked her to undertake the book reviews but soon extended her job to include a regular weekly column. Under the heading 'Poetry and Prose, From the Notebook of an Eccentric', Mary Ann wrote a series of articles on assorted subjects, purporting to be extracts from the pocket book of an old friend. It was a clever device because it gave her the freedom to write on any subject which took her fancy without running short of material. As was customary, articles were anonymous, but even at this early stage in her writing career, Mary Ann Evans found it advisable to hint that the author was a man.

Since Mary Ann's journalism for the Coventry *Herald* between 1846 and 1849 was anonymous, it is difficult to be sure which articles can be attributed to her. Those positively identified contain a noticeably satirical element. One humorous article entitled 'Hints on Snubbing' reassures readers that there is always somebody lower down the social scale who can be snubbed, for at the bottom the shoe-black may snub the dog and cat in a variety of ingenious ways. Editors of provincial newspapers can always snub their opponents, the writer continued gleefully, knowing that Bray regularly abused his opposite number through the columns of his paper. None of her articles are outstanding in style or content, but they are quite respectable newspaper contributions and marked the next stage in the evolution of the novelist.

Although Mary Ann had succeeded in discovering an outlet for her talents, she had not found an ideal one for her affections. Much as she loved Bray, there was no future in that relationship and her family continued to make her aware of the terrible disgrace of spinsterhood. Though she railed against their persistent attempts to introduce her to 'suitable' husbands, she had to admit that she did find men irresistible. In any gathering she would be found talking to the men rather than the women and, when challenged, she claimed most women she met were boring whereas most men were well read and took an interest in life outside the home. There was much truth in what she said, but an equally compelling reason, which she of course never mentioned, was sexual attraction. Several years earlier Maria Lewis had complained

that Mary Ann was obsessed by the opposite sex.[15] Then she had
retaliated with the thrust that it was a pity Maria's only interest was
minding other people's business. However, when Sara Hennell also
made similar comments, Mary Ann was forced to consider their
words. Though Charles could get away with love-affairs all over the
place, he was male and such freedoms were not permitted for a
woman. She would have to try and find love within the conventional
framework of marriage.

Mary Ann's cynicism about the state of matrimony was matched by
the lack of suitable male partners. Cara did her best for her friend by
taking her into the society of free-thinkers in Coventry in the hope
that that might produce a husband. She also took her to stay with her
family in London and invited Mary Ann to accompany them on an
annual summer holiday, all without result.

Cara was not the only person who thought they ought to help Mary
Ann find a man. Her half-sister Fanny, married to a bailiff and living
near Coventry, decided that this younger sister would be less
troublesome if she had a husband to control her. In the spring of 1845
Fanny invited her sister to stay for a few days and contrived to
introduce her to a local man who was restoring pictures up at the hall.

'They passed two days in each other's company, and she thought
him the most interesting young man she had seen and superior to
all the rest of mankind,' Cara reported to Sara in a flurry of
excitement.

> The third morning he made proposals through her brother in law
> Mr Hooton [sic] – saying, 'she was the most fascinating creature he
> had ever beheld, that if it were not too presumptuous to hope etc
> etc, a person of such superior excellence and powers of mind, etc',
> in short, he seemed desperately smitten and begged permission to
> write to her. She granted this, and came to us so brimful of
> happiness; – though she said she had not fallen in love with him yet,
> but admired his character so much she was sure she should: the only
> objection seemed to be that his profession – a picture-restorer – is
> not lucrative or over-honourable. We liked his letters to her very
> much – simple, earnest, unstudied.[16]

Though the love-affair looked promising, for the young man was
extremely eager to marry Miss Evans and visited her home to be
vetted by her father, Mary Ann took fright.[17] Events were passing out

of her control. Fanny had selected the man, her father had approved him and arrangements were going ahead though she felt she hardly knew him. As she had seen happen so often to others, she found herself being pressured into marriage. She wrote to tell him that she feared she had misled him and wished their relationship to cease. Crossing with her letter came one from the suitor making formal application to Mr Evans for his daughter's hand in marriage. To put an end to the matter once and for all, Mary Ann explained to her father that at their last meeting the gentleman in question had behaved so strangely, she was sure there was madness in his family. She therefore could not possibly go through with the engagement.

With the benefit of hindsight, it is clear that Mary Ann made the right decision, though it cost her some painful migraine headaches and much heartache. For some time afterwards she pondered the unfortunate affair and regretted her hasty decision; should the man come wooing again, she decided she would accept. Only by marrying could she put an end to the continual family pressure and relieve herself of uncertainty about her future after her father died.

She began to fear it would be her lot to experience passion vicariously, only through the novels of George Sand. The writings of the daring French woman, who dressed mannishly, smoked cigars and took lovers as freely as a man drew Mary Ann's admiration. George Sand's novels were not considered respectable reading matter. When they appeared in England in the 1840s they could be read only by those with a knowledge of French. Suggestions that these 'erotic' novels should be translated into English were firmly resisted on the grounds that they would lead to mass profligacy if they became accessible to ladies. Those women like Mary Ann, who had taught themselves French to a high enough standard to be able to read Sand's novels in the vernacular, could hardly be considered ladies. It was George Sand's concern with the relationship between a man and a woman, 'with love – nothing but love' as Sand put it, which upset some Victorians. But for Mary Ann Evans, George Sand's writing was both liberating and reassuring because it proved she was not alone in questioning convention. Many of Sand's novels highlighted the evils of a marriage system which removed a woman's rights and left her no better than a slave. As if vindicating Mary Ann's rejection of the picture-restorer, Sand maintained it was immoral for a man or a woman to enter into marriage with a person they did not love, and, more contentiously, she argued that a woman had the right to give her body to whom she chose and only for as long as she loved that person.

Mary Ann was elated by such bold writing and referred to Sand as 'my divinity'. She had discovered a woman who shared her concern about socialism, revolution and, more particularly, the inherent immorality of a marriage system which could bind two people together in an intimate physical union without any concern for the union of their minds.

Sara Hennell did not share Mary Ann's desire to read about the passionate struggles of a woman and a man, and Cara found George Sand rather strong meat for her palate. Charles Bray could be relied on to share Mary Ann's enjoyment in Sand's work, because the novelist was only stating in writing what he had been practising for years – namely the right of the heart, not the law, to dictate personal relationships. Discussions about the idealism and immorality inherent in the writings of George Sand occupied the quarterly magazines equally as much as they did Charles and Mary Ann whilst walking Bray's spaniels over the Radford fields.

One of the chief supporters of the French novelist in the press was George Henry Lewes. He proclaimed her as the most remarkable writer of the century and defended her writings against English critics' charges of immorality: 'Because she was herself unhappy in marriage,' he wrote, 'people assumed that she wrote against it; the truth being that she advocated marriage, but not its abuses' (prophetic words indeed from someone who was to find himself trapped in an unhappy marriage).[18] Long before they met, Mary Ann found herself in total agreement with this anonymous writer who so vigorously defended George Sand.

Mary Ann also enjoyed reading *Jane Eyre*, published in 1847 under the authorship of Currer Bell. Some suspected that the author was a woman masquerading as a man, but Mary Ann was more concerned about the relationship between the man and woman in the book than about the sex of the author, and took exception to the way Currer Bell dwelt on the sanctity of marriage. Commenting on Mr Rochester's faithfulness to his mad wife Bertha, she told Bray: 'All self-sacrifice is good – but one would like it to be in a somewhat nobler cause than that of a diabolical law which chains a man soul and body to a putrefying carcase.'[19]

Ironically, while Mary Ann was questioning a law which did not permit divorce, George Henry Lewes was busy writing to Currer Bell with the sole intention of unmasking the author as a woman. In the *Edinburgh Review* he announced: 'It is now scarcely a secret that Currer Bell is the pseudonym of a woman', and went on to criticize the book for being coarse, masculine and unladylike. Not surprisingly Charlotte Brontë was furious at such prejudice and what she regarded as treachery: 'After I had said earnestly that I wished critics would judge me as an *author*, not as a woman, you so roughly – I even thought so cruelly – handled the question of sex. I dare say you meant no harm and perhaps you will now be able to understand why I was so grieved,' she wrote back to him.[20] But Lewes never fully understood Charlotte Brontë's annoyance until faced with similar attempts to unmask George Eliot.

When Lewes did meet Charlotte Brontë at a dinner party in London in 1850, he amusingly described her in terms which he might well have applied to Mary Ann Evans: 'a little, plain, provincial, sickly-looking old maid'. Nevertheless he was impressed by her: 'What passion, what fire in her!' he was to say, 'quite as much as in George Sand, only the clothing is less voluptuous.' The quiet vicar's daughter from Yorkshire was not endeared to this extrovert who leaned across the table and said knowingly to her, 'There ought to be a bond of sympathy between us, Miss Brontë, for we have both written naughty books.'[21]

'Naughty books' had to be set aside in 1848 as did much else for Mary Ann found her time fully taken up with nursing her father. She received little assistance from her brothers or sisters and any time she spent away from him was resented. When Cara had taken Mary Ann off to Scotland for a holiday in 1845, knowing her friend to be desperately in need of a break, they arrived in Edinburgh to find a letter waiting for them from Isaac. Mary Ann must return immediately as her father had fallen and broken his leg, and needed Mary Ann to look after him. None of Robert Evans's other four children ever offered to assist with their father; Mary Ann was unmarried and therefore it was her job. As her father's health deteriorated, she had to give him mustard baths, keep him entertained by reading aloud and take some responsibility for the business papers which arrived at the house.

In the twelve months before his death in June 1849, Mary Ann gave up all thought of herself and her future and nursed a man who was not the easiest of patients. There were times when she complained bitterly about her lot and sent angry letters to her brothers and sisters, but then had to write and apologize. After the complaining and the depression, Mary Ann entered a period of calm, finding pleasure in caring for her father; 'the one strong deep love I have ever known', she wrote sadly.[22] As her father grew weaker he became less cantankerous and more appreciative of her efforts; but, as Cara remarked with great perception, 'he takes opportunities now of saying kind things to M. A., contrary to his wont. Poor girl, it shows how rare they are by the gratitude with which she repeats the commonest expressions of kindness.'[23]

During the night of 31 May 1849 Robert Evans died at the age of seventy-eight, and Mary Ann was free. At that moment she did not see it that way, for at twenty-nine she feared life had passed her by. 'It is so in all the stages of life – the poetry of girlhood goes – the poetry of love and marriage – the poetry of maternity – and at last the very poetry of duty forsakes us . . . it seems to me as if I were shrinking into that mathematical abstraction, a point.'[24]

CHAPTER 7

Metamorphosis, 1849–1850

The death of Robert Evans destroyed the core of Mary Ann's existence. Gone was the person she loved above any other; gone was her purpose in life, even her very home. Isaac made it clear to Mary Ann that she must now look to her own devices. The family had done their best for this recalcitrant member who had persistently resisted their efforts on her behalf; they could not be expected to do any more. The house, which Isaac had always felt to be an absurd extravagance, was promptly placed in the hands of agents to be re-let, and work began on apportioning out the furniture as Robert Evans's will dictated.

The bulk of the estate was divided between Robert Evans's two sons. Robert, the elder son, was then forty-seven, and he inherited the Derbyshire properties which he had administered for his father for many years. Similarly, Isaac at the age of thirty-three gained possession of the cottages and farms his father had been accumulating in Warwickshire. At a stroke both Evans sons were set up as small landowners with both freehold and leasehold estates and went on to build up little empires of their own.

As was customary, the daughters of the family fared less well in their father's will. Each was assigned a thousand-pound settlement on their marriage (in the case of Fanny and Chrissey this had already been taken up). Having seen the shocking way in which Edward Clarke had run through Chrissey's dowry, Robert Evans had taken the exceptional step of stipulating that the thousand pounds payable in the event of Mary Ann's marriage would be independent of any husband she might marry and not be subject to his debts, control or engagement.[1]

The lesson to be drawn from Chrissey's experiences had made a deep impression not just on Robert Evans, but on Mary Ann as well. Only when her father's will was read out did she become aware of the true extent of her brother-in-law's debts. In addition to the marriage settlement it was Robert Evans's intention to leave each daughter a further thousand pounds invested to yield a small annual income that would prevent any of them ever being left destitute. In Fanny's case there were no complications, but when it came to Chrissey, no legacy was available. Her husband had an outstanding loan of eight hundred pounds from Robert Evans on which neither interest nor capital had ever been paid. The resultant debt added to the rent on their premises in Meriden, which it transpired had also been paid by her father for the last seven years, more than exceeded Chrissey's inheritance. The only good thing to come out of Robert Evans's will from the Clarkes' point of view was the wiping-out of the excess.

Not having required her dowry, Mary Ann inherited two thousand pounds from her father's estate. This money was to be invested, with the trustees making twice-yearly payments to her. The fact that Isaac was one of the trustees proved a bugbear, for whenever she offended him, he delighted in exercising his power by arranging the transfer of this vital money as slowly as possible. Though Robert Evans left his other daughters some family mementoes – Fanny receiving silver forks and his prized set of Walter Scott novels, Chrissey silver spoons and her mother's two-volume Bible – Mary Ann was not permitted any such relics. As the one who had stayed at home the longest and devoted her life to her father, she was hurt by his apparent heartlessness.

After her father's funeral, Mary Ann was utterly bewildered. The months of twenty-four-hour nursing, the lack of sleep and the emotional stress of losing her father had left her numb. Her family seemed to present a blank wall. Isaac moved round the Foleshill house assessing the value of the contents and arranging for their speedy disposal; Fanny continued to show detachment towards Mary Ann because she did not want her half-sister to consider billeting herself on the Houghton household at Baginton, and Chrissey, the only one to show her any warmth, was bowed down with her own family problems and yet another pregnancy.

With great thoughtfulness Charles Bray appeared on the scene, collected up Mary Ann and her few possessions and took her to stay at Rosehill. He guessed how upsetting it must be for her to sit there while the house was emptied around her by unsympathetic brothers, and he invited her to make her home with himself and Cara for as long as she wanted. Gratefully she leaned on Charles and allowed herself to be organized. For so long she had shouldered the responsibility of the house, her father's welfare, even his business commitments towards the end. Total abdication was bliss.

In the warm atmosphere of Rosehill, Mary Ann passively accepted the Brays' plans to take her away to the Continent. Having often heard her speak wistfully of such a thing, Cara suggested this might be the opportune time for her to realize her ambition. Charles planned the itinerary around places he had heard Mary Ann mention. Paris was the obvious choice because she had heard accounts of the city from Miss Rebecca Franklin and the Brays, and was convinced it must be the centre of European culture. Her daydreams had also incorporated Switzerland after reading George Sand's dramatic accounts of the country in *Lettres d'un Voyageur*. 'O the bliss of having a very high attic in a romantic continental town, such as Geneva,' Mary Ann had fantasized only the previous year.[2] Since most large European towns were connected by railway, it was realistic to consider travelling through several countries in the space of a few weeks.

Forestalling any arguments Mary Ann might raise about the cost of the expedition, Bray pointed out that it was possible to live more cheaply on the Continent than in England. She might also consider the tour an investment in her future since it would improve her languages and enable her to undertake further translating or obtain a high-quality teaching post. All of this was apart from the obvious curative effects such a change of scenery and air would impart.

Still in a trance, Mary Ann obeyed. Foreseeing that their friend might prove a trying companion in her emotionally charged state, the Brays tried to arrange for others to join the tour. Sara wanted to but could not take time off from governessing, and though Cara's beloved Edward Noel did agree, he backed out at the last minute as did several other seasoned travellers. In the end Charles and Cara had to cope with Mary Ann by themselves for nearly six weeks, as she alternated between miserable inertia and peevish fault-finding.

The trio crossed the Channel on 6 June 1849, five days after Robert Evans's funeral, and headed for Paris. After two days in the French capital they worked their way down to the south of France and into Signor Brezzi's homeland of northern Italy, which Mary Ann had often expressed interest in visiting. From there they journeyed across the Alps into Switzerland, intending to come up through Germany and back to England. Cara soon realized the folly of their decision to bring Mary Ann away so soon after her bereavement for, despite the spectacular scenery, she remained oblivious to her surroundings. Not until they reached Switzerland late in July did anything permeate her shell of indifference; as they emerged from a mountain pass into a breathtaking valley she stood and drank in the view: 'It seemed to me like an entrance into heaven,' she was to write later in her short story 'The Lifted Veil'. Four days were spent wandering round Geneva, followed by a leisurely progress round the Swiss lakes before they started the journey home.

Talk of home suddenly brought Mary Ann to life and she demanded that Charles take her back to Geneva. She was not going back to Coventry, she said imperiously, she wanted to stay in Switzerland. It came as a relief to the Brays that their morose fellow traveller had come alive and reached some decision about her immediate future, albeit an unexpected one. As demanded, Charles escorted her back to Geneva, while Cara rested at the far end of the lake. He found her a respectable *pension*, ensured that she had sufficient funds and stayed long enough to see her settled before he collected Cara and headed back to England.

It was very brave of Mary Ann on her first visit to Europe to decide to stay on alone in a strange country where she knew no one and, though well read in literary French, had considerable difficulty in understanding French as spoken by the Swiss. In fact she acted impulsively with no consideration of how she would pass her time, nor how long she would stay. All she knew was that she did not want to go back to Coventry.

With plenty of tourists in Geneva that summer, Mary Ann was not as isolated as might be thought. Her subsequent letters to the Brays describe the English and American guests in the *pension* like a Victorian *Hôtel du Lac*. The sombre spinster, thin and pale and dressed in heavy mourning, spent her time sitting in the drawing room or down by the shore watching her fellow guests; the future novelist with a keen eye for detail and a sympathy for the little foibles of human nature penned to her friends at Rosehill glorious thumbnail sketches of the inmates of the Campagne Plongeon during the late summer of 1849. Despite her own morbid state the characters tumble out of her letters with a wonderful sense of the ridiculous. There is the middle-aged American lady, 'kind but silly', with her daughter, 'silly but not kind', and 'both of them chatter the most execrable French with amazing volubility and self-complacency. They are very rich, very smart, and very vulgar,' Mary Ann decided as she observed the two women engage in a one-upmanship contest with an elderly English woman.[3]

Then there was Madame la Marquise, 'a very good-natured person evidently, but she has the voice almost of a market-woman', with her husband the squinting Marquis, 'the most well-bred, harmless of men. He talks very little – every sentence seems a terrible gestation, and comes forth fortissimo,' Mary Ann noticed.[4] Other amusing vignettes filled her letters to the Brays and gave them cause to hope that their miserable fellow traveller was regaining her old spirit.

Those who saw the silent figure at the *pension* were not attracted to her. One guest told Mary Ann later that when she first set eyes on her, she thought: 'That is a grave lady. I do not think I shall like her much.'[5] Another elderly matron decided that some marriage counselling might not come amiss and warned Miss Evans that too much study was bad for her. It gave others the impression she was a cold person. Most of the visitors to the *pension* appear to have had no other interest than watching other guests and telling them what was good for them. Mary Ann was the recipient of all kinds of unsolicited advice. The Marquise decided that her appearance was all wrong and tried to smarten up the dowdy spinster by insisting she send home for her best dress. Equally the French woman thought something had to be done about Mary Ann's outdated hairstyle. Wearing the hair parted in the centre and dressed in ringlets might have been fashionable in the Regency period, but this was the middle of the nineteenth century. As Mary Ann reported to Cara, the Marquise 'has abolished all my curls and made two things stick out on each side of my head, like those on the head of the Sphinx. All the world says I look infinitely better so I comply, though to myself I seem uglier than ever – if possible.'[6]

The interest in her appearance and her welfare made a welcome diversion for Mary Ann for a while, but soon the triviality of these strangers' concerns irritated her and she longed to be rid of them. Increasingly she took walks alone by the lakeside and tried to discourage conversation by burying her head in a book or keeping to her room. She became rude and disdainful of the pathetic small-talk over meals and everyone's continual obsession with everybody else's business. She was clearly feeling better and it was time to move. Mary Ann still refused to contemplate Coventry: 'I have no yearnings to exchange lake and mountain for Bishop Street and the Radford Fields,' she told the Brays, requesting instead that her boxes of books be sent out to Switzerland so that she could make use of her freedom to study.[7] Her new address, she told them, would be 107, rue des Chanoines, for she had found herself new lodgings. As she departed from the Campagne Plongeon at the beginning of October, one elderly English woman, whom Mary Ann thought a shrewd judge of character, said prophetically, 'You'll be quite another person if you get some introductions to clever people – you'll get on well among a certain set, that's true.'[8]

At that time Mary Ann had no desire to belong to any set; she merely asked to be left alone so that she could heal emotionally. As she began to feel stronger and take notice of life around her, she thought about the family she had left in Warwickshire. Though she had written regularly to each in turn during her travels and sent them the address of the *pension*, she had received only silence. Worried lest some tragedy might have befallen one of them, Mary Ann asked Charles Bray to visit Fanny Houghton and report back. The answer came back that Fanny presumed Isaac would write to his sister. Weeks turned into months and still there was no word from any of them. 'I suffer greatly from it,' Mary Ann wrote, as she bombarded Fanny with yet another letter.[9] Eventually it was Chrissey who broke the silence with a sad note which apologized for not writing sooner, but her children had had scarlet fever. The letter went on to explain that seven-year-old Clara, Chrissey's eldest daughter, had died of the disease and the rest of the children were ill. Though nothing so heartrending was happening to Isaac or Fanny, their correspondence was infrequent and cold. 'It is five months at least since I heard from you,' Mary Ann protested to Fanny. 'Are you too ill, or too wretched or too indifferent to write to me?'[10] When Mary Ann departed for the Continent, the Evans family had thankfully shelved the problem she presented and had no wish to encourage her back home again.

In marked contrast to the indifference of her own family, Mary Ann found she was the centre of attention at her new lodgings. By chance

thinkers. It was Sara's remarks about meeting Harriet Martineau again which reminded Mary Ann of the novelist's insistence that it was necessary to live in London in order to get literary work. Sara was detailed to find out the charges at Mr Chapman's boarding house because Mary Ann had decided to try her luck in the capital.

Once in England Mary Ann headed for Rosehill and four days' rest while she steeled herself for the visit to Griff House and Isaac. The promised warm welcome was a profound disappointment; Mary Ann told Fanny that she was made to feel more of an outcast at Griff than she had all the time she had been in Geneva. 'O the dismal weather and the dismal country and the dismal people. It was some envious demon that drove me across the Jura to come and see people who don't want me,' she lamented. [16]

It was, however, a new Mary Ann, or rather Marian, as she now decided to call herself, who had returned from the Continent. Her time in a strange country had proved to her that she could survive without the rest of the Evans family and be happier. 'I am delighted to feel that I am of no importance to any of them, and have no motive for living amongst them,' Marian wrote defiantly. [17] After thirty years of being at other people's beck and call, the time had arrived for her to control her own life.

CHAPTER 8

The Wicked *Westminster*, 1851

T here could not have been a more exciting time to be in London than 1851, when the eyes of the nation were focused on its capital. In an article at the beginning of May *The Times* enthused with some hyperbole about 'a sight the like of which has never happened before, and which in the nature of things, can never be repeated', claiming it to be 'the first morning since the creation of the world that all peoples have assembled from all parts of the world and done a common act'. It was in this mood of celebration that Her Majesty Queen Victoria opened 'The Exhibition of the Works of Industry of all Nations' on 1 May that year.

The immense exhibition, housed in what *Punch* christened the Crystal Palace, captured public imagination. The glass pavilion itself was remarkable: it stretched a third of a mile along Prince's Gate, towered above the other buildings and covered fully twenty-six acres of Hyde Park, incorporating even the old elm trees which grew in that part of the park. A crowd of twenty-five thousand gathered round the sovereign for the solemn service of dedication and a further six million reportedly passed through its doors during the six months the exhibition was open. The vast display of British and colonial goods – and to a lesser extent goods from other foreign parts – symbolized the mood of mid-nineteenth century pride abroad in the country, typified also by Edwin Landseer's painting 'Monarch of the Glen' exhibited the same year. Britain was congratulating itself on successfully weathering the threat of revolution which had rocked many European states. Chartist agitation had died down and, since the repeal of the Corn Laws three years previously, general peace and prosperity had settled on the country.

Marian Evans was infected with a similar optimism when she went to London on 8 January 1851 fresh from her stay in Warwickshire, where conversation had been dominated by the Great Exhibition and the selection of ribbons to display on the Bray stand. Another subject discussed that Christmas was Marian's future; Charles Bray's enthusiasm and confidence bolstered her determination to seek work in the capital. It had been his efforts the previous autumn which had secured her a commission to write for a national periodical. Bray had recommended to the publisher John Chapman that Marian was the best person to review *The Progress of the Intellect, as Exemplified in the Religious Development of the Greeks and Hebrews*, written by Robert Mackay and recently published by Chapman. She was delighted to be entrusted with the task, completed it promptly and took the initiative to deliver the manuscript in person. Once in London she decided to remain a further fortnight to discover whether this was really where she wanted to live. On previous London visits, Marian had stayed with the Hennells but this time she sampled Mrs Chapman's boarding house in the Strand, the same building from which John Chapman operated his publishing and bookselling businesses. The accommodation proved comfortable, the company most congenial, so it was settled that Marian should return in the new year for several weeks to hunt for work.

In this Marian Evans was consciously following in the steps of Harriet Martineau, who had once boarded with the Chapmans and still visited the family regularly. Like her, Marian was able to go to London with some publishing achievements behind her. There were the Strauss translation five years previously, and miscellaneous articles for the Coventry *Herald*, but, far more impressively, Marian could now say that, like Harriet Martineau, she had written for the *Westminster Review* because the January 1851 issue carried her review of Mackay's book. Chapman, as good as his word, had secured a place for the review in one of the leading quarterlies and further promised Bray that should his protégée Miss Evans choose to come to London he would help her find work. It was this offer which finally tempted her to take the plunge. John Chapman's friendship was worth a great deal because he had many acquaintances among the London literati and his regular weekly parties were attended by many well-known writers and radicals from Europe and America, as well as Britain.

When Marian exchanged the pure air and tranquillity of Rosehill for the smoke and bustle of the Strand in 1851, it was like entering another world. The London street was a hive of activity, a noisy thoroughfare where horses, carriages and carts clattered past the house all day and half the night. Pea-soup fogs were a part of everyday life for half the year, followed by an appalling stench from the drains – or lack of them – during the warmer months. Mrs John Chapman's boarding house, upstairs from the bookshop, blended in between Twinings the tea merchants and a fishmonger's who displayed an appetizing selection of eels wriggling on the slab. On the opposite side of the road was the Lyceum Theatre and the offices of the *Economist* newspaper, originally founded as the mouthpiece for the Anti-Corn Law League. Sustained only by cocoa, bread and cheese given him by the proprietor's wife, a sad little specimen of humanity swept the crossing in front of Chapman's bookshop.[1] One of the first warnings Marian received on her arrival was not to go into the side streets, for even in daylight women could be seen brawling and men sprawled out in a drunken stupor. After dark, who knew what horrors lurked there?

Mrs Chapman's advertisement offered 'Board and Residence at 142, Strand. 10 doors west of Somerset House', with the guarantee that 'sleeping rooms are all quite free from noise. . . . The central position of the House (midway between the City and West End, near the Theatres and Houses of Parliament, and within reach of the Thames Steamers and of Omnibuses to all parts of the Metropolis) affords peculiar facilities to Strangers and all who wish to economise their time.'[2] Just how peculiar those facilities were, Marian was later to discover, but her first impression was one of amazement at the sheer size of the house, for it was six storeys high with a further three floors below ground level. Originally 142 Strand had been built as an inn with extensive accommodation for lodgers. When a licence was refused, the proprietor hanged himself and the lease was disposed of at a much reduced price. Mrs Chapman, preferring not to advertise the suicide association, described the building as 'having been recently built for a First Class Hotel'. Most floors comprised nine rooms because the building was three rooms wide and three deep. This made for some very dark rooms in the middle which were lit by the ingenious method of having a skylight in the ceiling and a glass panel in the floor. The overall effect was gloomy, as Marian found out. She described being in a 'dim abode like a potato in a cellar' for her room had 'the light one might expect midway up a chimney, with a little blaze of fire below, and a little glimmer of sky above'.[3] These, however, were Mrs Chapman's second-class bedrooms costing two pounds five shillings a week full board – fires, boot cleaning and wines extra. Now in control of her own finances and acutely aware of their limitations, Marian was thrifty. She had to find herself work in London or her stay would be very short indeed.

The day following her arrival, Marian was flattered to find John Chapman seeking her out as a fellow writer for her opinions on the new novel by Eliza Lynn he was proposing to publish. He would particularly value Marian's views on 'a love scene which is warmly and vividly depicted, with a tone and tendency which I entirely disapprove', asking also whether she thought the passages might excite those of a sensual nature.[4] Such explicit questions from a man she hardly knew came as a surprise to Marian but, used to frank discussions at Rosehill, she was not embarrassed. She found it just as easy to discuss sexual matters with Chapman as she had with Charles Bray; indeed Chapman treated her even more as an equal than her Coventry friend had. The tone of their friendship was set from the beginning. To her delight, Marian found that though she had come in search of journalism, she was being given an insight into the day-to-day workings of a publishing house, invited to read manuscripts, to give an assessment of their worth and to accompany Mr Chapman on visits to authors.

What was even more to Marian's taste was the large amount of personal attention she received. Before her arrival Chapman had made a special point of enquiring about the rent of a piano for her room despite there already being one in the drawing room; when the train came in from Coventry, he was on the platform to greet her; a few days later he took time off from business to go with her to select a piano; the next morning he was to be found sitting in her room listening to her rendition of Mozart's Masses. Chapman also told her how envious he was of her linguistic abilities and how he longed to know German. Eager to please him, Marian offered to give him twice-weekly lessons in the language in her room. Chapman gratefully presented her with a season ticket for Newman's Geometry lectures at the Ladies College in Bedford Square as a token of his thanks. As it happened he too proposed to attend these excellent lectures and would be delighted to escort her. The pace of London life was clearly different from that in the provinces for all these events took place during Marian's first week in the Strand.

Marian was totally captivated by her host and responded warmly to his attentions. John Chapman was aged twenty-nine, two years her junior, over six foot tall, dark-eyed and extremely handsome. What endeared him to people was his charismatic personality. John Chapman and Charles Bray had much in common: both were extrovert and possessed an over-developed social conscience which attracted them to money-losing causes. But Chapman had none of Bray's arrogance or abrasiveness and consequently made fewer enemies. The two men shared the same flexible attitude to matrimonial ties, which in Chapman's case earned him various nicknames. Some called him the 'Raffaelle bookseller', others, taking into account his dashing looks and penchant for women, labelled him 'Byron'. In the Chapman family he was known as 'Straley Jack' to distinguish him from another cousin called John Chapman, 'Straley' because in his late teens Chapman had gone to Adelaide, South Australia, and set himself up as a seller of watches, chronometers and sextants. Despite being the son of a Nottingham druggist, John had been apprenticed to a watchmaker in the town but ran off before the apprenticeship was completed. He went to join an elder brother who was studying medicine in Edinburgh. This gesture of fraternal affection was not appreciated and John was put on a boat to Australia with sufficient capital to make a new life 'down under'. This was shortlived. By the time he was twenty, Chapman appeared in Paris where he practised as a surgeon. 'Practise' would seem to be the operative word since he began his medical studies at the same time. The next year he was back in England as assistant to a surgeon in Derby, at the same time paying court to a woman fourteen years his senior with a considerable inheritance from her father's lace-manufacturing business.

Mrs Chapman's money financed the couple's move to London and John's purchase of a publishing house. That had not been his intention when he called at John Green's, publisher of theological and philosophical works, opposite Newgate Prison. What Chapman actually hoped was to persuade Mr Green to publish the manuscript of *Human Nature*, which he had just written, but Green wanted to sell the business and refused to take on any further work. Impulsively Chapman made an offer to buy the business and become his own publisher. It transpired that he had purchased a publishing house, a bookshop and ownership of the *Christian Teacher*, a Unitarian quarterly. After a short period living in Newgate Street, where ghoulish crowds assembled to watch the public executions, the Chapmans preferred the quiet of an East London home close to the Hennells. There they added a 'superior' boarding house – for ladies and gentlemen of a literary disposition –to their list of activities and began entertaining on a lavish scale. In the summer of 1844, Chapman transferred his home and business to 142 Strand in order to be at the heart of London publishing. At the same time, with an eye to transatlantic business, he made an arrangement with a bookseller in Boston, Massachusetts, to supply any English publications they required, and in return Messrs Little & Brown undertook to recommend 142 Strand as the ideal base for American literary visitors to London. The plan was enterprising and moderately successful, bringing the great philosopher Ralph Waldo Emerson to stay in the Strand for three months in 1847. Thereafter there was a steady trickle of American guests but never enough to ensure that the boarding house ran at a profit. If possible, Chapman let rooms out to groups who wanted a base in the capital; during Marian's early months at 142 Strand, the Chemical Society operated from two rooms on the first floor. Later Robert Owen made enquiries about renting the whole of the first floor for the Federation of American and English Socialism. To Marian's relief, the project fizzled out and she did not have to face the doddery radical. During the ten years the Chapmans lived in the Strand, they were as much haunted by money problems as their friends the Brays; both families saw their capital evaporate in pursuit of well-meaning but financially disastrous schemes.

When Marian arrived at the beginning of 1851, a year which augured well for those in the hotel business because of the likely number of visitors to the Great Exhibition, she was one of only three paying guests. The house needed to have ten or eleven boarders to run profitably, but most of the time there were only four or five. Other residents included John Chapman, his forty-one-year-old wife Susanna, two of their children (a third child born deaf and dumb was brought up by a relative in the country), an elderly invalid aunt of Mrs Chapman's who required constant nursing but died at the end of 1851, and various relatives who turned up for free holidays. But by far the most interesting resident was Elisabeth Tilley. She was thirty-one and occupied an ambiguous position in the hierarchy. According to Chapman she was the lady who superintended the housekeeping.[5] His daughter thought she was 'a kind of companion – mother's help, good in many ways but rather opinionated'.[6] Miss Tilley also undertook some light secretarial duties for the head of the household by way of reading letters and manuscripts aloud to him, but her true status was as his mistress. Mrs Chapman, who was fond of her charming but errant husband, had been obliged to accept the situation, just as Cara Bray had, and for the most part the *ménage à trois* existed fairly amicably. Elisabeth Tilley was not Chapman's first extramarital relationship and she was certainly not his last. Until his death at the age of seventy-three, the man they nicknamed 'Byron' conducted numerous affairs either with female lodgers whom he contrived to have accommodated in a room adjoining his own or with other paramours he entertained in rented rooms in the city. Later he abandoned all subterfuge and moved in with his mistress, leaving his family elsewhere. When his children were old enough to realize what was happening they tried to help their mother and arranged a legal separation for her. 'It was a bitter thing for two young people, both under twenty-one, to have to do,' his daughter recalled, 'but we believed we were right.'[7] In 1851, however, the children were not old enough to understand their father's philandering. All they noticed was that the servants were rude to Miss Tilley, and she had no interest in looking after children as she was supposed to.

Marian had been unaware of the 'peculiar facilities' afforded visitors to the boarding house when she stayed the previous autumn but received two unsolicited letters from Miss Tilley shortly before she returned the following January. The letters have not survived, nor are their contents known, but when John Chapman learned they had been sent he was furious with his mistress. Tension mounted when Marian arrived at the house clearly undeterred by Miss Tilley's warnings. It says much for Elisabeth Tilley's perception that she should have recognized a rival in the unattractive woman from the provinces. The following morning Elisabeth cornered her lover. In an hysterical outburst she accused him of spending an unnecessary amount of time in Miss Evans's room and she would not listen to his claim that it was all quite innocent. The mistress decided a dramatic gesture was called for and, though Marian had been in the house barely twenty-four hours, Elisabeth announced her departure. Further quizzing revealed that she was actually giving nine months' notice of her intentions – long enough to prevent anyone calling her bluff and long enough for Chapman to mend his ways and prevent her really having to leave.

This piece of pure theatre so soon after Marian's arrival was only one of a number of histrionic scenes which characterized her eleven-week stay. Further drama was only averted in the first week by the presence of Sara Hennéll in the house, staying for a few days to help her young friend settle in. Well known to all parties for her prim governessy air, Sara kept them all on their best behaviour, and their charming host Mr Chapman insisted on abandoning his business for a while to take the two guests (with a tactful invitation to Elisabeth as well) to view the growing metal skeleton in Hyde Park. By January the iron semi-circles which would form the lofty central arch of the Crystal Palace were already in position and bystanders could watch teams of shire horses haul up the immense iron girders to make the sides of the structure.

Once Sara Hennell departed so did everyone's veneer of politeness. John Chapman continued to pay marked attention to the new lodger, inviting her to accompany him to watch Mr Michael Faraday demonstrate the magnetism of oxygen at the Royal Society. Marian thought it marvellous. Once again she had a male escort to take her to scientific lectures. There was nothing unladylike about the excursion, she reassured Mrs Bray: 'You must know Faraday's lectures are as fashionable an amusement as the Opera – so there was a store of ladies.'[8] The females at 142 Strand were not bothered about how many other ladies were present; they objected to John devoting himself to Miss Evans for the whole evening. While Elisabeth Tilley displayed far more jealousy than Mrs Chapman, who had long ago accepted that she would have to share her husband, John now found himself being attacked from both sides.

During the second week of Marian's stay, Chapman, gloriously oblivious to female emotions, asked Miss Evans over the breakfast table whether she would like to go for a walk with him in the park. Only too aware of the hostile glare from the other women, Marian was evasive. Elisabeth Tilley did not miss her chance and jumped in with the comment that if John wanted to go for a walk, she would be pleased to accompany him, and as Chapman noted in his diary:

> I then invited Miss Evans again telling her E[lisabeth] would go whereupon she declined rather rudely, Susanna being willing to go out, and neither E[lisabeth] nor S[usanna] wishing to walk far I proposed they should go a short distance without me, which E[lisabeth] considered an insult from me and reproached me in no measured terms accordingly, and heaped upon me suspicions and accusations I do not in any way deserve. I was very severe and harsh, said things I was sorry for afterwards, and we became reconciled in the Park. Miss Evans apologized for her rudeness tonight, which roused all E[lisabeth]'s jealousy again and consequent bitterness.[9]

For the whole of the three months Marian was there similar little dramas were re-enacted. But, having backed down eight years earlier when challenged about her amorous behaviour with Dr Brabant, Marian stood her ground. Now thirty-one and for the first time on the verge of gaining both love and work, she was prepared to fight, especially as John Chapman confessed he felt great affection for her. It had never been Marian's plan to share a man with others, but she was philosophical about that; anything was better than nothing.

Chapman regularly played the women off against each other. It no doubt boosted his ego to have three women vying with each other for his favours. With apparent innocence he would relay a piece of gossip one had said about the other or contrive to show one woman a note written to him by another. It was a virtuoso performance and ensured that passions and tempers ran high most of the time. The resident women temporarily shelved their differences and united in an effort to push out the intruder. This was not such an easy task because Marian Evans was no shy little girl from the country to be frightened off, but a mature woman who had survived ten years of Evans opposition to emerge more self-confident than before. The declarations and more physical manifestations of love she received from John Chapman gave her all the strength she needed to fight back. Marian never employed Elisabeth's wildly exaggerated accusations and tearful floods, nor Susanna's threats and complaints; instead she drew herself up to her full height and became haughty. The intelligent, experienced writer with a private income lorded it over Miss Tilley 'the domestic' and used her superior linguistic powers to annihilate 'the landlady's' arguments. Her supercilious response ensured that the wrangling continued unabated. Through it all John Chapman watched from the sidelines, as a 'serene spectator' he said, recording in his diary that his wife and his mistress were comparing notes on the subject of his intimacy with Miss Evans and had arrived at the conclusion that they were completely in love with each other. 'E[lisabeth] being intensely jealous herself said all she could to cause S[usanna] to look from the same point of view, which a little incident (her finding me with my hand in M[arian]'s) had quite prepared her for. E[lisabeth] betrayed my trust and her own promise. S[usanna] said to me that if ever I went to M[arian]'s room again she will write to Mr Bray, and say that she dislikes her.'[10] Through all the upsets, Chapman calmly continued his early-morning astronomical observations, recording excitedly: 'Saw for the first time Venus and Jupiter through a telescope. The crescent form of Venus was distinctly visible.'[11] If dawn was taken up with Venus in all her guises, dusk was occupied with more literary pursuits: Chapman noted that he had reached Canto 8 of his old favourite, *Don Juan*.

Although Marian's avowed purpose during the winter months of 1851 was to find work, she expounded more energy in the pursuit of love than of journalism. Chapman used his influence as promised. He showed Empson, editor of the *Edinburgh Review*, the article she had written about Mackay's book and suggested a similar one might be in order for the *Edinburgh*, if not the identical subject, perhaps another discussing C. C. Hennell's *Inquiry*. Borrowing Marian's actual words, Chapman said the author was prepared to write for love not money. But even with Chapman promoting her case and disguising the disadvantage of her sex ('you will be pleased to see that Mr C spoke of me to Empson as a man', she told Bray), it was useless.[12] She was disheartened to have failed even to give her work away but could console herself that she was gaining a useful insight into the book world. Following one of the many *contretemps* with his wife, Chapman asked Marian to take over the editing of an historical novel he had just had thrown back at him.

At Chapman's Friday soirées Marian made contact with writers, radicals and even magazine editors, but no work resulted. One of the less attractive figures, however, came to pay her court. Robert Mackay, whose book Marian had reviewed for the *Westminster*, was in his early fifties and a wealthy academic, but he paid no attention to his dress and regularly turned up with a flannel waistcoat worn on the outside of his coat. A popular after-dinner anecdote circulated about him going round to collect money for Mazzini and the Freedom of Italy group. He looked so scruffy that one subscriber mistook him for one of the less fortunate and said, 'Now I should think, my friend, you're a man who has seen better days.' Says Mr Mackay, very mournfully, 'I think I see about as good days now as I deserve.'[13] Keen to develop the acquaintance he had made with Miss Evans the previous year Mackay became a frequent caller at 142 Strand with invitations for Marian to walk with him or, in the chaperoning company of the Chapmans, to dine at his house, 'and not content with this he came in the morning to make himself quite sure we were coming and to tell us that he had had his piano tuned', Marian told Cara with amusement.[14] This gentleman, who was working on a book concerned with the origins of all divinities, was to emerge later in George Eliot's novel *Middlemarch* as the tedious scholar the Reverend Edward Casaubon, who was engaged in compiling *The Key to All Mythologies*. Needless to say, Mr Mackay could not compete with John Chapman's charms in Marian's eyes and his suit came to nothing.

After increasingly acrimonious exchanges with the two women at 142 Strand, Marian decided that the London experiment had failed and wrote to Rosehill telling them she was coming home. In her final week in London she gave herself up to the enjoyment of theatre, opera, concerts and art exhibitions. John took her to a spectacular magic-lantern show at the Coliseum which, with the aid of musical effects and dissolving images, portrayed 'A Grand Moving Panorama of Lisbon, and the Earthquake in 1775'. Instead of the Great Exhibition, which had not yet opened, she had to content herself with 'The Great Globe' in Leicester Square, which the Chapman children insisted she visit. As John's daughter Beatrice recalled:

It was a great ball with a map of the world and a winding staircase going round and round it inside. There were galleries with cases containing goods belonging to the different countries. . . . We didn't much care for the Great Globe; we didn't think the world ought to be inside; and it was much hotter at the North Pole than at the Equator, which we thought most improper! The only things we liked were the volcanoes, which were made by little red lights.[15]

John escorted Marian to the train. There on the platform of Euston station, away from the eyes and ears of Elisabeth and Susanna, Marian gave herself up to tears and embraces, pleading with John for some statement of his feelings that would sustain her in his absence. The desired declaration of love was given, then ruined when John added that he still loved the other two as well but in a different way. All too soon the train arrived and a tearful Marian was taken away.

That was by no means the end of the affair from a personal or a professional point of view. Once she had departed, John did not forget her. He realized what a useful person had slipped through his hands. A letter went to Rosehill suggesting that Marian might like to compile *An Analytical Catalogue of Mr Chapman's Publications* containing a synopsis of each book; she would be paid for the task. Marian was pleased that something positive had resulted from the London visit, even if not a proper job. Matters might have proceeded smoothly had not Chapman in his inimitable fashion decided to pass Marian's letters to Susanna, and vice versa. All the old animosities surfaced and Marian refused to undertake the catalogue, even though she desperately wanted the work. It took all John's charm and persuasion to make her change her mind and then she told him: 'on condition that you state, or rather, I should hope, *restate* to Mrs C the fact that I am doing it, not because "I like" but in compliance with your request. You are aware that I never had the slightest wish to undertake the thing on my own account. If I continue it, it will be with the utmost repugnance, and only on the understanding that I shall accept no remuneration.'[16] It was a deliberately arrogant reply, but Marian knew that her letters were dissected by both the leading ladies of the house. Although brusque letters like this travelled back and forth, there were often enclosures destined for the eyes of one person only – intimate folded notes from Marian so 'inexpressively charming, so quick, intelligent and over-flowing with love and sweetness' that once read they had to go on the fire.[17]

Apart from his personal feelings, John needed Marian to remain well disposed towards him because he was in the process of buying the *Westminster Review* and was looking for some cheap labour. 'The Wicked *Westminster*', as the scientist T. H. Huxley dubbed it, had once been the most prestigious of quarterly magazines, with a tradition for radical outspokenness. Founded in 1828, the *Westminster* had been on a par with the *Edinburgh Review* and the *Quarterly* as one of the great triumvirate of Victorian quarterlies. The magazine's zenith had been around 1840, when, under the able editorship of the philosopher John Stuart Mill, it received a great deal of moral and financial support from those with a vested interest in maintaining an effective radical mouthpiece. Thereafter the magazine lost its cutting edge, and shortage of money began an ever tightening spiral of reduced payments to authors, lower-quality articles and difficulties in attracting sponsors. When Chapman evinced an interest in purchasing it, only three hundred pounds were necessary to make him the proprietor. If the buying was easy, financing production was another matter. Chapman needed not only money to launch his first issue in January 1852 but also contributors and subjects of sufficient stature to restore the magazine's reputation.

At the time of purchase, the *Westminster Review*'s circulation was around a thousand copies, while the highest it had ever reached was 1,620. At six shillings an issue and with a philosophical content, the quarterly's appeal was limited to intellectual, radical middle-class readers. With payments to authors running at three hundred and fifty pounds an issue, it never paid its way despite carrying some advertisements, and it had always been kept afloat by regular injections of capital from sponsors.

'Mr Chapman hopes to confirm and extend the influence of the *Review*, as the chief organ of liberal opinion, by engaging the co-operation of the highest talent and culture,' Chapman proclaimed, confident that his influential circle of friends would not only write but finance the journal.[18] With an optimism worthy of Bray, he drew up a four-year plan, at the end of which time he calculated the magazine would be profitable – a bold aim for an enterprise which had never balanced its books in its life. A newly founded radical weekly, the *Leader*, was already suffering a cash crisis, so it would have required some very convincing talking on Chapman's part to raise the two thousand pounds he calculated were necessary to launch his new-look *Westminster*. He wanted money loaned over four years, in return for which the sponsor would receive a free copy of the *Review* and, at the end of the four years, have his capital repaid along with interest from the profit the magazine had made.

To attract that amount of money, Chapman required an exceptionally good prospectus. This was where he thought Marian might be of help. Her editorial skills had impressed him earlier in the year and he was confident that he could charm her into writing the prospectus for love rather than cash, the latter being heavily committed. Close contact had been maintained ostensibly because of the catalogue of his publications she was producing. A few weeks after he had completed negotiations for the *Westminster*'s purchase – and persuaded the retiring editor to publish the article Miss Evans had tried to give him earlier in the year – Chapman took the train to Coventry, where he found Marian 'shy calm and affectionate' and the Brays fully occupied with their other house-guests.[19]

The visitors at Rosehill during May and June 1851 were Mr and Mrs Thornton Hunt, whose experience of co-operative living was of particular interest to Charles Bray. For four years the Hunts had shared a house in Bayswater named Phalanstery with Mrs Hunt's brother and wife and her sister and husband. There on a small scale the six practised a form of socialism expounded by the French theorist François Fourier. *Inter alia*, Fourier claimed that society would benefit if men and women lived together as equals, without the fetters of marriage. Any resultant children belonged to the group (the phalanstery), not the individual. These and other aspects of his philosophy were debated frequently at Rosehill, and Marian found Fourier's ideas far more attractive than those of Robert Owen. Ultimately Fourier communes proved no more successful than the Owenite ones and, after four years, those living in the Phalanstery had gone their separate ways.

Marian had met Thornton Hunt earlier in the year in London as one of the founders of the *Leader*. With offices near the Strand, he was a regular visitor at the Chapmans' both socially and professionally. The needs of the *Leader* made Hunt's stay at Rosehill necessarily brief, but his wife Kate stayed on with Cara for six weeks, during which she and Marian also became firm friends. Marian thought her 'the most thoroughly unaffected being' she had met.[20] Before Mr Hunt's return to the capital, Marian joined the husband and wife in some part singing to entertain the others. This harmonious picture of the Hunts' married life remained in her mind until John Chapman enlightened both Bray and herself as to the true state of affairs.

She had always agreed with Charles that what mattered most was that individuals should follow their natural inclinations in matters of the heart and not be dictated to by others. Mr Hunt's natural inclinations, she learned, had led him to give Mrs George Lewes, wife of his business partner, a son. Not only that, but it was rumoured that both she and Kate were now pregnant with his children.

In this very liberated atmosphere, Marian found that her intimacy with Chapman was accepted without comment. The two were left together and no one raised an eyebrow when they decided to leave a concert at the interval to go home together. Whether the affair between Marian and John Chapman ever developed into anything sexual is not recorded and can only be the subject of speculation. That discreet biography composed after Marian's death by her husband John Cross censored John Chapman out of existence. Undoubtedly there were some intimate exchanges between Marian and John which went beyond holding hands and precipitated Marian's return to Coventry in March. However, it is unlikely they had become lovers by then. It is much more likely to have happened in the conducive environment of Rosehill at the end of May and beginning of June 1851 when the days were 'warm and beautiful, with a strong and balmy breeze, and towards evening a beautiful clear sky', as John recorded lyrically.[21] He always presumed he could have a sexual relationship with his chosen female and could muster the most wonderful arguments, as his later seductive correspondence with Barbara Leigh Smith demonstrates.[22] He argued that chastity was an absurd contravention of natural laws and, drawing on his knowledge as a medical man, claimed that prolonged virginity was unhealthy. The female body was designed for motherhood and various ailments would arise if it did not fulfil this function. He also knew some reliable methods of preventing conception should that be preferred. Marian would have found it hard to deny the logic of his argument and it is debatable whether she would have wanted to. Whatever the relationship during those thirteen days of early summer, they were never as intimate again. 'We made a solemn and holy vow which henceforth will bind us to the right,' Chapman wrote before he returned to London.[23]

The vow was evidently the result of Marian's appraisal of the situation. Along with paying her much loving attention, John had also asked her to help him with the *Westminster Review*. Initially the request had been for her to write a regular column on foreign literature for which she would be paid his new improved rates. Marian had no hesitation in accepting and was soon planning her return to London. Since John was adamant that Elisabeth Tilley had to remain, Marian suggested she take private rooms in the capital and nominated

October as a suitable month for her return, for it would give plenty of time for the preparation of their first issue in January 1852. Marian was ambitious; already her mind was running on beyond responsibility for one feature, and when Chapman suggested she might like to be 'an active cooperator' in editing the *Westminster Review*, she accepted with alacrity. Eager to prove her worth, Marian insisted that John hand over the prospectus he had been struggling with, which she then worked on through dinner to finish.

While she was engaged in that, Chapman discussed with Hunt and Bray the problems entailed in having a woman as editor, and all agreed that, for the sake of the magazine's credibility, the editor's identity and sex must be kept secret. Chapman also discussed with Charles Bray, whom he always regarded as Marian's 'minder', what pecuniary arrangements he should suggest. Weighing up Marian's private income against the costs of the *Westminster*, he decided a nominal salary plus free board and lodging were adequate recompense for her editorial expertise. If she wrote any articles then of course she would be paid at the standard rate. Though hardly the most generous of contracts, Marian never contemplated turning it down because she was desperate to get a toe-hold in the writing world. Even this was progress, since she had been prepared to give her work away just to see it in print. Moreover it would be possible to earn extra money by writing articles. John also spoke about the possibility of producing an abridged version of her Strauss translation for which she might be paid one hundred pounds, five times what she had received for the original translation. At last the future looked promising.

John Chapman returned to London and the welcome embrace of Elisabeth Tilley: 'I never saw her in such a rapture which continued all day,' he recorded happily in his diary. 'Susanna received me affection-ately but soon got into disagreeable talk about M[arian].'[24] Clearly things had changed little in his absence, and John had four months in which to make his harem accept Marian Evans as editor of the *Westminster Review* and a free boarder in the house.

Marian was sorry when John had to return but elated that she was to have a job as an editor. 'I am training myself up to say adieu to all delights, I care for nothing but doing my work and doing it well,' she wrote and though she had the whole of the summer in front of her, she was so keen to prepare that Charles Bray vacated his study for her.[25]

Chapman corresponded regularly, keeping Marian fully informed of developments and sending her the articles and letters he had received. She in turn read and appraised the material, suggested potential subjects to Chapman and drafted out replies to his correspondence in the most confident and professional manner. In an amusing reversal of roles, Harriet Martineau, whom Marian had previously been so much in awe of, found herself unknowingly at the mercy of Miss Evans for a commission to abridge a translation of some writings by the French philosopher Comte. While admiring Harriet Martineau's style, Marian told Chapman that she had less confidence in the calibre of her mind and recommended the work should go to a curate in Somerset, adding rather arrogantly: 'Miss Martineau disclaims any egotism in the affair, but she evidently thinks no one can be so fit for the work as herself. This I doubt – nor do I think her name in the title-page would be of much value now – at least not more than "a graduate of Oxford or Cambridge" as the case may be.'[26]

Marian's letters to John Chapman in the four months before she settled in London display a common sense and an understanding of business her father would have been proud of. She urged John Chapman, who too often played one person off against another, to be more honest in his dealings with people or he would discredit the *Westminster*. She might have been the lowly paid, anonymous assistant but she quickly found her feet and was organizing the magazine and its proprietor. Chapman, who had his hands full with other branches of his publishing and bookselling activities, recognized Marian's abilities and gratefully let her take charge.

Another person who met her at the Brays in the summer of 1851 also recognized her qualities and urged Chapman to make full use of them. George Combe came to stay at Rosehill in August 1851 and was invited to examine the skulls of Charles Bray and Marian Evans. Combe recorded in his notebook that he found Bray had an excellent intellect but great combativeness and destructiveness and very deficient concentration. Miss Evans, however, was the most extraordinary person of the party at Rosehill, exhibiting 'great analytic power and instinctive soundness of judgement. We had a great deal of conversation on religion, political economy, and political events, and altogether, with the exception perhaps of Lucretia Mott, she appeared to me the ablest woman whom I have seen, and in many respects she excels Lucretia,' he wrote. 'She is extremely feminine and gentle; and the great strength of her intellect combined with this quality renders her very interesting.'[27] Marian would have liked that description, but not perhaps his comment about her being a farmer's daughter of about forty (she was actually thirty-one but managed to lose a year off her age so that for most of her life she was believed to be younger than she was; even her coffin plate bore 1820 as the date of birth). Impressed by her outstanding intelligence and the likelihood that the *Westminster* would become a radical mouthpiece once more, Combe was persuaded to become a sponsor. With a vested interest in the quarterly's future, he felt it a duty to urge Chapman to pay more attention to his editor. 'I would again very respectfully recommend to you to use Miss Evans's tact and judgment as an aid to your own,' he wrote. 'She has certain organs large in her brain which are not so fully developed in yours, and she will judge more correctly of the influence upon other persons of what you write and do, than you will do yourself.'[28] Phrenology might have no scientific basis, but Combe analysed the personalities correctly.

As her professional life at last took shape and all at Rosehill congratulated Marian warmly, the Evanses were less effusive. 'The wicked *Westminster*' was just the sort of subversive and irreligious publication Mary Ann (as they still called her) would get involved with and they had no wish to be associated with it. It was a known fact that the journal was not permitted in many circulating libraries and had been condemned by clergy. When Marian did the rounds of her family to bid them farewell, the reception was cool. The only good Isaac could see was that his sister would be off his hands. Chrissey as always was the most affectionate but she was troubled by her husband's poor health and mounting debts. Fanny, whom Marian spent a few days with to prepare her wardrobe, was impressed by her younger sister's success, but did not show it. The atmosphere was so strained that Marian felt obliged to write and apologize to her elder sister.

The summer passed quickly with a holiday in Devon chaperoning Cara, who wanted to stay with Edward Noel but was concerned about appearances, and visits to London in the company of the Brays to see the Great Exhibition and to make peaceful overtures to the women in Chapman's household before Marian took up permanent residence on 29 September. From then on the capital was her home, though she still sought sanctuary at Rosehill when town life became unbearable.

CHAPTER 9

The Man Question,
1852–1853

Marian walked straight into heated discussion about the 'woman question' when she arrived at Chapman's. This Victorian riddle, which nobody succeeded in solving (few thought there even was a question), might in present parlance be called feminism. Arguments about the rights and wrongs of the issue had rumbled on at 142 Strand since July 1851 when an article on 'The Enfranchisement of Women' appeared in the *Westminster Review*. These were given fresh impetus a few months later by news of the imminent arrival of Frederika Bremer, a Swedish feminist writer.

The 'woman question' was not new to Marian: she had read George Sand and others on the subject and discussed the issues endlessly with the Brays. At Rosehill there had been unanimous agreement about the need for better female education, but a difference of opinion about other changes. On feminist matters Charles Bray was less enlightened than might be expected, maintaining that it was an essential part of nature's design that men should be of a higher order than women. Sara Hennell, who argued with her brother-in-law on principle, thought that that was rubbish and advocated equality in educational and political opportunities.

Bremer's works, which had been circulating in translation in England for eight years, had been read by all at Rosehill, and the Swede's contention that women should be freed from the legal and educational restraints which limited their horizons to marriage provoked some heated debate. The great lady's arrival at Chapman's proved an anticlimax. According to Marian, the woman she had always venerated for her powerful writing was a physically repulsive creature who looked far older than her fifty years. She was so small and wizened, with rheumy eyes and bad teeth, that Marian avoided conversation over the dinner table.[1] During the month Fredrika Bremer lodged with Mrs Chapman, Marian came to repent her hasty judgement based on outward appearances, for she discovered that the novelist had a sweet personality and was a fine musician and artist. None of this, however, was sufficient to persuade Marian to join the ranks of the Bremer disciples who converged on Chapman's. These young women who came to pay homage to their figurehead were sure the scholarly Miss Evans from the Midlands would share their convictions.

Marian thought differently. The editorship of the *Westminster Review* was the culmination of a personal battle for independence; she did not regard herself as striking a blow for women's rights just because of her job. Among those she encountered at the court of Miss Bremer was a new breed of women, slightly younger than herself, the wealthy daughters of radical politicians with plenty of confidence and money but limited experience of the world. Arising from their fathers' interests they were brimful of the philosophies of John Stuart Mill, well read in the risqué fiction of George Sand and vociferous in their condemnation of the doctrine that marriage was a woman's profession. Marian felt she had little in common with these twenty-year-olds, whose path through life had been so different from her own. Their hours spent in opulent homes in Savile Row or Blandford Square, punctuated by tours of the Continent, afforded them no conception of the way most women in the country had to live.

The first of these crusading young women Marian was introduced to was Elizabeth Rayner Parkes, known to all as Bessie, daughter of the Birmingham MP 'Radical Joe' Parkes, and great-granddaughter of Joseph Priestley. As the only child of wealthy parents, her future was assured and she was able to indulge her whim to become a poet. There was no necessity for her to marry simply to have someone to provide for her; in fact, as Bessie well knew, if she did marry she would be worse off through losing her legal existence and control of her fortune to her husband. Armed with this knowledge, her mission in life was to fight the restrictions women faced.

Not surprisingly Bessie wanted to meet Miss Bremer as she passed through London on her way to Sweden after a successful American tour. The writer's incredible ugliness struck Bessie too, but unlike Marian she was able to ignore it and greet her idol warmly. For much of an evening in October 1851 Bessie was content to watch the interesting company Chapman had assembled.[2] Edwin Chadwick, the public health reformer, deep in conversation with the Swedish novelist on the subject of sanitary reform; an American guest, Mrs Follen, putting her case for the abolition of slavery to Mr Wilkinson, author of a book on human anatomy; Cara Bray and the novelist Eliza Lynn exchanging opinions on literature, and Marian Evans in the middle of a group of men and a dispute about gravity and astrology. Bessie Parkes was surprised to meet Marian Evans in these surroundings because their one previous meeting had been at the home of Mrs Bray in Coventry where Bessie had been taken to meet 'the learned Miss Evans', who had translated the Strauss work for her father. Neither woman had had any opportunity for conversation since Charles Bray had held the floor with his usual ebullience; nevertheless Bessie had gone away with the impression that Miss Evans knew a bewildering number of languages, modern and classical, and wrote for magazines. When the opportunity presented itself at Chapman's soirée, she cornered Marian and poured out her plans for a campaign against female injustices and the part Marian, as a writer for the *Westminster*, could play.

Although Bessie reported to her mother that Miss Evans was a wonderful woman who was bound to be the author of everything philosophical and perceptive in the *Review*, Marian was less impressed by Miss Parkes.[3] She resented being told what to do by someone she hardly knew (a bored little rich girl, who needed a social cause to pass the time until her marriage, was Marian's cynical assessment). Marian treated the younger woman coolly; she had come to London to work and had no intention of getting tied up in Miss Parkes's crusade, no matter how worthy the cause.

Some interpreted Marian's behaviour as haughtiness and were quick to criticize the newcomer. Eliza Lynn, already established as a professional writer, turned her tongue and later her pen to attacking Marian. She called her provincial manners uncouth, her unfashionable clothing unkempt, and her person unwashed and unbrushed.[4] In fact Miss Evans, she declared, was distinctly underbred. More revealingly the writer, whose literary reputation was later to be totally eclipsed by that of George Eliot, wrote in her autobiography that Marian Evans 'assumed a tone of superiority over me which I was not then aware was warranted by her undoubted leadership. From first to last she put up my mental bristles, so that I rejected then and there what might have become a closer acquaintance had I not been so blind, and so much influenced by her want of conventional graces.' Marian found life in London no easier socially than in the Midlands. Those of her own sex were either against her because she rejected their way of life or were jealous of her success, and few men would tolerate a woman who was so independent.

The actual identity of the editor of the *Westminster Review* remained a secret to all but those most closely involved in the quarterly's production. It was given out that Miss Evans assisted John Chapman, but his reputation as a philanderer and the fact that Miss Evans was always to be seen by his side meant that people believed the word 'assistant' was a polite euphemism. Paradoxically, the mistaken belief that Marian was Chapman's mistress did not imply social ostracism. Many of Chapman's friends had mistresses tucked away in the background and thus quite happily included his 'assistant' in invitations to dinner.

Bessie's father Joseph Parkes was one such person, who began by asking Chapman and Marian together to his house in Savile Row. On discovering that this woman hailed from his own county of Warwickshire and was quite prepared to dine without being chaperoned by Chapman, he indulged in her excellent company. Parkes was in his fifties and, like most men Marian met, conducted extramarital affairs. Soon after he married in the 1820s, he decided that he and his wife were not suited and he was therefore justified in taking a mistress. This was easily effected by the purchase of three houses in London. His wife and daughter were installed permanently in one, his mistress in another and he was free to be accommodated wherever his 'parliamentary commitments' dictated. Bessie was used to her father's comings and goings and her mother's compliance, so she grew up without any knowledge of her father's secret life. When a few years later her father castigated Marian for immorality, Bessie had no idea he was applying double standards.

Marian already knew of Parkes's proclivities because Chapman and Bray were inveterate gossips, but it made no difference to her friendship with him. Parkes was much taken by the intelligent Miss Evans, with her quiet wit, who never seemed overawed by a predominantly masculine gathering. Marian had a manner which naturally flattered men; Bray thought it lay in her ability to turn whatever was said to the speaker's best advantage, but that was only one facet. Bessie Parkes, who observed Marian often during these years, noticed that the older woman had a presence which pleased men and caused her father to be 'much attached to her'. Whenever there were any celebrities or noted intellectuals to be entertained, Parkes would insist Marian dined with him. 'I can see her descending the great staircase of our house in Savile Row, on my father's arm,' Bessie recalled, 'the only lady except for my mother, in the group of remarkable men, politicians and authors of the first class; she would laugh softly, and look up into my Father's face respectfully.'[5] The facial features so often ridiculed when Marian became a public figure were scarcely noticed. In Bessie's memory, 'abundant brown hair framed a countenance which was certainly not in any sense unpleasing and very sweet and kind in expression. Her height was good, her figure remarkably supple. In all movements it had an almost serpentine grace.'[6]

Marian enjoyed the masculine dinners with their political controversies, their anecdotes and uproarious laughter and had no desire to attend the glittering functions held for ladies. After declining the first of Mrs Parkes's invitations to one of her balls at the Savile Row house, Marian privately told Bessie that she could not attend because she possessed nothing suitable to wear. 'It would be a crucifixion of my own taste as well as other people's to appear like a withered cabbage in a flower garden. At a dinner-party, when people think only of conversation, one doesn't mind being a dowdy, but it is the essence of a dance that every one should look fresh and elegant – at least as to their garments.'[7]

Even without attending the Parkeses' balls, her social life was exhilarating, exceeding anything she had experienced at Rosehill. At Chapman's gatherings there were, in addition to British journalists and politicians, leading figures from abroad – always of the most radical, even revolutionary persuasion. In 1852 the visitors included Giuseppe Mazzini, the republican leader from Genoa, who was in exile in England attempting to raise moral and financial support for the next stage in his campaign to liberate Italy. Marian had been inspired by his nationalist activities in the 1848 Italian uprising but never dreamed she would meet the romantic leader. The Italian she had learned with Signor Brezzi was put to good use assisting Mazzini shape up his article on 'Freedom and Despotism' for the April edition of the *Westminster Review*. His revolutionary plans to rid Italy of the 'curse of the Papacy' so intrigued Marian that she went to hear him address a meeting of the 'Society of the Friends of Italy'. There his oration was received with wild enthusiasm, but it was Marian's belief that he put his ideas more forcefully on paper.[8]

Another political refugee to arrive at 142 Strand was Pierre Leroux, who had played an active part in the Assemblies established after the 1848 Revolution in France. A coup d'état two years later forced Leroux to flee to England and, like other exiled revolutionaries, he landed up at Chapman's. Marian spent two hours deep in French conversation with this friend of George Sand discussing everything from political and social organization to the origins of Christianity. He was, she pronounced with great admiration, 'a dreamy genius'.[9]

That his sister had progressed from mixing with English radicals to European revolutionaries would have scandalized Isaac Evans. Fortunately for everyone's peace of mind, this gossip from London did not reach Griff House and Marian took care not to enlighten any of the family in her letters. Aside from their political persuasions, Isaac would have been impressed by the moneyed upper-middle-class circles his sister was increasingly to be found in. She became friendly with Peter Taylor, nephew of the silk baron Samuel Courtauld and chairman of the Society of the Friends of Italy, who had been responsible for bringing Mazzini to Chapman's. Taylor was pleased to introduce her to his wife Clementia, for the two women were of similar age and interests and, it transpired, similar backgrounds. Although Clementia had married into money, she had met her husband while governessing his sisters. She was largely self-educated, fiercely independent and, despite her marriage, was organizing a national campaign to fight the legal injustices women suffered. Marian found herself drawn more to Mrs Taylor's practical approach to the woman question than to Bessie Parkes's well-meaning but idealized notions. 'I do sympathize with you most emphatically in the desire to see woman socially elevated –educated equally with men, and secured as far as possible along with every other breathing creature from suffering the exercise of any unrighteous power,' she told Clementia.[10]

Friendship with this woman brought invitations to attend some of Mrs Taylor's salons where she encountered a few daring young women who dressed like George Sand and could even be seen smoking cigarettes. However, this in no way rivalled the attractions of the company who assembled for Chapman's soirées. There she was introduced to Thackeray, basking in the fame of *Vanity Fair* published in 1848, and Charles Dickens, editor of the journal *Household Words* and author of the enormously successful *David Copperfield* published two years previously. Initially Marian decided Dickens was a phrenological disappointment, for he lacked a suitable anterior lobe, she told Bray. On closer acquaintance she forgot about this defect, discovering instead a highly entertaining companion.

There were very few women writers in London and the unmarried ones tended to live, as Harriet Martineau did, with a mother or aunt to lend respectability to their unconventional calling. Marian Evans, living and working in the Strand at the heart of the masculine world of journalism, was well aware that she was in a decidedly equivocal position and took great care there was nothing in her behaviour to invite scandal. Her dress was always sober and businesslike (Bessie Parkes noticed how Marian always wore black velvet when she came to dine at their house even though black was the colour for matrons). At thirty-two Marian believed she was unlikely to receive any marriage proposals, although she did not give up hope. What mattered more to her was to do the job she had fought for really well.

She was meticulous in every detail and, as a result, six months after she joined the *Westminster Review*, it was being described as 'the most important means of enlightenment of a literary nature in existence'.[11] One of the proofreaders at Chapman's remembered Marian in typical informal working pose in her room at the Strand: her chair usually pulled up sideways to the fire, her feet swung over the arm and her hair hanging loosely on her shoulders rather than tightly scraped back as fashion demanded, on her lap the manuscript she was studying.[12] Having found a job where she could make use of her learning, Marian responded in true Evans style. Not only did she set herself high standards but she expected the same of others. In that she was destined to be frustrated. John Chapman had a kind heart and was always trying to find work for impoverished radicals irrespective of their suitability for the job. One needy European freedom-fighter who arrived at 142 Strand in search of work was given the job of doing the accounts. With no knowledge of such matters and limited command of the language he caused chaos. To her annoyance, Marian found herself regularly called in to sort out similar messes. In her early days at the Strand she willingly assisted with everything from editing and proofreading manuscripts to the last-minute packing of boxes of books for shipment to America. But after six months of Chapman's 'bungling', as she called it, Marian became less tolerant. She did not object to working hard if it would pull him out of the mire, but it seemed to her that he deliberately courted disaster. He commissioned articles from the wrong people and upset the right ones. Out of the verbose rubbish he often presented for editing, she was expected to extract high-quality prose yet give no offence to the author, who believed his writing was perfect.

Quite early on she dissuaded Chapman from writing for the magazine himself because his enthusiasm outstripped his abilities. With admirable subtlety she advised him not to weaken his position as editor-in-chief by being known as a contributor.[13] Most of the correspondence connected with the quarterly passed through her hands and even though she could not send out letters herself, since officially she did not exist as an editor, Marian tried to control Chapman's replies.

It was an uphill battle and, though the *Westminster* gained in stature under her editorship, its finances were permanently in a critical state. Chapman, like Bray, was irresistibly drawn to worthy but costly disputes. In 1852 he challenged the powerful Booksellers' Association to permit books to be sold at a discount and won his case, but victory was costly. Chapman also had a habit of casually using the funds of the *Westminster* as petty cash when his personal finances were at a low ebb, so that by the time the third issue of the quarterly was due there was a problem finding two hundred and fifty pounds due to contributors.

Five months of the disorganization of 142 Strand were sufficient for Marian to confide in Charles Bray that she was looking for new lodgings. Though she would be at a financial disadvantage because she received a very small salary for her editorial work and took the rest as free board and lodging which Chapman could not afford to make up in cash, she believed she would be better off in the long term. Away from the chaotic domestic and business arrangements at the Strand, Marian would still be able to undertake editorial responsibility for the *Westminster* but not feel obliged to help with all the other activities. If she needed extra money to supplement her earnings and annuity, she would have the time and confidence to write for other periodicals. Now that she knew many of the editors personally there was a high chance of her work being accepted.

Another reason for Marian's wish to move out was that she had recently made a friendship which she hoped with careful nurture might develop into a more permanent relationship, and she did not want her chances spoiled by interference from the inmates at Chapman's. Her attention had focused on Herbert Spencer, the editor of *The Economist*, who was the same age as herself and, like her previous amours, tall, good-looking, intelligent and a free-thinker. However, there the similarities ended. Herbert Spencer was quite the opposite to Bray and Chapman, being introspective, unemotional and distinctly prudish when it came to sexual matters. He had an obsessive concern about his own mental and bodily welfare, the sort of person Marian labelled 'a monomaniac'. Even at thirty-two, this hypochondriac was marked out as an eccentric, who would take up the latest health fad, be it vegetarianism or mesmerism. To the amusement of his companions, Spencer was wont suddenly to cease what he was doing and check his pulse. On other occasions he would deliver his opinion on a subject, then clap on his earpads because his medical adviser had warned him it might be bad for his health to get involved in disputes. Over and beyond his idiosyncratic behaviour, Spencer had a brilliant innovative mind which had already led him through various careers from teaching to civil engineering during the railway boom and to inventing all manner of objects – he developed a velocimeter for use on the railway; designed, produced and sold a pin to bind loose music; designed but never managed to get off the ground a machine for aerial locomotion. All were the products of an inspired technician rather than a mad scientist – but by the time Marian encountered him, Spencer had embarked on another career, working as a journalist and writing philosophical books in his spare time.

With offices on the opposite side of the road to the *Westminster* at 340 Strand, it was not surprising that the editor of *The Economist* became a regular visitor at number 142. Spencer had never found it easy to make friends and was grateful for the company offered at Chapman's, even if it was more bohemian than he would have liked. He was also prepared to put up with the teasing he received there. Among the servants he was known as 'Spontaneous Fission', following a chance remark one of the maids overheard. Mrs Chapman told him he was 'pernickety' and could fill a page in the *Westminster* with fewer words than anyone she knew because he always used such dreadfully long ones. 'Oh, you always do say funny things about me, I think, Mrs Chapman,' came the glum reply.[14]

Having heard hilarious accounts of Spencer's foibles from the others, Marian was soon entering into the spirit of the game. Since Spencer was always asking people whether he ought to get married or not, she and Chapman decided to have some fun. They offered to work out the ideal wife for him from his own philosophies set out in his book *Social Statics*, published by Chapman. Since Spencer took it all seriously, the joke lasted for two months, during which time they told him they had worked out the best woman for him would be a young poetess and an heiress. Some time later they introduced him to Bessie Parkes. When confronted by a possible wife, Spencer became agitated and told Marian that the lady was too highly intellectual and possessed too much self-esteem. Anyway, he concluded lamely, 'I do not think the spirit will move me.'[15] The whole episode provided great entertainment at Chapman's, and Spencer accepted it all with his usual resignation.

Although Marian had enjoyed the joke hugely, she felt guilty about it, knowing that it could equally well have been played against her. That made her realize how much she and Spencer had in common: not only were they the same age and from the Midlands – Spencer having been born in Derby – but, more significantly, neither fitted the mould others deemed right for them.

Spencer was lonely. He was always asking either Mrs Chapman or Elisabeth Tilley or Marian to accompany him to the theatre or opera when he received complimentary tickets for performances which the promoters wanted to see reviewed in *The Economist*. Marian was only too pleased to accept these invitations and he, grateful for her friendship, called regularly to talk to her. 'We see each other every day and have a delightful *camaraderie* in everything,' she wrote to Cara Bray in the early summer of 1852. 'But for him, my life would be desolate enough now, with poor Mr C so occupied and so sad.'[16] The letter went on to tell Cara how Chapman spent most of his time sitting around in the bookshop in a state of perpetual anxiety about money and spoke of staff cuts. It was a dismal prospect for Marian, who could see her position as editor being further watered down by shop work. Letters she received from Rosehill told her that life was changing there and it might be harder for her to look to the Brays for the same support as before. Sara and Mrs Hennell had moved from London to the small cottage in the grounds and expected Charles to keep them, although Sara and Charles had regularly been at daggers drawn. The ribbon-weaving business faced ruin while the proprietor concentrated his efforts on the next round in the battle for secular education. Circulation of the Coventry *Herald* was similarly declining as Bray used the paper to wage his personal vendettas. Marian could see that she was not likely to be able to depend on Rosehill as her base for much longer; that was another good reason for looking towards somebody else to provide her with that home.

Although Marian had always been outspoken in her condemnation of marriage and the way in which women lost their identity, deep inside she still longed for the security and respectability which that state would bring her. Marriage to Herbert Spencer, she felt sure, would be a marriage of equals because he was a firm supporter of freedom and equality and had proclaimed in his *Social Statics* that 'equity knows no difference of sex', thereby advocating political and civil parity for women. Marian believed that she and Herbert were of comparable intellectual calibre and shared the same love of music and science. What she closed her eyes to were the enormous differences that separated them. Herbert Spencer was indeed a believer in the independence of women, but was such a dogmatic individual that no one, be they male or female, was ever permitted to volunteer an opinion in his hearing on pain of the earpads being used. Like Marian he was passionately addicted to music, but that and theatre were the only art forms he tolerated, being scathing of literature and art. His pathological hatred of the German people, their culture and philosophy conflicted sharply with Marian's admiration of German language and thought, which she held to be the most advanced in Europe. Nevertheless their friendship was 'deliciously calm' because nothing ruffled Herbert Spencer.[17] Chapman claimed that nobody had ever heard him swear, though privately most people at 142 Strand thought Spencer would be a better fellow if he did swear now and again like the rest of them.

As the friendship with Miss Evans deepened, Herbert Spencer became concerned lest she might think he was building up to a marriage proposal, whereas he saw their relationship merely as a pleasing companionship with no obligations. 'The greatness of her intellect conjoined with her womanly qualities and manner, generally keep me at her side most of the evening,' he told a friend.[18] To Marian herself he stressed the freedom such higher minds as theirs were able to enjoy. It was so refreshing to be able to talk to a woman or go to the theatre with her, without everyone marrying them off, he said. Since Marian was such an intelligent liberated woman, there was no earthly reason why they could not spend as much time together as they liked. Spencer was so confident in his ideas that he never looked at the face of his companion to see what impact his words were having, and Marian, terrified she might destroy what little she had gained, quietly agreed. Herbert Spencer was sufficiently egocentric to believe that Marian found his company so stimulating that she liked to be seen about town with him. Her manner of looking adoringly up into his eyes, hanging on his every word or polishing up his rare witticisms were all received as proper obeisance. Her invitation to call her Pollian, a name reserved only for her closest friends, merely caused Spencer to compose one of his few jests about her 'diabolical descent' from Apolyon, a character in the Book of Revelations; the invitation to greater intimacy passed unnoticed. Marian was far more sensitive to every nuance in the relationship and, though secretly pleased to hear people talk of her and Herbert as though they were engaged, was terrified he might be frightened off. Charles Bray could not credit that his warm-hearted Marian should have chosen a cold fish like Spencer, who needed a nursemaid not a wife. However, eager to help, Bray invited both of them to Rosehill for a few days. Marian panicked: 'We certainly could not go together for all the world is setting us down as engaged – a most disagreeable thing if one chose to make oneself uncomfortable. "Tell it not in Gath" however – that is to say, please avoid mentioning our names together, and pray burn this note, that it may not lie on the chimney piece for general inspection.'[19]

Despite Marian's precautions, rumours of an impending Evans–Spencer engagement reached Herbert's ears when the earpads were off. His horror was not assuaged when Marian tried to reassure him that it was mere idle chatter, so she set about organizing a summer break for herself to take the heat out of the situation. She thought not only that the tongues would find something else to wag about in her absence, but that Spencer would realize how much he missed her when she was not there. She chose Broadstairs, recently popularized by *David Copperfield*, as the place to gather her thoughts while enjoying the sea air, rather than return to the highly charged

The charismatic John Chapman, watchmaker, surgeon, bookseller, publisher and gynaecologist. Marian adored him and helped him edit the Westminster Review.

A self portrait of Barbara Leigh Smith, Marian's closest female friend, who campaigned for married women's property rights and helped found Girton College, Cambridge.

John Chapman's long-suffering wife, Susanna, portrayed in a pastel sketch in the early 1850s.

A sketch of Bessie Parkes, probably drawn by Barbara Leigh Smith. Both young women were frequent attenders at Chapman's soirées where they met Marian Evans.

A painting of the brilliant though egocentric Herbert Spencer, by J. B. Burgess. In 1852 Marian fell in love with this one time railway engineer and inventor who turned journalist and philosopher. The intensity of the thirty-two-year-old woman's affections terrified Spencer, who extricated himself as fast as he could. He died a bachelor in 1903.

Marian Evans Lewes photographed in 1858 after she had written Adam Bede. *The photographic artist has tactfully straightened the subject's nose. Although several copies of this picture were printed, the novelist continued to maintain: 'I have no photograph of myself, having always avoided having one taken.'*

George Henry Lewes, with whom Marian lived for twenty-three happy and unmarried years. It was his encouragement which led her into novel writing and his entrepreneurial skills which made George Eliot the richest novelist of her day.

The many faces of Marian Evans. Above, as sketched by Cara Bray in the late 1840s, the left hand sketch is copied from a photograph and the right hand one from a phrenological cast of Marian's head which was kept at Rosehill.

A recently discovered photograph of Marian, taken when she worked for the Westminster Review.

A more matronly sketch by Samuel Laurence in 1860. This did not meet with the subject's approval and was abandoned as the study for a painting.

Left: John Blackwood, the Edinburgh publisher of Blackwood's Magazine *and most of the novels of George Eliot. He showed great personal kindness to Marian and did his best to be tolerant of what he regarded as the Leweses' incredible avarice.*

Below: The drawing room at the Priory, showpiece of the Leweses' house, designed and extended by Owen Jones to accommodate the increasing number of George Eliot worshippers.

The only surviving photograph of John Walter Cross (seated on the right in this photograph). His marriage to the famous novelist was short and disastrous.

Number 4, Cheyne Walk, Chelsea, purchased by John Cross as a home for his bride. In the event, Mrs Mary Ann Cross moved in on 3 December and died there on 22 December.

The Heights at Witley in Surrey. Marian preferred the tranquillity of the countryside to life in London and hoped to settle here permanently.

The sculptor, John Letts, working on the statue of George Eliot in his studio at The Old School, Astley, near Nuneaton. The finished bronze was erected in Newdegate Square, Nuneaton in March 1986, paid for by public subscription and sponsored by The George Eliot Fellowship.

atmosphere of Rosehill. Thus to Spencer's immense relief, early in July 1852 Marian departed for a stay of unspecified length. Writing politely to enquire about her health, Spencer praised her cool handling of the situation in London, to which she retorted sharply: 'No credit to me for my virtues as a refrigerant. I owe them all to a few lumps of ice which I carried away with me from that tremendous glacier of yours.'[20] His remark that he was considering spending a few days in Kent himself received a spirited rejoinder: 'We will not inquire too curiously whether you long most for my society or for the sea-breezes. If you decided that I was not worth coming to see, it would only be a piece with that generally exasperating perspicacity of yours which will not allow one to humbug you.'[21]

Nettled by her taunts, Spencer decided he would spend a few days in the hotel she mentioned near her cottage, but the experience put a great strain on his health. Marian was overjoyed by what she interpreted as a sign that Herbert could not live without her, and she responded with an uninhibited display of affection or, as Spencer viewed it, 'much painful emotion'. The tears, the pleas and the blatant declarations of love made his pulse race and, in a temper, he walked out of Chandos Cottage and headed for London. What awaited him there was a tragic missive from one desperate for love:

> I know this letter will make you very angry with me, but wait a little and don't say anything while you are angry. I promise not to sin any more in the same way.
>
> My ill health is caused by the hopeless wretchedness which weighs upon me. I do not say this to pain you, but because it is the simple truth which you must know in order to understand why I am obliged to seek relief.
>
> I want to know if you can assure me that you will not forsake me, that you will always be with me as much as you can and share your thoughts and feelings with me. If you become attached to some one else, then I must die, but until then I could gather courage to work and make life valuable, if only I had you near me. I do not ask you to sacrifice anything – I would be very good and cheerful and never annoy you. But I find it impossible to contemplate life under any other conditions. If I had your assurance, I could trust that and live upon it. I have struggled – indeed I have – to renounce everything and be entirely unselfish, but I find myself utterly unequal to it. Those who have known me best have always said, that if ever I

loved any one thoroughly my whole life must turn upon that feeling, and I find they say truly. You curse the destiny which has made the feeling concentrate itself on you – but if you will only have patience with me you shall not curse it long. You will find that I can be satisfied with very little, if I am delivered from the dread of losing it. I suppose no woman ever before wrote such a letter as this – but I am not ashamed of it, for I am conscious that in the light of reason and true refinement I am worthy of your respect and tenderness, whatever gross men or vulgar-minded women might think of me.[22]

It was a very brave letter, which cost Marian much heartache, but it fell on stony ground. Herbert Spencer was embarrassed to receive such an open declaration of passion but relieved to see that she was not intending to make a public exhibition of her feelings. Much as he liked her – better than any woman he had met – he was uneasy in her company. Most of the time she was calm and rational but occasionally he glimpsed a powerful sensual spirit which unnerved him.

Drained of energy and emotion by the Spencer affair, Marian was in no hurry to return to London and stayed on at Broadstairs until late August. Charles Bray, with his usual nose for gossip, heard of the end to Marian's dreams and hurried down to the quiet seaside resort to comfort his friend. Nobody could have been more welcome to Marian at that time. Though never able to organize his own life, Bray could be relied upon to drag Marian out of the depths of despair and provide her with the necessary impetus to carry on. Since the sultry late summer weather had also brought swarms of insects which made daily life tiresome, Marian agreed to return to the smoke and noise of London, feeling 'plucky' rather than happy, she told her old friend Cara.[23]

It was a subdued Miss Evans who returned to the Strand, a contrast to the excited one of twelve months earlier, but as before she determined to immerse herself in work to the exclusion of all else. This time she found it harder. She no longer had faith in John Chapman's abilities, knowing him to be his own worst enemy. While he navigated the *Westminster Review* on to the rocks, she had no intention of going down with the sinking ship; indeed she could not afford such a fate. Instead, she decided to take on freelance work. Spencer continually talked of giving up his editorship of *The Economist* and said he knew several freelance journalists who easily earned five hundred pounds a year. The plans were bold enough, but Marian found them hard to put into practice when Chapman pleaded with her not to abandon him at such a crucial time. As always, she found him most persuasive and did not have the heart to refuse; she set Christmas 1852 as the date of her departure.

In a bid to forget the unhappy summer, Marian returned to her editing with grim determination. Spencer, unabashed by what had passed, was back on the scene again enquiring if she might like to accompany him to the theatre because he had some free tickets and wanted an escort. Marian gave him short shrift and looked towards cultivating some of the women she had met. One friendship begun in the autumn of 1852 lasted throughout her life and was the most intimate Marian ever had with a woman, reaching a deeper level of understanding than she achieved with either Cara Bray or Sara Hennell.

Barbara Leigh Smith was twenty-five, eight years younger than Marian, and came from a rich radical family like her friend Bessie Parkes. Barbara's personality was quite different from the plodding Bessie's, for Barbara was a bright young woman bubbling with exciting ideas. As the daughter of Benjamin Leigh Smith, bachelor MP for Norwich, Barbara had learned to stand up for herself. Quite early in life she discovered that not everyone would recognize Leigh Smith's bastards; even her cousins, Florence Nightingale on the one side and the Bonham Carters on the other, had no wish to be associated with the taboo Leigh Smith family. This rejection on account of their illegitimacy caused all five Leigh Smith children to grow up with a pride in being unorthodox. Polite society had rejected them and so they did not feel beholden to its absurd conventions, a stance Marian admired greatly. Barbara never forgot that wealth alone had bought her acceptance in radical circles, and she developed a strong social conscience which, even before she came into her full fortune at twenty-one, led her to work for the disadvantaged. One of her main concerns was the lack of education, and she financed and taught in an infant school in Westminster, which operated on enlightened principles. There was nothing fashionable or fickle about Barbara's causes. Her concern for education was lifelong and in later years was channelled into further education for women, most notably helping to found Girton College, Cambridge, so that women could be offered a university education.

When Marian met Barbara in the autumn of 1852, the younger woman had already developed strong opinions about the 'woman question' and persuaded Marian to give the subject more consideration. Barbara Leigh Smith and Clementia Taylor succeeded where Bessie Parkes had failed, because their approach to feminism was practical and supported by plenty of common sense, which always appealed to Marian. Both wanted to change the laws which made women economically dependent on their husbands.

The plight of the married woman was brought forcibly to Marian's attention in December when a thick black-edged letter arrived announcing the death of Dr Edward Clarke. Marian instantly set down her pen and caught the train to Coventry to be with her sister Chrissey and her six children to offer whatever assistance was necessary. The tragedy was made worse by the terrible financial situation Chrissey was left in. Her husband had long ago run through the money she had brought with her on marriage, and he had sold the cottage she subsequently inherited from an aunt. Moreover he had borrowed money against his future inheritance from the Clarke family. With his death coming unexpectedly, Chrissey found herself virtually destitute. Surprisingly Marian never regarded her brother-in-law as feckless; she had sympathized with his burning desire to improve conditions in the workhouse, even though other Evanses thought him foolhardy. Writing *Middlemarch* twenty years later, she portrayed Edward Clarke as Dr Lydgate, the earnest young doctor who struggled against perpetual money problems and bankruptcy to bring better health care to a charity hospital.

Chrissey, always the most mild of the Evans sisters, was crushed by her experiences and looked helplessly to her family for assistance. Although Marian could offer comfort to her bereaved sister, she knew that that was not enough and in the time she was at Meriden she tried to sort out what money could be raised to support Chrissey and her children, who ranged from one to fourteen years of age.

After ten days at Meriden, Marian was of the opinion that she could best help Chrissey by returning to London, working and sending money regularly. This did not meet with the approval of Isaac, who hated to find his independent-minded sister at Meriden, organizing affairs as if she were a male. He could not contain his temper and flew into a violent rage, saying that he hoped Marian would never ask him for anything, a comment which, she reported wryly to Cara, was 'almost as superfluous as if I had said I would never receive a kindness from him. But he is better than he shewed himself to me and I have no doubt he will be kind to Chrissey, though not in a very large way.'[24] Magnanimity was never Isaac's strong point, and the most he was prepared to do was offer Chrissey rent-free accommodation in one of the pokey little labourer's cottages he had inherited from his father. By a cruel twist of fate, it was the same cottage Chrissey had once owned herself, but which her husband had sold to Robert Evans to raise capital. The rest of the family were expected to furnish the cottage with their cast-off tables and chairs, in much the same manner as Gwendolen Harleth's family in *Daniel Deronda* were obliged to accept hand-outs of furniture from relatives when they became poverty-stricken.

The year 1853 opened with Marian putting aside all thoughts of herself and considering her new purpose in life: to support the Clarke family financially. This gave her a constant motive for work and economy. It was at that moment when she was least concerned with hunting for a partner that the genial George Henry Lewes hove into sight.

CHAPTER 10

I Am a Heathen and an Outlaw, 1853–1854

'I am a heathen and an outlaw,' Marian jokingly remarked to Bessie Parkes in the summer of 1853, never imagining how prophetic those words would be.[1] At the time she was concentrating all her attention and meagre resources on providing for her widowed sister and six children. Unlike other Evans relatives, Marian took Chrissey's plight to heart and put aside all thought of her own future until her sister's burden was eased.

Marian's own cosmopolitan experiences caused her to look for bold solutions to the problems of Chrissey's widowhood, like allowing the eldest Clarke boy to accept an offer of employment in Australia. Chrissey, however, was a more cautious person than Marian and, having recently lost her husband, could not face the possibility of never seeing her son again. Isaac's heartless suggestion that her two youngest children, aged one and three, should be sent to the Infant Orphan Asylum upset her greatly and incensed Marian. However, John Chapman's talk of the wonderful opportunities he had seen 'down under' led Marian to wonder whether Australia might be the answer for the whole of the Clarke family. She offered to give up her job and accompany them but made it clear that, once they were settled, she would have to return because she did not believe there was any future for a writer in such a remote continent. Chrissey could not be tempted; she had never lived more than a dozen miles from Griff in her life and clung with childlike simplicity to the belief that if she stayed near her home and kin everything would work out. Eventually, through the kind auspices of friends and neighbours, suitable employment was found for the two eldest children, schooling arranged for the next two, and the two little ones remained with their mother.

Although Marian's ambitious plans for an Australian future did not come to pass in 1853, ten years later after his mother's death, one of the Clarke boys decided to emigrate. Assisted by his aunt 'Polly' and his uncle, Henry Clarke, who shared the cost of his passage, Christopher Clarke went to New South Wales. He was fortunate to inherit the financial skills of his grandfather Robert Evans, rather than the disastrous propensities of his father, and his branch of the family went on to become successful merchant bankers.

Trying to work out the best solution to Chrissey's problems dominated Marian's thoughts until April 1854. At the same time she continued her editorial duties, but the pleasure was no longer there: 'I am out of spirits about the WR,' she told Charles Bray. 'The editorship is not satisfactory and I should be glad to run away from it altogether. But one thing is clear – that the review would be a great deal worse if I were not here. This is the only thought that consoles me.'[2] Again she announced her intention of quitting Mrs Chapman's lodging house on the pretext that the incessant din and dirt of the Strand was almost unbearable, only for John Chapman to turn on the charm once more and dissuade her from going until after the appearance of the next issue of the quarterly. By then, he told her with wonderful optimism, the business would have improved. Marian did not believe him but she gratefully abandoned the dismal prospect of hunting for lodgings. She knew it was unlikely that Chapman's affairs would ever get better, bungler as he was. Although the literary status of the *Westminster* had been restored, its finances were as precarious as ever and Chapman possessed the unfortunate knack of bringing their collapse ever closer. Despite what he said, his heart was no longer in the enterprise, and Marian suspected that he was surreptitiously diverting funds from the magazine into books and equipment for the medical studies which were increasingly occupying his time. The lodging house never proved a success and Mrs Chapman spoke of moving somewhere smaller.

One highlight in Marian's life was the regular visit of Charles Bray, forced to spend an increasing amount of time in London trying to stimulate ribbon sales. As always his presence was a great comfort to her: 'You are the dearest, oldest, stupidest, tiresomest, delightfullest

and never-to-be-forgotten-est of friends to me,' she wrote affection-
ately in January 1853. 'I am sure nobody cares for nobody more than I
care for you.'[3] Although he too faced bankruptcy, he remained as
cheerful and extravagant as ever, suggesting he would put up the
money to save the *Westminster* and protect Marian's job. She was at
once horrified and touched by his generosity, but urged him to put
such wildly impractical ideas out of his head and concentrate on
keeping the ribbon factory alive. Life was difficult enough for him
now that Sara Hennell and her mother were installed at Ivy Cottage in
the grounds of Rosehill. All his actions were subjected to the closest
scrutiny and he received abundant gratuitous advice about how he
ought to manage his firm, his newspaper and his marriage. Such a plan
as he proposed for the rescue of the *Westminster* would be courting
disaster on all fronts.

Light relief came in the surprising guise of Herbert Spencer, one of
Marian's few friends not burdened with money problems. Indeed,
since the death of a wealthy uncle, Spencer was contemplating giving
up *The Economist* to pursue his own interests. Nevertheless he
continued to call at Chapman's to discuss himself, his philosophies
and occasionally the ideas of others. His supply of tickets for the latest
plays and operas had not dried up, but Marian became circumspect
about accepting them lest the hated gossip should restart. Spencer also
took care to prevent another pulse-racing confrontation by acquiring a
chaperon for himself. Hardly the sort to form a close association with
anyone, Spencer had struck up a friendship with George Lewes,
literary editor on the new radical weekly paper the *Leader*. The sharp
differences in their personalities made them the most unlikely of
companions: Spencer was cautious and introspective, Lewes daring
and extrovert, but mutual loneliness and a common interest in
scientific investigation overcame these contradictions.

Marian had known Lewes from her earliest days in London. The
offices of the *Leader* were close by those of the *Westminster*, and he
wandered in at odd times to exchange ideas and material with
Chapman. She also knew he was a popular figure at Monday soirées,
where he entertained everyone with hilarious impersonations and
outrageous stories. During her eighteen months in the capital she had
found him difficult to get to know because he always put on an act,
and she had an idea he was probably not worth the effort anyway.

Lewes was proud of his theatrical background, his grandfather having been a famous actor at the turn of the century and his father 'Dandy' Lewes having managed the Theatre Royal in Liverpool. Dandy's son had theatrical aspirations too, after appearing in a few comedies at the Whitehall Theatre and touring with Charles Dickens's company, but the real highlight of his stage career he regarded as his performances in his own play, *The Noble Heart*, on the London stage and later in the provinces. George Lewes accepted the fact that he would never be a great actor and had moved into the field of journalism, where he had become a well-respected literary critic. Under the pseudonym 'Vivian', Lewes penned some lively and perceptive comments about the London theatre world. Journalist he might be but his appearance still had something of the showman about it. He was small, agile, flamboyant in his dress and manner, always the life and soul of the party and hence a popular name on many guest lists. Lewes never had any qualms about pushing himself forward. In his early days as a dramatist he contacted a leading critic to say he thought they ought to know each other; his cheek secured him an invitation and off he went armed with a copy of his latest play to read to the great man. He also made it his business to meet John Stuart Mill, when the philosopher was influential at the *Westminster Review*. Friendships had been shamelessly cultivated with other literary people, like the critic Thomas Carlyle and novelists Charlotte Brontë, William Thackeray and Charles Dickens; indeed there were few distinguished authors in London Lewes could not claim some personal acquaintance with. He did not restrict himself to English writers: as soon as George Sand's novels began to appear in England, he started corresponding with her, enclosing some of his own work. Although Lewes never met Sand, he managed so successfully to convey the impression that he was a key figure in the London cultural scene that she told a friend planning to visit England that a call on Lewes was essential because he knew many eminent people and was himself distinguished. He developed other connections among the European intelligentsia and was said to have the charisma to worm his way in anywhere.

Mr Lewes was not welcome in all social circles. One Victorian matron complained that 'he had neither shame nor reticence in his choice of subjects, but would discourse on the most delicate matters of physiology with no more perception that he was transgressing the bounds of propriety than if he had been a learned savage. I heard more startling things from Lewes,' she continued, 'in full conclave of young and old, married and single, men and women, than I had ever dreamt of or heard hinted at before and . . . it was all very embarrassing and shocking.'[4] Having been initiated by Bray and Chapman, Marian was far from embarrassed and enjoyed Lewes's ribald stories to the full. Nevertheless what she did find disconcerting was his bold and familiar behaviour towards women. He was quite likely to shout out a teasing comment across a crowded room, drawing all eyes on to the unfortunate female, or lean over and kiss an unsuspecting lady who came to take her leave. Despite being married with five children, he revelled in his reputation as a rake and would fuel it with talk of his latest conquests. Mrs Carlyle, writing of one visit Mr and Mrs Lewes paid her, expressed surprise that George Lewes should have spent the whole time raving about the delights of 'Julia' who had taken his soul captive with her 'dark luxurious eyes' and 'smooth, firm flesh'.[5] Eventually his wife Agnes rounded on him with contempt to enquire how he knew so much about Miss Paulet's flesh. Had he been feeling it? Cynicism and contempt had dominated the Lewes marriage long before, as Marian knew from juicy snippets Charles Bray enjoyed relating to her.

In public Lewes was still the genial entertainer, but in private he was lonely and disillusioned. It was in this mood that he found solace in the company of Herbert Spencer whose advanced ideas about evolution took him on peaceful plant-hunting expeditions to Kew Gardens.

Marian was astounded to discover the misandristic[6] Sara Hennell held a high opinion of George Lewes. Sara was hardly likely to tolerate Lewes's risqué jokes, but in fact she saw a different facet of the man – the well-informed intellectual. In the cloistered atmosphere of the Hennells' London home she had met him as a friend of her adored brother Charles Christian, and Lewes's behaviour on these occasions was impeccable. He gave the impression of being a cultured European who could speak French like a native, having been at school in Nantes for a time, and could converse in German equally well after two years as a tutor in Berlin and Dresden. He even flattered Sara by seeking her opinion of Goethe for his biography of the great German writer. From her brother, Sara heard that Lewes made a comfortable living from writing articles for magazines, in addition to publishing two plays and two novels, but, for her, his best work would always be the erudite *Biographical History of Philosophy*, of which four volumes had been published and two more were on the way.

These conflicting accounts of Lewes were known to Marian before the man himself and she imagined him as a dashing Byronesque figure. Her romantic image was shattered when she encountered him in a bookshop in Piccadilly. The person Chapman introduced her to was an ugly little man who looked out from a tangle of beard, hair and moustache and resembled in her words more 'a miniature Mirabeau' than any statuesque Byron.[7] To her amusement, Chapman reported that the Carlyles had nicknamed Lewes the 'Ape' because he always looked shaggy and could never sit still for five minutes. Marian found it hard to credit that this was the womanizer Bray had told her about. Lewes's wiry body lacked any obvious physical attractions and those parts of his face which showed through the curly mass of hair indicated a complexion ravaged by smallpox. She admitted he had expressive eyes; moreover his manner of addressing her conveyed the impression he had singled her out particularly for attention. Marian, wiser as a result of her experiences with Chapman, was not taken in. Over the following weeks she observed Lewes at various social gatherings turning exactly the same charm on all women he met. She dismissed him from her thoughts.

Lewes was fascinated by the unconventional woman who appeared at 142 Strand, the more so because she seemed impervious to his advances. He had heard she was a protégée of Bray's and, knowing of Bray's and Chapman's extramarital activities, doubted whether the dowdy spinster was as virginal as she appeared. She was two years his junior, had a good figure, was taller than average for a woman, but would hardly rate as a beauty, her looks being ruined by a conspicuous nose and a jutting chin. Her face was transformed when she smiled, and she had an endearing way of gazing with rapt attention on anyone who came to talk to her, whatever the topic. Lewes knew of Miss Evans's reputation as a brilliant scholar, thought her Strauss translation masterly and was impressed by her ability to converse intelligently on subjects as diverse as chemistry and French literature. Everything pointed to her being a quite exceptional woman. During the months that followed, he watched the progress of the *Westminster* with a professional eye, aware of Chapman's limitations and of the real brains behind the quarterly. Marian's skill in restoring the magazine's literary reputation he thought truly astonishing.

Lewes was quite prepared to accept a woman as his equal if her abilities warranted it and, from what he saw of Marian's editorial work, he judged she could do the job as well as himself. His keen sense of fairness had been applied to his own marriage from the start. Lewes encouraged his wife to continue her education and, since she had a flair for languages, suggested she might translate articles from European journals which he would get published for her. Victorian double standards infuriated him: that it was perfectly proper for married men to have extramarital affairs, even a full-time mistress if they could afford it, yet demand total fidelity from their wives, was an anathema to him. His wife was permitted the same freedom as himself. Love alone had brought them together and alone should bind them, he said, not any archaic laws or religious rituals. Should the love or inclination of either party alter, then they were free to act as they believed fit. The one restriction the Leweses placed on their 'open marriage', to call it by a modern name, was that there should be no irresponsible production of bastards: the only children permitted were to be their own offspring.

Contraceptive practices were widely known to men and women in the radical middle classes. John Chapman, whose medical studies predictably centred on gynaecology, was an advocate of a rhythm method of birth control expounded by one Ricirovski, and he kept a careful record of the menstrual cycle of his wife and many of his female lodgers in his personal diary. The condom, vaginal sponge and *coitus interruptus* were also used to prevent conception at this time, and George Lewes expected his wife to ensure the use of one such method if necessary.

The Leweses' honeymoon period lasted several years before each began to think about their agreed freedoms. George was assured of plenty of pretty and willing partners in the theatre whereas Agnes, bored with academic pursuits, turned her talents to a more interesting subject – namely Thornton Hunt, her husband's business partner. Hunt, the attractive olive-skinned son of Leigh Hunt, who had been a great friend of the amoral Shelley, was more than delighted to incorporate Agnes into his phalanstery. Superficially the Leweses lived together harmoniously with Lewes's widowed mother, but in practice each enjoyed other sexual partners – George a great many others.

Bray told Marian that Mrs Lewes had broken her side of the bargain by bearing a child by another man, but Marian paid little attention to the information. The Leweses had got exactly what they asked for, she said, and could hardly complain. Her sister Chrissey, on the other hand, did not deserve what fate had doled out, and Marian, so preoccupied in sorting out affairs there, failed to notice that George Lewes was determinedly seeking her out. Simultaneously he cultivated a friendship with Charles Bray in an effort to learn more about the extraordinary Marian. To her annoyance, she discovered that everything she had ever said or done at Rosehill appeared to be known to Lewes.[8] Irritating though that was, Marian could not help but enjoy Lewes's company; he was always around and such good fun. In fact, she admitted to Bray that Lewes had quite won her liking in spite of herself. To her mind he was simply a colleague, albeit an exceedingly able one. 'The editor of editors', she dubbed him.[9] It never crossed her mind to consider him as a possible lover. Sometimes he visited with Spencer, at other times alone, but either way in the bleak early months of 1853 Marian was grateful for a sympathetic ear to the troubles with her sister, the *Westminster Review* or her general dispiritedness. Not only did Lewes listen and offer practical advice, but best of all he could make her laugh. 'Like a few other people in the world, he is much better than he seems – a man of heart and conscience wearing a mask of flippancy,' Marian concluded.[10]

Once Lewes permitted the mask to slip, he found it comparatively easy to tell Marian he loved her. She was astounded. After years of unsuccessful man-hunting, she had concluded that she was such an oddity that she must lead her life alone. The circumstances with Charles Bray had been such that long ago they had agreed their intimacy could exist only on a mental plane. Any sexual attraction she had felt for him had been transformed into an intense sisterly devotion. It was not the most satisfying arrangement for a woman who desperately wanted a sexual partner. Consequently Lewes's declaration of love was met with a torrent of passion and emotion. Marian never had the slightest hesitation in giving herself completely to him. The fact that he was already married never concerned her. All that mattered was to enjoy what had been so long coming.

The summer of 1853 turned glorious once Marian took a lover. Her headaches disappeared and her spirits rose. Others sensing a change in her found her excellent company and invited her to join them. Would Marian like to spend two months on the Continent with Mr and Mrs George Combe? Or might she like to go on a tour of the south coast with Bessie Parkes and Barbara Leigh Smith? Either would have been gratefully accepted a few months earlier but now, basking in George

Lewes's affection, Marian was reluctant to move out of London. Even her planned sojourn by the sea in late July and August, when the *Westminster* was quiet and the Strand noisome, was no longer an attractive proposition until Lewes persuaded her. Continue with the holiday, he urged, and he would keep in regular contact by letter. Since St Leonards was an easy rail journey from London, he would come and stay frequently. There, away from the public gaze, they could spend time together.

Marian agreed. She had been so swept off her feet by the rapid progress of events that she welcomed a quiet period in which to reflect. Nevertheless she would not have gone without George's assurance that they could be together some of the time. In the same peaceful seaside resort where she had once taken her father to convalesce, Marian contemplated her future. George had never promised her marriage; indeed he had been open about the fact that such an arrangement was impossible. He had a wife living and English law was such that divorce was virtually unobtainable. In the past, Marian had had lengthy discussions with the ardent young feminists Bessie Parkes and Barbara Leigh Smith about the unfairness of a law which refused to accept adultery on the part of the husband as suitable grounds for divorce unless it was combined with intolerable cruelty or 'unnatural practices'; even then the best a wife could get was a separation order from her husband, not a divorce. However, adultery on the part of the wife was treated very seriously because a man owned exclusive rights to his wife. Moreover her adultery might cause his property to be handed down to children who were not legitimately his. In such a case divorce was possible but entailed petitioning Parliament at a cost of around seven hundred pounds for an Act to dissolve the marriage. Even if Lewes possessed the money he could not have secured a divorce because he had condoned his wife's adultery in the first instance by giving his own surname to the two children he knew had been fathered by Thornton Hunt. By law the Leweses were bound together, for better or for worse, until death parted them.

It was not just in the fictional world of *Jane Eyre* that people found themselves trapped within sham marriages. Marian knew full well that Thackeray was bound to an insane wife he could not be free of. Gossip circulated in London that the middle-aged critic Ruskin's marriage had broken down irrevocably; Mr Ruskin, it was said, detested his beautiful young wife and ignored her completely. She in turn was increasingly being seen with her husband's handsome young protégé, the rising artist John Millais. In London as in the provinces, Marian had seen that archaic marriage laws caused great misery. She had no hesitation in ignoring them.

During the six weeks she was out of London, Marian considered what options she had. She totally discounted any idea of giving George up; neither did she want to carry on a secret affair, snatching odd moments together. Past experience encouraged her to be bold. She had once braved her father's wrath to demand religious freedom and survived; similarly, despite family disapproval, she had gone off to London and led a successful, independent life. She was quite prepared to set up home with Lewes should he suggest it and continue her journalism as before. There would be criticism she knew, but few men of her acquaintance led blameless lives and were hardly in a position to criticize her or George.

Lewes admired Marian's courage but urged caution. His own philandering had always been treated as a joke, but Agnes's, he knew, had been criticized. There was one rule for the man and another for the woman, and he was reluctant to subject this latest girlfriend to ostracism. Lewes had also been taken aback by the strength of Marian's attachment to him and the lengths to which she was prepared to go. For his part he was very fond of her and flattered by her undoubted devotion to him; but he had never contemplated a permanent future with her and was wary of enmeshing himself in another relationship. If he lived openly with her, she would become a pariah, unable to get her work accepted by any editor. The only future for them, he said, was on the Continent. There, everyone knew that marriages were arranged by parents when their children were young merely to ensure the succession of property; nobody pretended these were love matches. Instead, everyone had the freedom to enjoy whatever *affaires de coeur* they wished. Only in that sort of environment would a liaison such as theirs be understood. But, Lewes knew, they could not live abroad permanently. It was unlikely that they could obtain sufficient work to keep themselves and pay for Agnes's and the children's upkeep in London. He believed the only solution was for Marian to be his mistress, living and working from her own establishment in London. That way she would retain her all-important good name and they could be together as much as they chose. He privately favoured such an arrangement because it would not tie Marian to him permanently. If he tired of her, as he always had of previous women, he could extricate himself from the relationship without any more serious damage to her than a broken heart.

Marian listened to his arguments about a possible future on the Continent for them and agreed. She had enjoyed her time in Switzerland and would have had no hesitation in returning there. If they settled in Germany, she could assist George in the research for his Goethe book. As to a future in England together, she could see the difficulties. Even in the enlightened capital city, people's hypocrisy and prejudice were no different from those in Coventry. In her heart of hearts, Marian knew she could not vanish abroad and leave Chrissey, nor walk out on her job at the *Westminster*. George too had responsibilities and genuinely cared about his own three children. If he and Marian were to go away together it could not be immediately. Marian was not disheartened by difficulties and suggested they look towards leaving early in 1854. In the intervening six months they could ease themselves out and make provision for their various dependants. To make life more tolerable she would take private lodgings. Away from the all-seeing eyes at Chapman's, they could be alone together and not provoke scandal. It was a compromise which Marian disliked, but there was undoubted logic in George's argument.

Now that she had discovered true love at the advanced age of thirty-three, she had no intention of letting it slip from her grasp. She was hardly likely to get another chance.

Early in September when she returned to the Strand, Marian announced once again she was moving somewhere quieter. John Chapman's request to postpone her departure fell on deaf ears because she was out most of the time inspecting new premises. To his amazement, she even talked of advertising if nothing suitable came up.[11] In the evenings she was also out accompanying George Lewes to the opera and theatre, even going backstage with him to meet the performers. Friendship with Lewes opened many doors but it also raised a few eyebrows. Joseph Parkes noted privately that Miss Evans had been out of her depth ever since she arrived in London and had mixed with men of the worst morals. Some members of that set, he added self-righteously, had no principles at all, either social or religious.[12]

Marian was oblivious to all this. In her new mood of determination, it took her only a few weeks to locate suitable lodgings in a street quietly tucked away on the north side of Hyde Park. Two small rooms on a ground floor permitted the unobtrusive entry and exit of visitors. From then on George Lewes spent most of his time with Marian, even bringing his work there in the day. The birth of Agnes Lewes's third child by Hunt, soon after Marian had settled into 21 Cambridge Street, seemed to the lovers to endorse the morality of their unorthodox union.

'I begin this year more happily than I have done most years of my life,' Marian recorded on her thirty-fourth birthday in November 1853.[13] Although the location of her new home was inconvenient for an editor of the *Westminster Review*, being a three-mile walk to the Strand, it had other advantages. Marian was no longer at Chapman's beck and call, nor the recipient of all the odd jobs he relied on her doing and which she never had the heart to refuse. None the less Chapman was a frequent visitor, bringing work and attempting to woo her back to his abode. But she would never consider it: 'When I put my head into the house in the Strand I feel that I have gained, or rather escaped, a great deal physically by my change,' she wrote ambiguously, enabling Charles and Cara Bray to interpret her words according to their respective knowledge of her lifestyle.[14] To Bray and Chapman alone she admitted that Lewes was her lover, because she knew both men would understand and not condemn her. If she had not told them, they would likely have guessed and, knowing their penchant for gossip, make matters worse. As it was, she only entrusted the information to them in exchange for a guarantee of silence about her conduct.

Although no longer at the hub of literary activity, Marian found that many of the friends she had made at Chapman's still came in search of her. Harriet Martineau, Herbert Spencer, even her old admirer Robert Mackay, now wedded and looking cleaner round the collar, she noticed, visited her poky rooms in Cambridge Street.[15] Bessie Parkes and Barbara Leigh Smith called regularly, bringing their poetry and paintings for Marian's perusal as well as news of Barbara's proposed publication to advance the cause of women's rights. Ostensibly the pamphlet advocated changes in property laws for married women, but Marian was interested to note that the whole tone of Barbara's arguments dismissed matrimony as having no advantage for women.

Inevitably rumours of Marian's involvement with Lewes circulated, aided by innocuous remarks from Chapman, who 'happened' to
mention to one person that he had seen proofs of Lewes's forthcoming
book on Miss Evans's table. This hint left plenty of room for
speculation. Though many guessed Marian was Lewes's current
mistress, it made no difference to her social acceptability. Invitations
to dine with the Parkes and other notable families continued to roll in
and, provided Miss Evans did not advertise her liaison, nobody
minded. Joseph Parkes did, however, take it upon himself to suggest
to Marian that she was playing with fire, but she made no response. It
infuriated her that Parkes should preach morality to her when
everybody knew that, while his wife lived in one of his London
houses, his mistress resided in another. Marian also suspected that this
holier-than-thou MP had pocketed the profits from sales of her Strauss
translation, since she had never received any royalties.[16] If he was an
example of the values of London society she was very happy to reject
them.

Having left the Strand, Marian still had to wean Chapman from
dependence on her. She told him bluntly that he must look elsewhere
for a new editor as she intended to become freelance, but Chapman
had heard this all before and took not the slightest notice. There was in
any case no money in his coffers to pay the wages of a male editor and
he did not know any good female ones who would come cheaply.
Marian was cross that he ignored what she said, but she was far more
annoyed to discover that Chapman had advertised two forthcoming
publications by the translator of Strauss. One was to be a translation of
Feuerbach's *The Essence of Christianity* and the other a non-fiction
book entitled *The Idea of a Future Life*; neither had even been started.
Ideas for both books had been discussed by Chapman and Marian
earlier in the year but nothing had been finalized. Since then Marian
had made other plans and, knowing Chapman could neither afford to
commission or to publish the works, presumed the matter closed. She
was furious to find him irresponsibly proclaiming the appearance of
these books and bitterly regretted that she had allowed herself to be
associated with the series in the first place. With all the pomposity of
her father, she told him: 'Friendship is not to be depended on, but
business has rather more guarantees.'[17]

Despite believing Feuerbach's book to be '*the* book of the age',
Marian started work on the translation with ill-grace in December

1853. She suspected John Chapman of deliberately trying to keep a hold on her by committing her to such a lengthy literary task; she had told him that her proposed book on the after-life was bound to take a year to write and the translation could easily take the same time. They were both profitless tasks from a financial point of view because there was to be no payment for the Feuerbach and the other book was to be on a 'half profits' basis (precisely o/o was Marian's prediction). These tasks not only diverted her from earning money for Chrissey, but even worse actually cost her money because reference books were needed. Surely, she demanded of Chapman, if he was not prepared to pay for the work, at least he could pay her book bill or her subscription to the London Library.[18] Because the study of the after-life would require more books, Chapman suggested they postpone publication of that to some unspecified later date. Marian was dismayed by his cavalier attitude and said he ought to regard the whole thing as a matter of personal honour, rather than merely think of his pocket. She felt a responsibility to the reading public to keep faith with the announcement and would produce a translation of the Feuerbach, but she could hardly be expected to edit the *Westminster* at the same time. Very cleverly she took the opportunity to manoeuvre her resignation for 1 January 1854.

Despite her intention of being free to leave for the Continent early in 1854, Marian did not find it as straightforward as she had anticipated. By applying herself single-mindedly for long hours, she had the Feuerbach text ready for printing by the end of March; it had taken her three months. Lewes meanwhile had been tying up the ends of his various theatrical and journalistic enterprises in a leisurely fashion, making some temporary provision for the welfare of his mother, wife and children and pondering on going to Weimar. If they went at the end of May, he thought, the summer could be spent in collecting further information on Goethe and completing the manuscript of the biography.

By early April it was apparent that Lewes was in no state to travel. The carefree playboy had found the strain of a complicated business and private life too much and he collapsed from exhaustion. A close friend collected him up and took him off to recuperate in Hampshire, well away from deadlines and domestic entanglements. It was a terrible blow to Marian, who could see the vision of her future happiness disappearing. Nevertheless for both their sakes, Lewes had to get better, and she agreed to help her lover by taking over his weekly book review column in the *Leader* along with other odd pieces of work she had continued to accept for the *Westminster Review* despite her resignation. Lewes was intensely grateful to Marian and had no doubt that her work would be of a high enough standard. He had in the past accepted her contributions under the 'Vivian' pseudonym when he had been too hard-pressed to produce the reviews himself. For a month she valiantly struggled to generate copy and edit proofs for the *Leader*, lend assistance with the *Westminster Review* and watch the Feuerbach translation through the printing stages. Without the advice and comfort of George, Marian found the sheer volume of work onerous and the outlook bleak, but in the belief that hard work was an excellent antidote to depression, she toiled on. To her delight George returned to London in mid-May, though still far from well. A severe headache, toothache and a ringing noise in the ears persisted, which his doctor insisted required the Malvern water cure and further convalescence in the countryside. With a sinking heart Marian saw him off once more. Was happiness destined to elude her?

A month later he was back in town, slightly better but still in need of convalescence. Marian took the initiative. The best thing for his health would be to go to Europe, she said. Astounded at this woman, who had already undertaken his work and was now prepared to compromise her good name for him, Lewes agreed. Few women he had known would have given so much.

The final preparations for departure were made hastily and in the fervent hope that no one would connect Marian's plans with Lewes's and place obstacles in the way. Fortunately Marian and George had not been seen together for several months, so gossip about them had died down. Marian knew that no member of the Evans family would ever understand or tolerate what she was about to do, so she let them assume she was travelling to the Continent alone, in the hope that she would retain the tiny fragment of love some of them had for her. Charles Bray was aware she was travelling with Lewes and promised to maintain regular contact with Chrissey, keep Marian informed and render any immediate assistance that might be needed. Arrangements were also carefully made for Isaac to pay Marian's half-yearly allowance directly to Charles Bray. By this method her exact whereabouts could be kept secret but the money would arrive on time. She knew Isaac of old and any excuse to delay payment to her would be fully exploited.

When it came to telling Cara and Sara about her intentions, Marian opted out. Neither would be able to comprehend her overwhelming desire to share her life with a man. For the first time she felt guilty, not about what she was doing, but that she was deceiving the two women who had been closer than sisters to her. They had loved and assisted her every step of the way, sharing her joys and frustrations, yet she felt they never fully understood her. Desperate to retain their affection, she said merely that she was going abroad and left Charles to reveal as much of the truth as he thought they could accept. The briefest of notes arrived at Rosehill on 20 July 1854 saying simply that her address for the next six weeks would be Poste Restante Weimar and afterwards Berlin.

CHAPTER 11

An Infamous Seduction,
1854–1855

There were several events in the summer of 1854 which captured the public's imagination far more than the disappearance of Miss Evans. Marian only had a small circle of acquaintances in London and few realized at the time that she had gone off to Germany with a married man. The fact that she was absent from the capital during the height of the summer was not exceptional, and the general assumption was that she had either returned home to the country or gone away to the seaside. The usual callers at 142 Strand were far too busy discussing the critic John Ruskin's impotence to concern themselves with the whereabouts of that serious middle-aged-looking assistant Chapman employed on the *Westminster Review*. Enormous interest had been generated by court proceedings started by Ruskin's wife Effie to annul their marriage on the grounds that it had never been consummated. All the intimate details of the Ruskins' sex-life were dragged out in court and the eminent art critic became too embarrassed to show his face around town.

The newspapers carried minimal details of the Ruskin affair, being preoccupied with momentous international events. Britain and France had declared war on Russia in March 1854 and, as the first major conflict for forty years, the Crimean War attracted enormous public attention. Developments in the use of the telegraph allied to an expansion in the popular press meant that this was the most publicized war ever, its campaigns discussed countrywide. Writing to his daughter in October 1854, Joseph Parkes first spent several sides of paper warning her of the social dangers of being associated with the unfortunate Miss Evans, and then devoted the rest of his letter to detailing Lord Raglan's account of the march around Sebastopol. Parkes's imagination had been fired by an account he had read in *The Times* which caused him to wax classical over military manoeuvres, claiming they were quite as glorious as anything in Xenophon or Tacitus, while the naval battles engaged such a host as had never been seen since the days of Xerxes.[1]

The other face to this war was not smothered in classical glory, but dominated by pain and ineptitude. At the request of a leading Cabinet minister, Barbara Leigh Smith's cousin Florence Nightingale had assembled thirty-eight nurses in the late summer of 1854 and was setting sail for the Crimea when news of the Evans–Lewes affair broke in London. Ironically her work in the Scutari hospital was to draw greater support for the feminist cause she eschewed than all the campaigning of her militant cousin. Miss Nightingale never wanted anyone to associate her with the author of the provocative pamphlet headed *A Brief Summary, in Plain Language, of the Most Important Laws of England concerning Women* which had been published that same summer. Not only was the booklet written by Barbara Leigh Smith, but it was totally financed by her. Its avowed aim was to state in the clearest terms the legal position of married and unmarried women, but Barbara employed such a clever unemotional style of writing that the reader was left in no doubt about the severe injustices women faced.

Marian had known about Barbara's proposed work for some time and had listened with quiet amusement to her young friend attacking English marriage laws. When the pamplet did appear, it ruffled few feathers despite its potentially contentious subject. The circulation was small and mainly among the already converted. Nevertheless, Barbara Leigh Smith's pamphlet did mark the beginning of a concerted effort to improve women's rights.

In 1854 it was the non-sectarian co-educational infant school she opened in a poor area of London which drew more public attention because of advanced ideas: girls and boys were taught the same lessons alongside each other and all punishments were abolished. Among the pupils at this very daring school were the children of John Chapman, the publisher, and Giuseppe Garibaldi, the exiled Italian revolutionary. Marian was deeply committed to the cause of girls' education and gave Barbara what advice she could, based on her limited experience of the Brays' school in Coventry. Before she left for Germany, she put Barbara in contact with Charles Bray.

It was not until the beginning of October, over two months after their departure, that a story began circulating about George Lewes running away to Germany with Miss Evans. When this reached the ears of Barbara Leigh Smith, she was full of admiration; her belief in the strength of Marian's character had been justified. With the exception of Herbert Spencer, no one else shared Barbara's admiration. The general attitude to the episode was one of disgust at the way Lewes had seduced that 'strong-minded woman' from the *Westminster Review*. News of the scandal spread round London with the virulence of cholera and even reached liberal circles in Birmingham, though it was never public knowledge in Coventry or Nuneaton.[2] Lewes was well known as a radical journalist, but the identity of his latest paramour was confused. At first it was thought he had run off with Harriet Taylor, who had written for the *Westminster Review* in the days of John Stuart Mill. At the time Mrs Taylor's frequent trips to the Continent without her husband, ostensibly in search of health but invariably in the company of Mr Mill, provoked much gossip. That Harriet Taylor went on to marry Mill after the death of her husband only confirmed in people's minds the idea that Continental jaunts were never as innocent as they seemed. Similarly, suggestions that Miss Evans had accompanied Mr Lewes to Germany to help him convalesce, or, as some said, to assist him in his Goethe research, were scornfully dismissed. Everybody knew exactly what Mr Lewes enjoyed studying.

Marian's work at the *Westminster Review* had always been kept as quiet as possible lest it upset the contributors, who might think it demeaning to submit their work to a woman. Once details of the Lewes affair came to light there was an even greater effort to dissociate her name from the journal. The real fear was that this scandal, coming on top of investigations by the quarterly's sponsors into Chapman's misappropriation of the review's funds, would do irreparable damage to the radical cause and sound the death-knell of the *Westminster Review*. Joseph Parkes flew into such a temper when he received the news about Marian that it was feared he would have a stroke. To his daughter he condemned those 'selfish and sensual acts' in the strongest terms he could use.[3] 'I call [Lewes's] concubinage with Miss Evans, (not his first amour of the kind) an infamous seduction,' he blustered. After a few platitudes about deeply pitying Miss Evans, whom he knew would be abandoned like Lewes's previous females, Parkes launched into his real worry:

> The event is most unfortunate as regards Liberalism. Individuals holding or professing their peculiar opinions and political principles ought to be especially careful in conduct. However extreme some of the views on social systems of this particular set may be, yet still Progress is their object; and it is a serious reflection on common Liberal principles, when two such highly gifted individuals bring such shame on their professions. In this light I heard it universally condemned and deplored in London. It is a great disgrace and drawback. Is there no friendship, no communion of minds, without this violation of marital and parental obligations?

Thus asked Parkes, whose own extramarital activities would never have stood up to close investigation.

Like the majority of people, Parkes believed Lewes had no business abandoning his wife, whatever the state of their marriage. No sensible middle-class man expected to love or be faithful to his wife; marriages were not contracted for sentimental reasons. It was understood that a man's pleasure was taken with prostitutes and mistresses, as Lewes had been content to do in the past. Private assignations of this nature were much preferable to public scandals, which set a bad example to the lower classes. As to Miss Evans, Parkes admitted her downfall was the more unfortunate because she was a clever woman and made such an excellent dining companion, but her behaviour amounted to social hara-kiri. It was all too likely that, come the end of the year, she would reappear totally penniless in London minus Lewes. Then her presence would be a great irritation and embarrassment to everybody. Both Joseph Parkes and Benjamin Leigh Smith were worried that Miss Evans might have infected their daughters with her immorality, for her brilliant arguing powers had made a great impression on the younger women.

The obsession with propriety of these two men, whose private lives she knew were anything but virtuous, infuriated Marian when word reached her. Years later, when she took up novel writing, she ensured that their like received their come-uppance; in most of George Eliot's novels there is a self-righteous middle-class male whose hypocrisy is exposed by a spectre from his shady past. In *Middlemarch* the banker

Bulstrode is embarrassed by the reappearance of Raffles; in *Daniel Deronda*, Grandcourt by the appearance of his mistress and children; whilst in *Felix Holt, The Radical* several respectable figures are haunted by past misdemeanours.

Despite the incessant sermons on moral behaviour which bombarded Bessie Parkes with every post, she did not sever links with Marian; instead she deliberately wrote to her in Germany. From the beginning of her acquaintance with Marian, Bessie had admired the older woman's refusal to conform and her desire for independence. To continue communicating with such an outlaw in the face of paternal displeasure became Bessie's gesture of rebellion. Despite their correspondence, relations between the two women gradually cooled, not because Bessie disapproved of the illicit love affair but because she disliked George Lewes intensely.[4] He was a thoroughly bad lot, she said, and she found it hard to understand why Marian with her lofty principles should idealize such a cad. Bessie retained that opinion of Lewes all her life even though she realized that this man was the centre of Marian's life and the inspiration for her authorship.

Public opinion was firmly on the side of Mrs Lewes, the abandoned wife, who was rumoured to be once again *enceinte* with another of 'those dirty sooty skinned children which have Th[ornto]n Hunt for father'.[5] Although the mixed parentage of Mrs Lewes's brood was common knowledge, even among respectable young women like Bessie Parkes, Mrs Lewes was still cast in the role of the wronged wife. Opinions as to who was the villain of the piece varied. Some believed it to be Lewes, the seducer, but others condemned Miss Evans as the one who had lured a married man away from his family. It was accepted that a man had powerful sexual needs which he struggled to keep in check, but a woman was not supposed to have such problems, being blessed with a highly developed moral sense which she was expected to employ under all circumstances. 'Love of home, children and domestic duties are the only passions women feel,' a manual for young ladies stated in 1862. Miss Evans had flouted the rules and brought shame to the name of womanhood, and consequently women were louder in condemning Marian's behaviour than men, pointing out that her sin had arisen from contravening God's law. A woman's place was in the home under the direction of a father or husband; in the case of a spinster like Miss Evans, she should have remained in the household of her brother. It was never ordained that a lady should be studious or that she should work for her living; a lady is simply a lady and does nothing else. To Marian's horror she learned that her behaviour had dealt a great blow to feminism. Everything Barbara Leigh Smith was fighting for was discredited by Marian's actions. Thereafter she was careful never to let her name be publicly associated with the Women's Movement, convinced it would do them more harm than good.

The furore which the Evans–Lewes affair caused in radical circles took Marian and George completely off guard and decided their future for them. When the two of them set off for Germany, it was not with the intention of cutting themselves off from their former lives. They were simply taking a holiday; admittedly they were living and sleeping together on a more regular basis than they had done before, but they never regarded their action as an elopement. Lewes had not decided to leave his wife for Marian. The last thing he wanted was another permanent relationship when his present one was causing him enough problems. Marian Evans, intelligent, considerate and extremely responsive, proved the ideal companion. Because she was a free-thinker, Lewes believed she would take a lover without worrying about conventions, and when the time came to admit the affair was over, he trusted her to be sensible and disappear without a fuss. He presumed she would then become someone else's mistress, but since Lewes lived essentially for the moment, he let the future take care of itself. His thirty-seven years had made him cynical; all romances eventually went sour, he believed. His own marriage had actually been a love match, despite the objections of his wife's wealthy parents, but after a few years the affection had dwindled. The only people he cared deeply about were his three sons, and Lewes assumed, once the German expedition was over, that he would return home and life would resume its monotonous pattern.

This was not Marian's vision of the future. She adored George with all the fervour of a thirty-five-year-old who believed herself to be on the shelf. She regarded Lewes as the love of her life, not merely a casual affair, and determined to fight tooth and nail to retain his love. She had never thought of their journey to Germany as an elopement, but, unlike Lewes, she did not expect life to carry on as before once the holiday ended. Although she had told Bray she might stay in Germany for twelve months, keeping herself by writing and teaching, once she had tasted the pleasure of being with George, she abandoned that idea.[6] Marian was determined to live with Lewes permanently and openly, not to be a clandestine mistress visited only when he had time. When she gave herself to a man, it was for life and she demanded the same commitment in return.

Their stay on the Continent turned into an idyllic honeymoon. No one expressed the slightest surprise that they travelled together despite not being man and wife. This had been something which had concerned Marian beforehand, but her fears were allayed early on when she was recognized by a passenger on the cross-Channel steamer. Fortunately this was Robert Noel, brother of Cara's beloved Edward Noel and as tolerant an individual as Marian could have wished to meet. He was returning home to his aristocratic German wife, but since this relative of Byron had himself engaged in some spectacular liaisons with women like Goethe's daughter-in-law, he was scarcely in a position to pass judgement. Indeed Noel proved a most considerate travelling companion, leaving the two lovers alone on deck to watch the setting sun and only joining them at their insistence. He also volunteered useful information on people and places Lewes ought to visit for his Goethe research, including Ottilie Goethe, the woman Noel had once loved.

A chance meeting with Dr Robert Brabant on the train to Cologne was not welcome to Marian. She had encountered him at Chapman's on numerous occasions since the unfortunate fiasco ten years earlier, so she no longer felt uncomfortable in his presence. Nevertheless Marian did not like or trust him, and guessed that some version of his encounter with them would soon be circulating in London with all the innuendoes Brabant so enjoyed. Forced to endure his presence in their railway carriage for some considerable time, Marian deliberately steered the conversation along safe literary lines and stressed her role as the translator of German texts required by Mr Lewes for his Goethe biography. Brabant, equally keen to demonstrate his broad-mindedness towards the 'runaways', as he believed them to be, was especially congenial. Because it was late when the train arrived at Cologne, Marian found it impossible to be rid of Brabant. He stayed the night in the town, though to Marian's immense relief not in the same hotel; nevertheless, immediately after dinner the doctor's dapper figure reappeared in their hotel bursting with excitement. Friedrich Strauss, author of *Das Leben Jesu*, was also staying in Cologne, and since Dr Brabant had been instrumental in organizing the English translation of this book in the first place, he wanted the honour of introducing the author to the translator.

In the event, the meeting was an anticlimax. Marian had built up her own picture of this influential European theologian and found the real Strauss a great disappointment. He was a gloomy individual who seemed to have found torment rather than freedom in his religious questioning. Although there was so much Marian wanted to ask him, their conversation was strained. Strauss spoke no English and her German, usually employed on paper, was not fluent in speech. It was a great relief to all parties when the interview came to an end.

After Cologne, Marian and George were on their own as they travelled down to Goethe's birthplace at Frankfurt, and in early August they arrived in Weimar where the great German writer had spent a major part of his life. George proposed they stay on for several weeks to enjoy a holiday as well as work on the book. Marian had arrived at such a perfect sense of well-being and contentment that she would have agreed to anything George suggested. 'I have had a month of exquisite enjoyment, and seem to have begun life afresh,' she wrote to her old friend Charles Bray, and then went on to relate how they were regularly in the company of Liszt.[7] The introduction had come through Lewes, who had no qualms about seeking out the famous pianist and reminding him of an acquaintanceship made several years earlier in Vienna.

Liszt was delighted to reopen the friendship and extended warm hospitality to Lewes and his female companion. Marian was captivated by the composer: 'Genius, benevolence and tenderness beamed from his whole countenance, and his manners are in perfect harmony with it,' she wrote in her journal.[8] Basking in the love of Lewes, she could not have been in a more receptive mood to listen to a performance by this extraordinarily talented pianist. Positioning herself close to the piano in order to watch his hands and face as she listened, Marian was convinced that for the first time in her life she beheld real inspiration. From her earliest years music had possessed the power to stir her deeply, but in her heightened emotional state these performances by Liszt were some of the most memorable and sacred experiences of her life.

There was a quite different aspect of Liszt's life in Weimar which interested Marian, namely that he lived openly with the Princess Caroline Sayn-Wittgenstein, wife of a Russian prince. Everyone

accepted their relationship as normal and this gave Marian hope that
once back in England she and George could also live together openly.

The summer passed blissfully and both felt themselves restored to
full health as a result. 'I am happier every day and find my domesticity
more and more delightful and beneficial to me,' Marian wrote to John
Chapman. 'Affection, respect and intellectual sympathy deepen, and
for the first time in my life I can say to the moments "Verweilen Sie,
Sie sind so schön [Stay, you are so beautiful]." '9 In Weimar she
received her first letters from home. There was news from Chrissey,
Charles Bray, John Chapman and Bessie Parkes, and no evidence
from any of their correspondence that her liaison with Lewes had
caused problems, which gave Marian further grounds for optimism.
Lewes communicated with his wife and was pleased to hear news of
his sons' progress, but Mrs Lewes never bothered to enlighten her
husband about her latest pregnancy. Such news would be sure to
anger him and she feared the cessation of her money supply.

Free from worries and in better health than he had been for a long
time, Lewes made great progress with his Goethe biography both in
research and in drafting. Marian delighted in assisting her lover with
his work by translating documents from German and editing his
manuscript. She had long cherished the notion of a perfect relationship
being one which achieved a mental and physical bond. In her opinion,
it had been the absence of this unity which had ruined the Bray and
Chapman marriages, and Marian Evans was determined not to make
the same mistake. While intent on furthering her own career, she was
quite prepared to employ her intellectual skills to assist the man she
loved. Her naive overtures in the past had led to misunderstanding and
embarrassment, but when the Brabant episode had been forgotten,
Marian had enjoyed working anonymously for Bray and Chapman,
though she had never received the full measure of their affections
she would have liked. So desperate was she to retain the love of
George Lewes that she offered to subjugate all her own literary
ambitions to undertake the menial tasks and hack-work which would
free him for greater things. To her amazement George did not ask that
of her; he was the first man she had ever encountered who believed
enough in her ability to suggest they had an equal partnership of mind
and body. Although Marian gratefully agreed with George's proposition, the idea of a woman giving up her own ambitions to channel her
energies into the greater glory of her man never left her. When she

began writing fiction, this formed the core of a short story called 'Miss Brooke', later woven into the novel *Middlemarch*.

John Chapman wrote to offer the commission for an article on the French philosopher Victor Cousin's book *Madame de Sable* for the *Westminster Review* to either journalist. George encouraged Marian to accept it because he knew that after years of editing the work of others she longed to have the opportunity to put her own views in print. As he pointed out, employing an argument guaranteed to make sense to Robert Evans's daughter, it would be sensible for Marian to earn some money to keep them since a large proportion of his income went on maintaining his household in London.

The pattern of their working partnership, which began in Weimar, remained for the rest of their lives. In the mornings they worked until lunchtime. Since both had learned to apply themselves single-mindedly and professionally to their tasks, a great deal was achieved in the space of a few hours. The work of one was always read, appraised and edited by the other, before it was sent out. Similarly they enjoyed bouncing ideas off each other before putting pen to paper. Afternoons were frequently passed in walking, visiting friends or attending recitals. Some evenings were spent at the theatre, opera or concert hall, but by preference were passed at home together reading. In addition to their individual books read for relaxation, Marian and George always chose a more erudite tome, from which they took turns in reading aloud. By this means they extended their knowledge and reinforced their intellectual bond.

While George worked on drafts of his Goethe biography, Marian spent the month writing Chapman's article and mulling over the idea of translating Spinoza's *Ethics*. Offered a forum in the *Westminster Review* to air her own ideas with the safeguard of anonymity, Marian made full use of the opportunity. The *Madame de Sable* article was widened to include a consideration of the elevated status of women in eighteenth-century France when compared to the servitude experienced by women in nineteenth-century England. Writing as though the author were a man, which Marian always did, she went on to deal with another subject close to her heart, the hypocritical attitude of the English towards marriage. Referring to the French 'ideal programme' of a woman's life which started with a marriage of convenience at fifteen, was followed by a series of passionate affairs between the ages of twenty and thirty-eight, then settled to penitence and piety, Marian wrote sardonically: 'Heaven forbid that we should enter on a defence of French morals, most of all in relation to marriage!' However, her comments on English conjugal relations were scathing. Marriage rarely fostered sufficient passion to win or retain any woman, she stated, it merely condemned her to a life of perpetual embroidery or domestic drudgery. As if justifying her own liaison, Marian opined that the best unions were those 'formed in maturity of thought and feeling, and grounded only on inherent fitness and mutual attraction, [which] tended to bring women into more intelligent sympathy with men, and to heighten and complicate their share in the political drama'.[10]

John Chapman received her punchy article with dismay, realizing that the topic he had suggested had been slanted towards the very subject he wanted to dissociate the *Westminster Review* from. Keeping his word, he paid up the agreed £15 and published her work in the next issue of the quarterly, but he was tardy about commissioning any more material from the lovers on the Continent. Publication of the article could not have come at a worse time, for it appeared simultaneously with stories of the Evans–Lewes scandal. Chapman found himself bombarded by questions about the authorship of the article, Marian's whereabouts and her relationship with Mr Lewes. At the same time, meetings of the journal's creditors were taking place and Chapman wished heartily he had not got himself involved in any of it. He did his best to keep his promise to Marian and say nothing, but when the tales circulating about the pair became wildly outrageous, he tried to tone them down. Similarly when he heard Lewes being condemned as a violator of virgins, Chapman felt obliged to intervene and let slip a few hints about Marian's previous intimacy with Charles Bray and himself. That stoked the fires wonderfully, and to his horror Chapman received complaints from Bray in Coventry who had got to hear of these rumours and guessed their origin. Terrified of Marian's wrath if she found out, Chapman pleaded heavy business commitments and his letters to Marian ceased for several months as he waited for the dust to settle.

When Marian heard that she was being attacked for her immorality, she fought back with the same ferocity and passion she had shown in the earlier conflict with her father. As before, her heart ruled her head and she hurled words around which she regretted later. Presuming Cara Bray and her sister Sara would be against her on account of her sexual involvement with George Lewes, Marian wrote defiantly to Charles Bray that she was quite prepared to accept the consequences of the step she had taken and, if it meant the loss of friends, so be it.[11] Her two female friends, who were only gradually uncovering the truth of Marian's activities in Germany, were deeply hurt when Charles showed them the letter. It seemed that their former intimacy counted for nothing. Although Marian had always placed great stress on being open and truthful, it emerged that she had deliberately misled them about the nature of her trip to Germany. She had told them she was going to Germany to study and, since Mr Lewes 'happened' to be travelling in the same direction for his health, would be escorted by him. Cara believed her and was perplexed when she received a letter from Mrs Combe, the phrenologist's wife, enquiring about 'the dreadful happening' with Miss Evans.[12] Innocently, Cara wrote back reiterating the story Marian had told them and reassuring Mrs Combe that she was sure that, if some terrible mishap had really befallen Miss Evans, they would have heard. When the truth emerged, Cara was angry that she had been duped by Marian and made to look naive and foolish in the eyes of her friends. The final insult was to be cast off by her proud friend for a judgement she had not made. It was a wound Cara did not recover from. Marian's name never appeared in her diary again, their correspondence was limited to essential pleasantries and them did not meet again for almost six years. No open rift was apparent between them, but their former intimacy was at an end. Cara could not help but be suspicious of the close friendship which had existed between her husband and Marian for so many years, since events had proved that both of them were equally capable of disregarding conventional etiquette if they so chose.

Sara was just as angry as her sister, though for slightly different reasons. Whereas Cara saw Marian's behaviour towards them as a betrayal of trust, Sara thought it insulting. Marian had been so arrogant as to prejudge Sara's reactions, then condemn her for them. It seemed to Sara that Marian was setting herself above them by claiming that she had confided her plans in Charles because he was a man, which implied that they, mere women, were not capable of understanding her dilemma. The letter to Charles was the final straw to Sara, for it seemed a boast that Marian did not need their friendship any more. Cara licked her wounds sadly, but Sara with her characteristic hot temper dashed off an impassioned reply accusing Marian of overweening pride.

The vehemence of Sara's letter took Marian even more by surprise than the reports of Cara's profound sadness. Both reactions had been brought about by Marian's thoughtlessness and she felt extremely guilty that, in her own happiness, she had paid so little attention to the two who had looked after her for so long. Marian's reply was a desperate bid to heal the wounds she had inflicted with lines like 'you, Cara and Mr Bray are the most cherished friends I have in the world', repeated a little later on as 'Cara, you and my own sister [Chrissey] are the three women who are tied to my heart by a cord which can never be broken and which really *pulls* me continually.'[13] The letter was designed to smooth things over but, though it ended with yet another reiteration of love, Marian made it clear that such a love as she felt for the two sisters would always be second best to that of a man's love.

Sara was able to accept her old friend's apology and friendship between the two of them began again, but she could not help adding: 'I have a sort of strange feeling that I am writing to someone in a book and not the Marian we have known and loved so many years.'[14] Never again were there affectionate valedictions to their letters suggesting they were husband and wife. Marian's behaviour had introduced a carnal element into life which Sara preferred to ignore. Their friendship could only be rebuilt on grounds of common intellectual and academic interests.

Letters from Rosehill cast a slight shadow over Marian's happiness, and letters from Chrissey telling of new family troubles added further darkening. One of the older nephews, whom Marian had tried so hard to place in a suitable position, had got himself into 'unmentionable' trouble and had had to be swiftly packed off to sea. The thought of her poor sister having to cope with this new problem made Marian homesick. There really was a cord attached to her heart when it came to Chrissey, and it wrenched in a way Marian could not ignore.

Troubles also began to settle on George late in 1854. He learned from his close friend Arthur Helps, who had assisted with his convalescence earlier in the year and came to visit the lovers in Weimar, that Agnes was pregnant again. Moreover, there had been such a hue and cry over reports that Lewes and Miss Evans had eloped together that there was no way the pair of them could ever resume their former lives. They had made their bed together, and they would have to lie on it.

As the weather grew colder, they moved on to Berlin, the last town on their itinerary. Money was running low and word came from Isaac (via Chrissey, because he could not be bothered to communicate with his sister directly) that problems with the investment of her legacy meant that she could expect less money next time. Articles which George or Marian put forward for publication in London were not as readily accepted as they had been, so despite working hard they were receiving little financial reward. The difficulties and the opposition they faced, however, served to unite rather than divide them. Marian's adoration of George never faltered; she worked hard, cared for him and found happiness in everything they did together, which made him look at their relationship in a new light. In Marian's company for eight months, he had been more contented than he had been for years, in better health and producing better writing. It augured well for their future together. When plans were made to return to England in March 1855, Marian was adamant that she would live with him no matter what anybody said. That none would receive her socially was a small price for happiness; after all she had always moved freely in society before and had never experienced the intense satisfaction she did now. In the future, Marian emphasized, they would be all in all to each other.

CHAPTER 12

A New Era of My Life,
1855–1857

Marian stepped ashore at Dover in March 1855 with mixed feelings. The crossing had been so rough that she was relieved to land, but ahead of her was the struggle for survival. She knew most people would shun her for flouting one of the cardinal rules of society. Such ostracism would present professional problems. If she could not move freely in intellectual circles as before, how was she to get work? Work meant money – a vital commodity now that others depended on her. Chrissey, overlooked by her affluent brother Isaac, relied on Marian to pay for some of the children's education. Most of George's income passed to his wife Agnes to pay for her keep and that of the six children she had produced, so it fell to Marian to provide for George as well as herself. It was an awesome responsibility, yet Marian thrived on challenges. She summoned up all her Evans pride and determination; no Evans was frightened of hard work and no Evans backed down. With George beside her, exuding confidence and clowning around to revive her flagging spirits, Marian believed she could ride out the storm.

The euphoria of living and loving with George kept Marian's worries at bay until they docked and she was on her own. It was harder then to keep her spirits up. Lewes left her in lodgings in Dover while he returned to the capital to test the climate and put his affairs in order before Marian joined him. As they predicted, Lewes was still received in polite society even though his extramarital affair was frowned upon. Marian was the scarlet woman whom nobody mentioned by name. Back in London Lewes was appalled to discover that Agnes had not only gone through his money in record time but had also run up large debts. As her husband, he was legally responsible for settling these bills and any more she might incur. She was exacting her revenge in a manner he had never anticipated. Fury at Agnes's behaviour prompted Lewes to arrange a legal separation from his wife, but as the law stood that would make no difference to his liability for all her debts. He could only hope that as a 'separated woman' she might not enjoy the same social freedoms she had as a 'married woman'. His intense anger at laws which not only prevented him from getting a divorce from his adulterous wife with her increasing brood of bastards, but held him legally responsible for her spendthrift habits was manifest to Marian's friend Barbara Leigh Smith. Barbara was drafting out the terms to be included in a parliamentary Bill to reform married women's rights. On the strength of Lewes's experiences, the Bill was altered to limit a man's liability for his wife's debts.

Arranging his tangled domestic life, the submission of his Goethe manuscript and the search for new lodgings proved far more tiresome than Lewes had foreseen. For five dreary weeks Marian was on her own in Dover. She attempted her usual antidote to despondency, namely hard work, but it became less effective as time dragged on. Regular letters arrived from George detailing his activities and reassuring her that he would return to collect her, but in her bleaker moments Marian mused on the plight of a woman cast off by her lover, a theme which was to find its way into many of her novels when she started writing. Maggie Tulliver in *The Mill on the Floss* found herself a social outcast after her absence with Stephen Guest.

As Marian trusted, George eventually reappeared to take her to some cheap lodgings he had found on the outskirts of London where they were not known. From henceforth it would be easier for her to be called Mrs Lewes, he said, because the lodgings had been taken for a married couple. Although Marian had always been appalled at the way other people allowed themselves to be dictated to by social pressures, she found herself doing just the same. George told her that in London people spoke euphemistically of their 'elopement', so if society wanted to view it that way, then this would be his second marriage and there was nothing to stop her calling herself Mrs Marian Evans Lewes. In the past Marian had enjoyed altering her name to make believe she had taken on a new identity. Could this not be merely an extension of that game, she asked herself. But at the back of her mind she was well aware of the hypocrisy implicit in the new name.

A different label did not solve anything. It was still not possible for any woman to call on the self-styled Mrs Lewes without compromising her own respectability, and there were few men who would wish to have their name linked publicly with a fallen woman. Nevertheless a few true friends made the trek out of London to the suburban villages of Bayswater, East Sheen and Richmond where the Leweses took lodgings for a few weeks at a time. John Chapman was an early visitor whose appearance was doubly welcome; he was not only an old friend but also brought the promise of work. The inopportune timing of Marian's previous article condemning marriage was forgotten, as he urged both journalists to submit to him as many articles as they could. This was prompted not just by affection for Marian, but by expediency. Chapman knew the Leweses to be two of the most professional journalists in London, capable of writing to order on any subject at any length. Their submissions were a pleasure to receive because they arrived on time, fitted the designated space and did not require editing. Now that Chapman was spending most of his time on medical studies, he needed writers of this calibre to keep the *Westminster Review* afloat. As a further inducement to Marian to resume her former role, Chapman offered to pay her more than the standard rate for any work she did. But she was not so easily bought. While agreeing to supply the *Westminster Review* with regular articles at the higher fee, Marian also made it clear that Chapman did not have an exclusive right to her services and neither would she ever be his editor again. George advised her against working solely for Chapman, for rumour had it that the *Westminster Review* was once again heading for disaster, and in any case one quarterly would never generate enough money for them to live on. What Lewes proposed was that, in addition to articles for Chapman, Marian should write other pieces which he would try to place with some of the journals that always took his work. His former contacts in the literary world were easily resumed and with articles always appearing anonymously there was no problem. Marian continued to write as she had always done, as though she were a man. This enabled Lewes to pass the copy off as his own if need be, or as 'the work of a friend'. Such was the quality of Marian's work that it sold itself.

A few women proved to be good friends to Marian by risking social disgrace and visiting her. One of the first was Rufa Hennell. Widowed after Charles Christian's death in 1850, she was still as unconventional as ever and seeing a great deal of John Chapman. Ostensibly that was because they both had young children who liked playing together, but gossip was rife about the rich widow and the philanderer. Marian had never been particularly fond of Rufa, even though she had been bridesmaid to her many years previously, but the older woman's kindness to her in April 1855 was never forgotten and indeed marked the beginning of a new closeness.

From Rufa, Marian heard about life at Rosehill, where she sensed a growing coolness towards her. Rufa was able to reassure her that Charles had gradually come to accept Marian's action and had said he would visit her next time he was in town. Surprisingly the unmarried Sara Hennell had shown a more sympathetic understanding of Marian's behaviour than any of them, but was hurt that Marian had not taken her into her confidence. However, Sara seemed to have got over that, Rufa said, and was quite prepared to resume their former intimacy. No such heartening news came from Cara. Whenever Marian's name was mentioned, Cara went silent. The bedroom so long set aside for Marian and furnished with the oddments she had brought from her father's house had been rearranged as though to exorcise her spirit. A few days after the conversation with Rufa, Marian received a parcel of her linen, sent from Rosehill with the briefest of notes from Cara, which spoke volumes. This once kind friend was demonstrating unequivocally that Marian would no longer be welcome at Rosehill and every last vestige of her existence was being removed. Marian was deeply hurt.

Back in Coventry Cara reviewed past events. She understood for the first time that though Marian had always written of her 'beloved trio', she had only ever had eyes for one person. If Charles had not been there, Marian would not have stayed. Cara was encouraged in her suspicions by George Combe, who was beside himself with anger at Marian for disproving his phrenological analysis of her character. He was quite prepared to ascribe all sorts of immorality to one who clearly had insanity in her family.[1] Cara was left wondering whether Marian, who had originally been the perpetual companion of Charles, had then lived with the notorious Mr Chapman and had eventually gone off with a married man, had ever been a friend to her. Or had Marian just been using her?

As the recriminations and suspicions mounted, Marian received a warm letter from an unexpected quarter. Ironically, Isaac, in writing to give details of investments made on her behalf with her father's legacy, welcomed her back from her European tour.[2] It was quite obvious that news of his sister's immorality had not percolated as far as Griff. Marian responded, giving as her permanent address Mr Chapman's, thus reinforcing the family's belief that she had taken up her former employment after the holiday.

News from Chrissey was as heart-rending as ever. An accident at sea had robbed her of her second son, typhus had killed one of her daughters and threatened to carry off another and even Chrissey herself. Since money was the immediate problem, Marian wrote to Isaac to ask that more of her next allowance be transferred directly to Chrissey. Hoping to prick his High Church conscience into doing more for their poor sister, Marian asked if he could see his way clear to advancing the money straightaway. In the meantime, she sent what clothes of her own she could spare for Chrissey to cut down for the children. At Christmas Marian returned to Warwickshire to see what could be done to ease her sister's plight. To her disgust she found that neither Isaac, Fanny nor the elder Robert, all of whom were prosperous, had troubled to do anything. Chrissey was ignored, having sunk so low in their esteem that she was considered a disgrace to the family. Even the visit which Marian persuaded Fanny to make to Chrissey's at Christmas when Marian would be there, was cancelled at the last moment. Fanny thought it was too inconvenient to go to Attleborough; perhaps Marian would care to call on her in Leamington? The reply went back: such a detour would not be worth it for one hour's visit.[3]

Equally blunt was the reply Charles Bray received from Marian. In answer to his invitation to call in at Rosehill while she was in the area, he received a note saying that he should have had the sense to realize she would not pay a call when the mistress of the house refused to see her.[4] Those who had known Marian in her younger days did not recognize the self-confident person who now presented herself. Secure in her relationship with George Lewes, she no longer needed her past anchorage.

Marian found life with Lewes stimulating in both a physical and an intellectual way, yet people rarely saw them together. In twelve months, Marian reckoned up that she had gone into London only twice. Their outings together took the form of walks on Hampstead Heath and similar country rambles, which they both adored. In contrast to Marian's isolation, Lewes was regularly seen in the Strand and at soirées. She understood that he was gregarious by nature and needed to attend male dinners as he always used to, go to gatherings which would further their work, and see his children regularly. Well used to her own company, Marian encouraged George to resume his former acquaintanceships and to accept the invitations of his good friend Arthur Helps to stay for a week with his family in Hampshire, as he had in the past.

Marian was happier than she had ever been in her life; she felt secure in George's affection and had a worthwhile career of her own. Her days were taken up with work. Knowing the monetary problems George faced with two homes to keep and his wife's bills to pay, she took up her pen with renewed vigour. Debt appalled Marian as it did all Evanses, and she was determined to keep George solvent. The translation of Spinoza's *Ethics* which had been undertaken in Germany was prepared for publication. George was convinced he could negotiate a better deal for Marian than she had ever received before. Turning to publishers to whom he had once casually mentioned the idea, Lewes pressed for a complicated deal whereby he would supply the text for one figure and earn half as much again by acting as its editor. The publishing house suspected sharp practice and turned the proposal down.[5] Despite his optimism, Lewes never succeeded in finding a publisher prepared to pay the large sum he thought Marian's work was worth. Her Spinoza manuscript, the fruit of a year's work, still lies unpublished.

Having wasted time and energy on unprofitable translations, Marian turned to writing freelance for as many magazines as she could. Such articles could at least be finished in a matter of weeks and turned into instant cash, which was the vital commodity. Between 1855 and 1857 she produced a prodigious number of articles of a high standard. The more she wrote, the more she developed confidence in her abilities and a new edge appeared to her writing. As one who never tolerated fools gladly, Marian was quite prepared with the safety net of anonymity to say just what she thought. One poetess's latest work was dismissed as 'sentimental doggerel' with nothing to recommend it beyond an etching of the versifier at the start that only proved Nature had tried to compensate for the imbecility of the writer. The highly respected Dr John Cumming, an Evangelical minister of the Church of Scotland, found himself subjected to a vicious tirade in the *Westminster Review* which condemned him for preaching drivel with 'unctuous egotism'. His ideas were ridiculed by the brilliant device of being expanded to their logical conclusion. In a sarcastic article which would occupy lawyers in a libel action for months if it were published today, Marian Lewes accused the eminent cleric of being ignorant, uncharitable and a liar whose accounts of his own experience were apocryphal.

George was delighted. He had had no idea Marian was capable of such powerful writing. Years later he said that the Cumming article had convinced him of her genius. Charles Bray also revelled in this attack on Evangelicalism and suspected Marian was behind it. 'We are keeping the authorship a secret,' she replied to Bray with great concern that he might wreck things in his usual tactless manner. 'The article appears to have produced a strong impression, and that impression would be a little counteracted if the author were known to be a *woman*.'[6] Similar censorious articles flowed from her pen, becoming ever more critical as they progressed. Even the venerable poet Tennyson was not immune. His newly published 'Maud' was judged as possessing much that was better not said, and Mrs Lewes concluded that on the whole it was best forgotten, like a bad opera.

As Marian and George grew increasingly competent at churning out marketable copy, both became disillusioned. George had always had his sights set on higher things. His biography of Goethe, published in 1855, proved outstandingly successful, selling over a thousand copies in three months. Not only was it popular, it was also heralded as a masterly piece of writing, which pleased Lewes immensely. Similarly his *Biographical History of Philosophy* was in such demand that it had sold out and a new edition was in hand. Yet his interest in the purely literary was waning. Shortly before he became Marian's lover, much of his spare time had been spent with Herbert Spencer dissecting plants. Work like this at the forefront of science held a greater fascination for Lewes than anything on the page. Like Chapman, he had originally begun a medical training but become so appalled by the butchery of early operations that he abandoned the profession, though not his interest in physiology. Encouraged by Marian, whose childhood on a farm ensured that she was never squeamish, he resumed this interest as a hobby. Marine zoology attracted him since few studies had been done in that field. Working holidays were arranged at the coast and while they both carried on their writing for magazines, their spare time was spent collecting specimens of sea anemones to study under the microscope.

Marian was keen to participate in George's studies, having been interested by scientific subjects since her teenage years. While other girls read novels, she studied treatises on chemistry and geology. Her own fiction reading had been limited, most having been undertaken for reviewing. Nevertheless her fantasies often contained the idea of being a novelist. Harriet Martineau had been her model from the time she had met the Hennells' famous relative in 1845. That Harriet Martineau had successfully made the transition from journalist to celebrated novelist had not escaped Marian's attention. A good deal more experienced eleven years later, Marian still looked up to this woman who had made many caustic comments about Miss Evans getting above herself at the *Westminster* and, more recently, about Miss Evans the husband-snatcher. In her Coventry days, Marian had shared in Cara and Sara's fantasy that they might all become novelists one day. Together the three had composed oddments; Cara and Sara usually chose to write pieces which would be suitable for children, while Marian, who did not share their teaching experiences, penned descriptive passages. Some of the Hennell sisters' efforts survive, illustrated by the exquisite watercolours of Sara.[7] Marian consigned her attempts to the bin. If they were not perfect, she did not want them.

A later effort, a description of a Staffordshire farmhouse, was based on memories of her youthful visits to an Evans uncle and turned up in papers she took to Germany. There she read it to George to hear his reaction. He was pleasantly surprised by her fiction style and suggested perhaps Marian ought to try her hand at this medium which often earned more than non-fiction. A series of short stories could be published in a journal first, then collected together and reissued in book form, thus earning a second fee. It was the lure of money and fame which caused Marian to take George's proposition seriously. She had always believed her future lay in non-fiction, but he convinced her that the rare combination of her writing ability and editorial experience might well be more profitable than she realized. Fears about tackling dialogue were soon dispelled, as he pointed out that with three novels and numerous plays behind him, he was qualified to help.

If she got her ideas down on paper, he could edit them and polish up the dialogue where necessary. They had worked together successfully before; it was quite possible they could produce a marketable commodity this time. Lewes did not expect Marian to produce a perfect story first time, but believed she would subsequently with assistance.

The title 'The Sad Fortunes of the Reverend Amos Barton' came into Marian's head one morning as she dozed in bed. Lewes pronounced it 'capital', although he had no more idea than Marian what the fortunes were going to be. She continued pondering the narrative as she worked at bread-and-butter articles. Fear that she could not invent a plausible plot led her to plump for the safe option of writing about something which had happened in real life. With a judicious changing of names, Marian set down the story of a curate she had known at Chilvers Coton, whose good name had been compromised. It made a good yarn, with the necessary ingredients of humour and pathos. Marian enjoyed herself hugely, sending up various people she had disliked in her youth, from snobbish neighbours to pompous bankers who visited her father.

Whether the story was true or not did not matter to George. It was witty, fresh and interesting. He was overwhelmed by the quality of Marian's work and believed she could be a second Jane Austen if marketed carefully. Her prose far surpassed his expectations and instead of suggesting massive rewriting, he edited the text and proposed trying it on a publisher. Blackwood's in Edinburgh was his first choice because one of the London magazines might recognize Marian's handwriting from her previous work. Also, within the claustrophobic world of London journalism, any hope of anonymity would be shortlived. Lewes had recently had successful dealings with Blackwood's over his seashore articles and decided to build on this connection. The *Maga*, as *Blackwood's Edinburgh Magazine* was popularly known, had an impressive national circulation on a par with any London-based journal.

Lewes sent the story out as the work of 'a friend'. He said he thought it was so good that Blackwood's ought to be given the first refusal. His dealings with the Edinburgh publishing house on this occasion and throughout *Scenes of Clerical Life* were masterly. He flattered them, kept them interested in his mysterious friend's work and made them pay up handsomely. By suggesting at an early stage that 'his friend' needed every encouragement and might easily be put off by criticism, Lewes persuaded Blackwood's to commit themselves to publishing this story as the beginning of a series, even though they had never seen the rest – nor indeed were the stories written at that stage. Whenever the publisher started to hint that Marian's stories had any faults, Lewes quickly warned him off with remarks about 'the shaken confidence of my friend who is unusually sensitive and unlike most writers is more anxious about *excellence* than appearing in print'.[8]

That was not true. Marian was not a timid writer and had plenty of experience to judge when her work was good and when it was not. Like most people she enjoyed praise, especially from her beloved George, and, since Lewes was also a competent professional critic, she had high regard for his judgement. She was quite ambitious enough herself to have seen her fiction through to publication, but was prepared to indulge her lover by playing the part of the fragile genius, reliant on a clever business partner. The longer the acting went on, the more those involved believed in the charade. What started as a ploy by Lewes to get Blackwood's to think positively about Marian's work developed into his obsessive desire to shield her from criticism. Later, Lewes went to absurd lengths to stop friends relaying adverse comments to Marian and to prevent her reading bad reviews in newspapers. Seeing this only as further proof of his love for her, Marian played along.

In their early dealings with Blackwood's, Marian knew exactly what the strategy was and watched Lewes's manoeuvres with amusement. The pair of them had great fun spinning yarns about Mr Lewes's mysterious clerical friend. When John Blackwood seemed to be getting too close to home, or if he began inferring a complete falsehood, then the tack was changed. 'When I referred to my "clerical friend" I meant to designate the writer of the clerical stories, not that he was a clericus,' Lewes wrote back, concerned lest the publisher might accuse him of deceit in the future. 'I am not at liberty to remove the veil of anonymity – even as regards social position. Be pleased therefore to keep the whole secret – and not even mention *my* negotiation or in any way lead guessers – (should any one trouble himself with such a guess – *not* very likely) to jump from me to my friend.'[9]

Although John Blackwood did respect Lewes's request for anonymity, it was difficult dealing with a nameless author, and once

'The Sad Fortunes of the Reverend Amos Barton' appeared in the January and February editions of the *Maga*, there was much speculation about the author. Remembering Lewes's insistence on praising the author, Blackwood wrote to 'My Dear Amos' to tell him how well his story had been received – it had even drawn Thackeray's attention, he said – and Blackwood encouraged 'Amos' to send in another manuscript.

Marian decided that for convenience she really must have some *nom de plume*, though cheques had still to be payable to Mr Lewes, she reminded Blackwood. The christian name she chose was George, as a tribute to her lover. As to the surname, she had no real reason for picking Eliot, she said, it simply sounded right. In fact Marian dredged from the depths of her mind a combination of names she had come across before. A George Elliot (*sic*) had been the clerk in a neighbouring parish which her father had dealings with, but more significantly there was a 'George Eliot's Close' shown on one of the old maps of Chilver Coton, kept in her father's office at Griff House.[10] Then, and as she was to do throughout her novels, Marian recycled a name from her past.

'Whatever may be the success of my stories,' George Eliot wrote in the first letter to bear her new name, 'I shall be resolute in preserving my incognito.'[11] Secrecy was vital on two counts. If it ever became known that the story was the work of a woman then it would be instantly devalued. Marian and George were well aware of that and had even advised Sara Hennell to sign one of her essays S. S. Hennell, in preference to penning her christian name. As Lewes was also quick to observe, the mystery element helped sales.

'I am a very calculating person now – valuing approbation as representing guineas,' Marian told Charles Bray early in 1857 soon after she had received a cheque for fifty guineas for 'Amos Barton'.[12] The story had been a month's work and earned her more than she had received for translating a whole book. Quite clearly her future was to be in fiction, and from then on she began gently to relinquish her freelance writing.

'Amos Barton' was followed by 'Mr Gilfil's Love Story', once again based on a real-life situation and in a place she knew well, the splendid Gothic mansion of Arbury Hall. With a wonderful sense of the ridiculous, Marian gave the Hall and the family a name from her own pedigree. A Sacheverel Evans had appeared on her family tree, so

Marian decapitated him and Cheverel became the pseudonym for the Newdigate family and Cheverel Manor replaced Arbury Hall. Feeling more confident and fluent the second time round, Marian wrote at greater length and 'Mr Gilfil's Love Story' was published in three parts in the *Maga*, earning its author eighty-eight pounds ten shillings.

Her new optimism and ambition showed in correspondence with Blackwood's, where she discussed the future publication of her stories in book form. 'I have no doubt we shall find it easy to arrange the terms,' she told Blackwood confidently.[13] At the time of her letter, though, she had only completed one story and only one-half of that had been published. But Marian had the bit between her teeth. The stories flowed from her pen effortlessly; equally importantly the money rolled in. Her third story, 'Janet's Repentance', which related the Evangelical disturbances in the Nuneaton of her schoolgirl days, was an even longer narrative and earned one hundred and twenty-one pounds from its five instalments in the *Maga*. She had planned a fourth story for the series, dealing with her brother Isaac's experiences under a clerical tutor in Coventry, but that was not to be. The business side of the partnership advised her to stop the series at three because that was the right size for publication as a single volume. Since her writing was highly prized by Blackwood's, Lewes believed the time was ripe for Marian to begin a full-length novel which could command a large figure.

Another good reason for halting *Scenes of Clerical Life* was that people had begun to recognize themselves and were not flattered. Questions were asked about the author. The successful identification of many characters in the story as real-life individuals was threatening to unmask 'George Eliot'. Blackwood heard that the real 'Amos Barton's' daughter, whom Marian had known well when she lived at Griff, had read the story and recognized their family history dating from the time when her father was curate at Chilvers Coton.[14] Other rumours emanating from Warwickshire suggested that a clergyman in the county had produced these caricatures of local inhabitants. After the publication of two of the four parts of 'Janet's Repentance', the Reverend William Jones wrote from Lancashire to find out just how many more parts of his unfortunate brother's troubles were going to be published. He would very much like to know who had 'revived what should have been buried in oblivion'.[15]

Blackwood's were delighted by the interest in their new writer's work and surprised by the booming circulation their magazine was enjoying in the Midlands. Everybody in the Nuneaton area seemed to have read the stories, even members of the Evans family. Marian and George fell about laughing at a letter which came from Fanny commending these stories to her sister's attention and letting her into the secret that a Mr Joseph Liggins, who used to live near Chrissey, was actually the author. Tongue-in-cheek, Marian replied to her half-sister: 'We too have been struck with the "Clerical Sketches" ', she wrote, deliberately getting the name wrong, 'and I have recognized some figures and traditions connected with our old neighbourhood. But Blackwood informs Mr Lewes that the author is a Mr Eliot, a clergyman, I presume. *Au reste*, he may be a relation of Mr Liggins's or some other "Mr" who knows Coton stories.'[16] News also came from Fanny that the favourite pastime in Nuneaton was comparing lists of names of people who had appeared in the book. Several of these lists have survived to the present and show a remarkable agreement about whom Marian had in mind for each person, right down to the names of some paupers in the workhouse.[17] Equally noticeable in these keys to *Scenes of Clerical Life* is the astounding interchange of names. Everyone recognized Mr and Mrs Hackit as Mr and Mrs Robert Evans (Marian's own parents), but there was also a real life Mr Hackit who appeared in the book as Mr Spratt. It was sufficiently muddled up to keep the drinkers at the Bull in Nuneaton (alias the Red Lion in Milby) entertained for months trying to unravel the tangle.

When challenged by Blackwood about her curate in 'Janet's Repentance' being identified as the Reverend John Edmund Jones, Marian bluffed her way out. 'Mr Tryan is not a portrait of any clergyman, living or dead. He is an ideal character, but I hope probable enough to resemble more than one evangelical clergyman of his day. . . . I shouldn't wonder if several nieces of pedantic maiden ladies saw a portrait of their aunt in Miss Pratt,' she concluded facetiously, knowing full well they would.[18] Miss Pratt was an uncharitable but very recognizable sketch of Miss Bond, the daughter of a well-known Nuneaton surgeon.

Despite Marian's nonchalant attitude towards people identifying themselves in her writing, Lewes thought she ought to be more careful about the transposing of characters directly from real life into 'fiction' because it could lead to her unmasking. Then the goose which laid their golden egg would be dead. Blackwood's were also becoming increasingly curious about the identity of the mysterious George Eliot. Specimens of handwriting from other contributors were fetched out of the cupboard and compared. When John Blackwood came down to London he asked around about Lewes's associates to see if he could find out who the writer was. No one thought it at all likely George Lewes would have a bosom friend who was a clergyman, since he 'lived in sin' with that strong-minded woman from the *Westminster Review*. That was the lead John Blackwood wanted. By the time he met 'Mrs Lewes' at her home in Richmond, he had already guessed she was George Eliot. Despite the majority of people believing George Eliot to be a man, Charles Dickens had told Blackwood at the start that only a woman could have written those stories, and he provided convincing evidence.

Even after Blackwood knew the truth, the secret had to remain intact because, as Lewes said, mystery was good for sales. Marian was amazed that Charles Bray never recognized her handiwork. He, who had known her so well and had heard her disparaging remarks about many of the people who appeared in *Scenes of Clerical Life*, was the one person she thought would guess her identity. He was also the worst person. Once Bray knew, so would the whole of Warwickshire.

Maintaining so many pretences became more of a chore than a game and, feeling confident in her relationship with George, Marian decided to tell her family she had married. In a carefully worded letter, drafted with all the precision of a magazine article and edited by George just as carefully, she informed Isaac that she had changed her name. Although Marian could not find a satisfactory way of avoiding the term 'husband', she did refrain from saying she had actually got married and confined herself to drawing a very sober portrait of Mr G. H. Lewes, a man older than herself with three boys away at school and himself 'occupied entirely with scientific and learned pursuits'.[19]

Fanny received a letter containing similar information and wrote back straightaway to congratulate her sister. Isaac, however, was never given to spontaneous gestures of affection. Instead he inaugurated a few enquiries of his own. Already he had heard whispers from Bray's sister, Mrs Elizabeth Pears, that Marian had been led astray in the evil city, but he did not have anything concrete to accuse her of. Believing that one who had renounced the Church was capable of the grossest immorality, Isaac persuaded the family solicitors to put the necessary questions. Mrs Lewes received their letter, couched in the sort of polite terms that Isaac had clearly never used, which said her brother was hurt at not being informed of his sister's marital intentions. The letter also demanded specific information about where and when the marriage had taken place.[20]

By the time she received the letter, Marian no longer cared. 'Our marriage is not a legal one,' she replied defiantly, 'though it is regarded by both of us as a sacred bond.'[21] The old Evans pride surfaced as she stressed she was not dependent on anyone for her income, having been earning her living as a writer for several years. Nevertheless she took the opportunity to restate the name of the bank account and branch where she wanted her allowance paid. 'I dare say I shall never have any further correspondence with my brother,' she told Sara Hennell, 'which will be a great relief to me.'[22] The unforeseen and most unhappy outcome of her letter was that neither Fanny nor Chrissey were allowed to communicate with their sister. The head of the family forbade it. The loss of Fanny Marian could bear, but not the loss of Chrissey. Although some of Marian's money could still be transferred to Chrissey, Isaac would not let her accept the parcels of clothing and other little luxuries Marian had been accustomed to send. Chrissey had not been cast in the same metal as her younger sister, and when Isaac further demanded that he handle all her money and dole out amounts for specific purposes, she had to agree. Once again Chrissey was the loser.

At the end of 1857 Marian looked back well pleased with what she had achieved in the two and a half years since her return from Germany. The book version of *Scenes of Clerical Life*, was being advertised ready for sale in the new year and a start had been made on a full-length novel. Significantly, one of her letters in December demonstrated the new businesslike approach of the novelist communicating with her publisher: 'Shouldn't we have "Right of translation reserved" on the back of the title-page?' she enquired about *Scenes of Clerical Life*.[23] She recorded in her journal at the end of the year her private hope that her writing might succeed and so give value to her life.

CHAPTER 13

I Certainly Care a Good Deal for the Money, 1858–1863

The publication of *Scenes of Clerical Life* marked the beginning of a brilliant writing career for Marian which not only exceeded her wildest dreams but also beat all records for money paid to an author. A year which started with the Leweses gratefully banking fourteen guineas ended with them receiving cheques for fourteen hundred pounds. Such was Marian's meteoric rise to fame and fortune.

The pair formed a powerful combination. Marian was undoubtedly a gifted writer. Her childhood memories served her exceptionally well; incidents selected with an eye to the absurdities of life were woven into an eminently readable narrative. Her novels appealed to the general reader, who simply required a good yarn, as well as to people of more discerning intellect, who demanded depth of character and a philosophy behind the plot. Excellent though her work was in its own right, it would never have succeeded so spectacularly if Lewes had not taken over the 'marketing' of George Eliot. He was well suited to the role, a born entrepreneur, without scruple about asking for money and never taking no for an answer. With plenty of charm and wit he drove a hard bargain but rarely caused offence. His experience as a critic stood him in good stead to recognize quality writing and his deep affection for Marian made him determined to do the best for her. He knew her driving ambition was to be famous and he was prepared to help her achieve this even at the expense of his own career. She had sacrificed so much to live with him that Lewes regarded the promotion of her career as a tangible way of repaying her. Although he knew himself to be biased, he was still convinced that her writing was the best on the market.

Lewes acted as Marian's editor and literary agent. He listened to her novel in its early stages and advised about the pace and direction of the plot. At the same time he began selling the unfinished work to a publisher. In the late 1850s literary agents were unknown and an author usually fended for himself. In having someone else to act on her behalf, Marian was as ahead of her time as she was in the sort of contracts she received. It was normal practice for a publisher to pay a single sum to purchase the copyright of a novel for a set number of years; no matter how many books sold or remained on the shelf, the author's receipts stayed the same. Once Lewes was convinced he was handling a bestselling author, he pressed for payment to be made on the basis of sales with no surrender of copyright – something which is standard today in the publishing industry.

In another way also the marketing of George Eliot anticipated future trends. Lewes went to great lengths to build up a sense of anticipation in the publishers, feeding them tantalizing morsels about the work in hand, encouraging them to believe they were going to receive a masterpiece, the like of which the world had never seen. In effect he was foreshadowing the 'hype'. Such was his persuasiveness, backed by the evidence of Marian's writing, that John Blackwood was willing to indulge Mr Lewes. When he asked for more money for each succeeding manuscript, Blackwood did his best to find it. When Lewes demanded publication in time to catch the Christmas sales or a reprint of a slightly larger quantity than the publishers intended, he got his way. His pressure was continual: what have you done about translation rights? he asked. What are the sales figures like? Don't you think you could do more to push *Scenes of Clerical Life*: the figures are disappointing? I have not seen any advertisement for Mrs Lewes's next book: do you not think it is time you placed one? To their credit, Blackwood's were extremely tolerant of the insistent Lewes. It was only when Marian herself started to handle correspondence with her publishers that the good relations soured.

Lewes carefully fostered the notion that George Eliot was 'so timid a creature' that he must be encouraged and humoured or the genius would vanish. Even after John Blackwood knew George Eliot to be Mrs Lewes, the pretence continued. Letters were still written to 'George Eliot' with all the indications that he was a male friend of Lewes's, in case anyone at Blackwood's Edinburgh office leaked the truth. Since the mystery stimulated sales, Lewes said it must be maintained. Marian herself took no pride in being thought shy and fragile and set about rectifying that idea. She possessed all her father's business acumen and longed to exercise it.

With contempt she dismissed any notion that it might be unladylike to discuss money: 'I speak to you without circumlocution, and I am sure you will like that best,' she wrote to John Blackwood. 'You know how important this money question is to me. I don't want the world to give me anything for my books except money.'[1] The letter went on to say that since *Adam Bede* had sold so well she had altered her expectations for the next book (*The Mill on the Floss*) and believed Blackwood's would probably not be able to afford her new terms, so she had not bothered to send them the manuscript. By that gesture and her failure to thank them properly for the ex-gratia payment of £800 they proposed to make on account of *Adam Bede*'s runaway success, Marian ruined the relationship. In an internal memorandum the normally quiet and gentlemanly John Blackwood declared he felt savage about the whole episode.[2] That George Eliot, who had been treated with 'unexampled liberality', should be so greedy filled him with disgust, he said. It was indeed poor thanks. The terms Blackwood's had given her were generous for a newcomer, and whenever one of the Leweses wrote, as they habitually did, asking for earlier payment because their 'exchequer was low' or they had miscalculated the accounting date, such payouts were invariably made.[3]

In a personal way also John Blackwood showed kindness to Marian. She had only to mention in his hearing her partiality for something and it usually found its way to her. Over the years the land agent's daughter from the provinces had developed some aristocratic tastes. She was fond of oysters, she admitted: Blackwood ensured she received a box. A little later she revealed her life-long desire to own a pug dog in the hope that some rich reader might indulge her whim. John Blackwood promised instantly she should have one, not realizing how expensive and difficult it would be to locate this rare breed. These gestures of goodwill on Blackwood's part were upset by Marian's avariciousness.

'Mr John has been most thoroughly hood-winked,' one of Blackwood's managers opined.[4] But Mr Simpson, who had never met Marian, did not realize the formidable power this strange-looking woman exerted over some men. John Blackwood was just as captivated by her as Bray and Chapman had been in the past. While in Edinburgh, Blackwood could agree with Simpson that Marian's behaviour was abominable. In London, face to face with the woman, he was once again her slave. Their differences were patched up because Blackwood's paid more.

Secrecy about authorship of the novels had to be maintained, Lewes ruled, but he found it increasingly difficult when Marian continued to write about people and episodes from her past. The guessing game which *Scenes of Clerical Life* prompted did not abate but only received fresh impetus with the publication of *Adam Bede* in 1859. Though the novel purported to be set in Derbyshire and Staffordshire, there was much in the book to link it with Mary Ann Evans. For example, Isaac recognized Adam Bede as his father. Marian strenuously denied there were any portraits in this second book, but the hero's career, his age, the dates given and the places mentioned (it did not require much intelligence to read Ashbourne for Oakbourne) matched Robert Evans's early life exactly.[5] Isaac kept his opinion to himself because he did not want his sister's immorality tarnishing his own reputation. Furthermore, *Adam Bede* contained a dreadful indictment against one of his employers, Colonel Francis Newdigate, lifelong friend of Robert Evans, who featured in the book as the young squire Arthur Donnithorne. Details of their youthful friendship were faithfully recorded right down to their joint cabinet-making venture, a product of which stood in Griff House for all to see. But Isaac knew Colonel Newdigate would not be at all pleased to read further in the book that Marian had turned him into a seducer of young virgins on the estate. As far as Isaac was concerned, Marian's secret was definitely safe.

Not everybody thought the same way. The great air of mystery which shrouded the author naturally invited speculation and attempts to uncover his identity. Even though letters were appearing in *The Times* and gossip was rife, George assured Marian they could sit back and laugh. The persistence of the Joseph Liggins myth, however, irritated Marian, and when his supporters began collecting money because, they claimed, Blackwood's had fleeced him over *Adam Bede*, her irritation turned to agitation. Letters of denial were sent to the newspapers, but nothing short of exhibiting the real George Eliot would silence the claimant.

Meantime the sales of *Adam Bede* boomed. Lewes urged Marian to work on her third book and have it published before she was unmasked. Although she had vowed not to use any more real people in her writing, the temptation proved too great. When *The Mill on the Floss* appeared the following year, Isaac was furious to find his Pearson aunts wittily caricatured as the Dodson sisters. The undying love of sister for brother in the book cut no ice with him; he knew that he would have to placate his brother-in-law. The Reverend Richard Rawlins, once a curate in Coventry and tutor to the young Isaac, was also attacked with a sharp pen. Drawing on memories of her childhood visits to Isaac at Foleshill vicarage, Marian created the Reverend Walter Stellings, a recognizable but unsympathetic distortion of Mr Rawlins. This public way of settling old scores became a worry to Isaac Evans. What else did she plan? Fanny, his half-sister, was also aware that Marian used characters from her past and writing to Isaac several years later said: 'I am on the tiptoe of expectation to see the forthcoming novel by Mary Ann. It is too much to hope that no member of her own family will figure in it,' she added, half-hoping and half-dreading her turn would come.[6]

Although the Evanses at Griff were silent on the subject of George Eliot, others beavered away at *Adam Bede* and broadcast their findings. One persistent member of the Warwickshire gentry succeeded in tracing the character of Dinah Morris in the novel back to Mrs Samuel Evans in Derbyshire and was convinced that George Eliot had copied this woman's diaries and sermons out verbatim. Not only were the investigations getting dangerously close to the truth but, what was far worse, Marian's real creativity was being undermined. She felt unable to quash the allegations. Her temper frayed, her health deteriorated, and those who had previously thought themselves friends of the Leweses received a cool reception. 'Pray tell "everyone" that we don't visit and don't desire to be called on,' George Lewes told their landlord.[7] His intention was to discourage nosey neighbours, but this attitude set the tone for most callers.

Spencer was well acquainted with Marian's ideas, having read most of her magazine articles, and he guessed she was the elusive George Eliot. Foolishly he confided his suspicions to John Chapman, who immediately proclaimed in the *Westminster Review* that George Eliot was a woman. That sealed Spencer's and Chapman's fate as far as Marian was concerned. She dashed off a terse letter of criticism to Chapman for his 'circulation of idle rumours and gossip' and then noted in her journal: 'I shall not correspond with him or willingly see him again.'[8] Chapman was subjected to the same Evans banishment as Isaac had inflicted on Marian. When Spencer was thoughtless enough to call on the Leweses, he was made to feel so uncomfortable that he stopped calling. Once Spencer became *persona non grata* at the Lewes lodgings, Marian became critical of this man she had once offered to devote her life to. He was an embarrassing bore, she said, whose absurd watching against disease was becoming a disease in itself.

Her Coventry friends fared slightly better because of the distance separating them from her. It never ceased to astound Marian that these old friends whom she had been intimate with for so long had never suspected she was the novelist. It was quite clear from the innocent pieces of gossip about Mr Liggins and the tittle-tattle about George Eliot's work which Sara relayed to Marian that it had not crossed her mind. Marian wanted to tell them before they learned the truth from anyone else and she chose a time when 'the beloved trio' would be together in London. Such occasions were rare but the Handel Festival at the Crystal Palace in June 1859 lured even the reluctant Cara to the capital. Correspondence between Cara and Marian had resumed now that Cara had recovered from the shock of learning her friend was living with a married man, but despite Marian's regular messages of love, Cara remained cool. The two had not met since that day in 1854 when Marian arrived at Rosehill to tell them she would be travelling on the Continent in the company of Mr Lewes. To mark their first reunion for over five years, Marian thought it would be a fine gesture of friendship if she shared her secret.

Sara and Cara came to the meeting with the intention of telling Marian about their own literary progress, for both Hennell sisters were in the throes of publishing their first books. Charles also intended discussing with Marian the new edition of his *Education of the Feelings* which he was preparing for publication. Suspecting that Marian at the hub of the London literary world would probably look down on her provincial friends, Sara and Cara hoped to demonstrate they were not to be outdone. With high expectations of the meeting on both sides, it was hardly surprising that it turned into a fiasco. Sara immediately pressed the manuscript of her *Thoughts in Aid of Faith* into Marian's hands, requesting a professional opinion once Marian had had time to study it. Cara, clutching the manuscript of her textbook *Physiology for Schools*, was more cautious. Before either sister had time to say more, the excitement which had been welling up in Marian gave voice. She confessed she was the author of *Scenes of Clerical Life* and *Adam Bede*; her friends could only stare in disbelief. 'This experience has enlightened me a good deal as to the ignorance in which we all live of each other,' she wrote calmly in her journal that evening.[9] But the encounter with her three friends was anything but calm. Sara became hysterical and had to be led away sobbing. Charles and Cara were so thunderstruck by the news they did not know whether to rejoice at Marian's success or be upset by the great gulf which obviously divided them. The evening was ruined; so emotional did everyone become that attendance at the planned concert was overlooked.

When the Rosehill friends called again a few days later there was still much awkwardness. Responding to Sara's request for a frank opinion about her theological discourse, Marian told her that neither she nor Lewes thought the work was very good and gave their reasons. Sara was surprisingly calm after her previous outburst, but Marian could see she was upset and cursed her own lack of tact. The much delayed reunion ended quietly and painfully, with Marian enjoining them to keep the confidence she had entrusted to them. After the visit each had second thoughts: Marian wrote to ask forgiveness for her thoughtless blundering and Sara to apologize for her histrionics. In a magnanimous letter, Sara admitted she had been foolish. 'I could not at once see that the wonderfully new circumstances made all different,' she explained, as she told Marian how she had assumed her friend to be still engaged on the philosophical book 'The Idea of a Future Life' which had been talked of ten years before. The reality had proved so different that she thought her friend was lost. 'I remain gazing at the glory into which she has departed, wistfully and very lonely,' Sara ended sadly.[10]

Despite the upset, Marian's idea of demonstrating her affection for her old friends proved a wise one. Relations between them, which had been strained since Marian's cohabitation with Lewes, were much more cordial after the meeting. Charles, Cara and Sara appreciated Marian's kindness and were able to indulge in a little fun of their own as the only ones in Coventry with certain knowledge of George Eliot's identity. When faced with questions like 'Did Miss Evans write those books?', Sara was gleefully able to pronounce in all honesty, 'No, Miss Evans certainly did not'.[11]

Charles delighted in Marian's success and was sure he could take the credit for setting her on the right road. He was not slow to realize that if Marian had written best-selling novels, she was probably in receipt of a considerable income. He, as ever, was on the way down financially. The ribbon-manufacturing business had been sold, and though they nominally lived at Rosehill, it was not in the large main house, but in the cottage in the grounds. Circumstances were such that they were even obliged to consider relinquishing that. To Marian's embarrassment, Charles wrote about some shares he was selling and suggested she might like to purchase them.[12] When this did not produce the desired response, he then wrote asking for money to help him out of a fix. Once again he had been involved in a lawsuit, ending up out of pocket by £150: could Marian assist him? The plea from one for whom she still cherished much affection could not be ignored. Marian explained that she could only manage a £100 loan in return for a promissory note; that was all she had available.[13] She failed to mention the £1,825 she was considering investing in the Great Indian Peninsular Railway and the £1,600 earmarked for the purchase of a house. Marian's income was at a level which would certainly have earned the approval and admiration of her father.

Barbara Leigh Smith, now Mrs Eugène Bodichon after her marriage to a French doctor, warned Marian of rumours flying around London that the noticeable improvement in the Leweses' standard of living had been provided by *Adam Bede*. With Liggins still muttering in the background, displaying a manuscript of *Scenes of Clerical Life* in his own handwriting, and a rival publishing house announcing the publication of *Adam Bede, Junior. A Sequel* by an unspecified author, Marian had had enough. 'You can tell it openly to all who care to hear,' Barbara Bodichon was advised in June 1859. 'The object was to get the book judged on its own merits, and not prejudged as the work of a woman,' Lewes explained to her, knowing that someone who battled to improve women's rights would understand.[14]

The timing of the disclosure was opportune. As George Lewes had hoped, George Eliot's fame was so well established that it only suffered a minor dent by the revelation that the author was Lewes's mistress. It was known that Queen Victoria had enjoyed *Adam Bede* so much that she had commissioned two paintings of scenes from the book. Mrs Poyser, a character in the book noted for her down-to-earth common sense, was even quoted in the House of Commons in 1859. Without doubt Marian's writing had succeeded in high places.

One who did not need to be told *Adam Bede* was by Marian was

Barbara Bodichon. She had read a review of the book when she was in Algeria with her husband, knew instantly that her dear friend Marian must be the author and wrote to congratulate the new celebrity. At one time Marian had thought Sara Hennell was the only woman who really understood her, but their recent meeting suggested otherwise. By contrast Barbara, whom she had known a shorter time, seemed in total harmony with her mind. Each sympathized with the other's desire to make a name for herself in her chosen field: Barbara in art, Marian in literature. While both wanted to see the lot of women improved, they agreed that women must demonstrate that they deserved the increased responsibility on grounds other than just their sex. The defeat of the Bill to reform married women's property rights in 1857 caused Barbara to be despondent, and her marriage, which followed soon after, removed her from the forefront of the women's movement. That position passed to the earnest, but less charismatic, Bessie Parkes.

Since her interest was in literature, in 1858 Bessie became the editor of a new magazine which, unusually, was aimed specifically at women. The *English Woman's Journal* was founded and financed by Barbara Bodichon, who believed that a magazine available to women all over the country would prove a more effective way of influencing women's views than the work of a small pressure group in Blandford Square. Bessie's approach to Marian for contributions met with a refusal on the ground that she did not have the time. This was partly true for she was working on a novel, but she was also disinclined to get involved in what she saw as an amateur production. Despite her enthusiasm, Bessie permitted all manner of errors to appear in the early issues. Marian was appalled: shoddy work was something she never tolerated. Moreover a public display of inferior work by women would do more harm than good, Marian told Barbara. Marian's unwillingness to help weakened the old bond of friendship with Bessie.

The need to protect the secret of Marian's authorship strained many existing friendships, and the illicit nature of her conjugal union hindered the formation of new ones. As compensation, family ties became important for Marian. All communication with the Evanses had been severed at Isaac's command, though Marian frequently wondered about the fate of her sister. In February 1859 word came directly from Chrissey that she was dying of tuberculosis and deeply

regretted ever breaking off contact with the one person who had
shown unfailing kindness to her and her children. *'Pray believe* me
when I say possibly it will be the greatest comfort I can possibly
receive to know you are *well* and *happy*. Will you write once more?'
she pleaded.[15] Marian was devastated: 'It has ploughed up my
heart.'[16] Her first impulse was to drop her pen and rush to
Attleborough for a final reunion with her sister, but Lewes dis-
couraged her. Marian was in the middle of a novel and had been quite
upset enough by the arrival of the letter. A visit to the dying Chrissey
would destroy all her concentration and jeopardize a Christmas
publication date. 'I almost wish the silence had never been broken,' he
confided in his diary. 'She had got used to that.'[17] As Marian
prevaricated, Chrissey's daughter Emily wrote to say her mother was
worse and longed to make her peace with Marian. Would she come? A
few shaky words at the end of the letter pencilled by a frail Chrissey
tore Marian apart. She would have to go to her sister but Lewes was
equally insistent that he could not be left alone for two days because of
servant problems. Once the domestic situation was resolved, Marian
could go to Attleborough with a clear conscience. As he hoped, the
meeting never took place: a few days later Emily wrote to say that her
mother was dead. Marian was beside herself with grief. Chrissey was
the only member of the Evans family she had really loved: 'I had a very
special feeling towards her, stronger than any third person would
think likely,' she told Sara Hennel. 'Chrissey's death has taken from
[me] the possibility of many things towards which I looked with some
hope and yearning in the future.'[18] Gone was the chance of bidding her
sister farewell, of confiding in her about the happiness of her life with
George and her successful writing career. Ironically, now that Marian
had the money to help Chrissey, it was too late. Chrissey's life, which
had held so much promise and had been lived in obedience to the
Evans rules, had ultimately proved tragic.

After Chrissey's death, Marian transferred her attention to the
orphaned Clarke children. Because they were male the needs of the
two surviving boys were adequately catered for. The elder, almost
twenty-one, was finishing an apprenticeship and the fourteen-year-
old attended a boarding school paid for by a Clarke uncle. Knowing
Chrissey's daughters would receive scant sympathy, Marian concentrated her efforts on them. A boarding school in Lichfield was selected
for fourteen-year-old Emily and eight-year-old Katie, and Marian
continued to pay the bills. Since she would not permit herself to

conceive a child because of the stigma attached to bastards, Marian decided that Emily and Katie Clarke would be her adopted daughters, joining Lewes's three sons to make up her unconventional family. Her nieces' welfare was taken seriously with visits by Marian to Lichfield to inspect the school and reassure the girls of her concern for them. Before the first anniversary of Chrissey's death came round, another black-edged letter arrived from Emily. Little Katie was dead. Was there to be no end to the suffering inflicted on the Clarke family? Katie's death had the effect of drawing Marian and Emily closer. Regular correspondence begun then between aunt and niece lasted throughout Marian's life and Emily knew she could look on her Aunt Polly as her mother.

The other part of Marian's surrogate family comprised Charles, Thornton and Herbert Lewes, the only legitimate children of George Lewes. 'I have four children to correspond with,' Marian told Sara proudly at the end of 1859. 'The three boys in Switzerland, and Emily at Lichfield,' but, predictably, 'our boys' became Marian's favourites.[19] George Lewes adored his sons and so, when Agnes's affair with Thornton Hunt threatened to become a public scandal, he sent them to the Continent for schooling. He had enjoyed a European education himself and believed they would profit from the more cosmopolitan environment. Although George was living with Marian throughout, he left the boys in ignorance of the breakdown of his marriage. In the summer of 1859, when his sons had been settled at the Hofwyl school near Berne for almost three years, Lewes paid his customary visit and ventured to explain the true state of affairs back home. To his immense relief the boys were unperturbed by the news that they had a new 'Mutter', as she was to be called, and were positively ecstatic when Mutter turned out to be the author of *Adam Bede*, a book whose fame had already reached Switzerland.[20] The Lewes boys were as charming and easygoing as their father, so when they met their stepmother the following year the relationship was a success from the outset: 'How truly they loved and prized Polly,' Lewes wrote with pleasure in his diary.[21] On Marian's part he needed to have no qualms; all her life she had found it easier to identify with males than with females and the Lewes boys rapidly overtook Emily in her affections. Emily's annual visits to Aunt Polly at Christmas were elbowed aside by the needs of 'our big pet Charlie'.

In the summer of 1860 Charles Lewes was almost eighteen and

George decided his school days were over. Charlie was to be found a job as a clerk in the Post Office, courtesy of Lewes's good friend Anthony Trollope. It would be necessary to pass the entrance exam, but that posed no problem. Marian was delighted to tutor her 'son' and he, wishing to please his new Mutter, was more assiduous than usual in learning his lessons. The result was he came out top.

The appearance of a young person in the Leweses' home livened things up and had a beneficial effect on Marian. Although she did less writing in 1860, she was more content. She lavished plenty of affection on Charlie and he showed no embarrassment in accepting it. The two enjoyed themselves hugely playing duets, accompanying each other's singing or hatching practical jokes to play on George. Being *in loco matris* suited Marian well. Others also noticed a softening in her manner; Blackwood was no longer plagued by demands for money. To his immense surprise he actually received a letter in which Marian admitted 'one is in danger of desiring money too much'.[22] Spencer found himself invited to visit the Leweses once more and warm letters were exchanged with the residents of Ivy Cottage, Rosehill.

The Mill on the Floss proved a financial success after its publication in 1860, though it was never as popular as *Adam Bede*. However, word came down the grapevine that the new novel had the royal seal of approval. With an ever-increasing bank balance, the Leweses were free to invest in shares, rent a larger house near Regent's Park to make it easier for Charlie to get to work and seek legal advice on the viability of a Continental divorce for George. Marian's vast income removed from George the necessity of writing copy simply to earn a living. Instead he was able to enjoy his physiological studies. Surprisingly the rakish Lewes settled into the academic life easily and even succeeded in making new discoveries about the nervous system in animals. Although Marian handled day-to-day contact with her publishers, Lewes remained her agent advising her on the progress of her literary career. Already she was the most sought-after novelist in the country, in receipt of offers to name whatever figure she chose to work for another publishing house. The only reason she was not tempted towards the Sirens was her lack of confidence about what she had to offer. She had tried to move away from her childhood experiences in a macabre short story entitled 'The Lifted Veil'. The combination of mesmerism, clairvoyance and a ghoulish scene where a blood transfusion resurrects a corpse makes the story resemble more the style of Edgar Allan Poe or Mary Shelley than George Eliot. Blackwood's were not enamoured with Marian's new venture and preferred to publish it anonymously in the *Maga*. Lewes also sensed that the story was taking Marian in the wrong direction and did not pressurize Blackwood's to issue the work in book form. Another novella written during these years was also an attempt to move away from specific childhood incidents but Marian never felt happy enough about 'Brother Jacob' even to show it to Blackwood's.

This did not apply to *Silas Marner*, written at the end of 1860. This short novel, comfortably set among squires, weavers and religious fanatics, came to her 'by a sudden inspiration'. Significantly, this story, like 'Brother Jacob', hinged on greed for money, but unlike the earlier work *Silas Marner* flowed effortlessly from her pen. Begun in November, finished the following February and published two months later, *Silas Marner, the Weaver of Raveloe* earned its author virtually £1,800 in the first year alone. But Silas was not the only one to be lured by gold.

After Marian's dalliance with short stories, George wanted her to settle to a *magnum opus* and during their Italian holiday in 1860 suggested she should try her hand at an historical novel. Knowing Marian's dependence on some actual event or person as a springboard for her imagination, Lewes mentioned as a possibility the life of Savonarola, a fifteenth-century Florentine hero. Although Marian readily accepted George's idea, it proved a mistake. Because the subject did not come out of her own subconscious, the resultant book, *Romola*, has been judged the least successful of her novels. Even when her writing was based on specific events and places Marian still liked to do some research to give her work verisimilitude. When confronted with a story set in an alien time and place, Marian panicked and began such intensive research that she became bogged down. The magnitude of the task overawed her; *Silas Marner*, which she claimed had *demanded* to be written, was actually penned during the early days of this research as a piece of escapism. But when the weaver's story was finished, Marian had no further excuse to avoid tackling *Romola*. Lewes as ever was optimistic: this new novel would be the best yet. Marian was more pessimistic than usual. Her heart was not in the work and it became drudgery. On several occasions she contemplated giving it up, but George was on hand to encourage and reassure her, and the song of the Sirens grew louder.

Clandestine negotiations began with Smith & Elder, a publishing house who had been wooing both Leweses for a year in the hope of netting the real prize: George Eliot's next best-seller. Smith & Elder had recently started a new magazine called *Cornhill* and appeared to have a bottomless coffer. Ten thousand pounds were offered to Marian for her new book, which was planned as a sixteen-part serial in their journal. Lewes was ecstatic: 'It is the most magnificent offer ever yet made for a novel,' he enthused and urged Marian to accept.[23] Marian was not swept away by the astronomical figure. Sixteen instalments would not suit the narrative, she protested, twelve would be better. Much as she liked money, she was not prepared to prostitute her art. *Cornhill* could have *Romola* only if the book was serialized as she wanted, not otherwise. Since that would occupy only twelve issues, she calculated that, by their terms, seven thousand pounds should be the selling price. Smith & Elder accepted instantly and rewarded the Leweses with seats at the opera. George Lewes himself was also given the post of Literary Adviser to the *Cornhill*, yielding 'a pleasant salary of £600' for minimal work.

John Blackwood fumed. He had been fed titbits of the new novel by Lewes and all the indications had been that the *Romola* manuscript would come to him on completion so that he could make an offer. When the contract with Smith & Elder was signed in May 1862, Marian wrote and told John Blackwood she had struck a deal with another publishing house. His reply was as polite as ever. With tongue-in-cheek, Blackwood said Mrs Lewes could rest assured that he was sure the change had been made with 'extreme reluctance'. Privately he said he had been expecting it. 'I am sorry for and disappointed in her, but with their extortionate views we could not have made an arrangement so all is for the best,' he philosophically concluded.[24] As John Blackwood predicted, the Leweses would find that the move was not a wise one in the long run, no matter how great the bribe.

CHAPTER 14

Changing the Image, 1863–1869

W hen Marian reached her forty-fourth birthday towards the end of 1863, she had good reason to celebrate. In the fourteen years since her father's death, she had successfully supported herself by her writing. Indeed her seven years as a novelist had earned her a staggering total of £16,000 together with an international reputation which no other British author but Dickens, with his greater output and longer period of writing, could rival. Moreover she still received half-yearly payments from her father's and aunt's estates as well as royalties from new editions and translations of her existing books. Marian knew that, even if she never wrote another word, with her undreamed-of wealth she could afford to live in the sort of luxury no member of the Evans family had ever experienced. But while George Eliot's name spelt fame, Marian Evans Lewes herself was infamous. She was not a woman received in polite society nor indeed by any person concerned about their good name.[1] But George Lewes had plans to change that.

In November of that year, for the first time Marian felt sufficiently confident to host a party for twenty people, although the proximity to her birthday was merely coincidental. She rarely recognized anniversaries and never those which reminded her of her family. What was actually being celebrated was Charlie Lewes's twenty-first birthday and a house-warming. Two weeks earlier the Leweses had moved into The Priory, 21 North Bank, just one street away from Regent's Park. It was a move which was to mark the final stage in Marian's rise to the top.

She had shown great reluctance in purchasing the smart house in St John's Wood, not just because the forty-nine-year lease would cost her two thousand pounds but because she believed it was foolish to tie money up in bricks and mortar. Remembering her father's views, always her guide in matters of finance, Marian preferred most of her money to be invested in stocks and shares. Such a strategy produced a steady income but still left the capital accessible should need arise; despite her changed circumstances, Marian retained the old Evans paranoia about debt. To George's amusement and occasional irritation, thrift was all-important to Marian, and if arrangements were left to her, the Leweses were quite likely to find themselves holidaying in the cheapest hotel or travelling by the most economical route no matter how uncomfortable. Marian thoroughly enjoyed managing her own financial affairs after years of being beholden to her father and Isaac. She could always account for every pound earned and every penny in her purse and expected everyone else to be just as meticulous in money matters. Barbara Bodichon was surprised to receive a letter from Marian reminding her that she still owed one of the Leweses' servants a shilling, lent to pay the cab driver. Would Mrs Bodichon please settle up with the housemaid as soon as possible?[2]

It took Lewes a long time to persuade Marian that a house of their own was to be preferred. He knew it was useless to suggest she deserved a little self-indulgence, with her previous asceticism only just under the skin. Instead it was his contention that to own a house would prevent the terrible time-wasting every time they moved. Since they customarily took a property on a short lease, the nightmare of house-hunting and packing up came round all too regularly. The upheaval always upset Marian's health and disturbed her concentration to such an extent that she could do no work for weeks afterwards. A house taken on a long-term basis and adapted to their specific needs would do away with all that. When Marian viewed the purchase in that light, she relented.

Apart from the cost, the house at North Bank was ideal, being conveniently close to the city yet situated in a quiet backwater away from the incessant clatter of carriages on cobblestones. They would be within a short walk of the Zoological Gardens, one of their favourite haunts: George went there to study animals for his research and Marian accompanied him either out of interest or simply for relaxation. The London parks were always havens for Marian because they gave her that much needed illusion of being in the countryside. The garden surrounding The Priory, with mature trees and sweeping lawns, would be restful and redolent of that garden at Rosehill with its many pleasant associations.

Surprisingly it was the high brick wall surrounding the property and completely hiding it from the road which finally clinched the deal in Marian's mind. The fame which authorship brought had not turned out as pleasurable as she had anticipated and she increasingly sought to escape from public gaze and the discussions about her personal conduct which she maintained was nobody's concern but hers and should not be used to judge her writing. In the nine years she had lived with Lewes, gossip had steadily gathered in strength rather than died down. Though she called herself Mrs Lewes and wrote under the name of George Eliot, whispers still persisted about the shameless Miss Evans who had stolen another woman's husband. The widespread popularity of *Adam Bede* and the secrecy of its authorship had served only to focus attention on Marian once the truth was out. On their regular trips to the Continent, there was usually someone in their hotel who managed to discover the identity of the couple and made the Leweses the centre of much unwanted attention. People were always intrigued by Marian and eager to volunteer opinions about her novels or ask about her future work; Lewes too was pestered for his autograph and one of his visiting cards as a memento.

The travellers they encountered on the Continent were annoying rather than hostile to Marian, but in London matters were rather different. Marian knew her literary achievements provoked as much jealousy among women as men. This meant she rarely dined out, only occasionally went into the city to shop and was never seen at any soirées. Since they were able to afford a private box, or were sometimes in receipt of a gratuitous one from a publisher, Marian and George felt able to resume attendance at concerts, plays and operas, but more commonly they spent evenings at home together reading or Marian played the piano for entertainment. One or two of Lewes's scientific friends called and Marian eagerly joined in the discussions, which usually centred on the implications of Darwin's recently published *On the Origin of Species*.

Once installed in The Priory, George planned to extend these evenings which Marian enjoyed into something far grander. Fortunately for him, when the decoration and furnishing of their new home was discussed, Marian had shown no real interest, being content to let him undertake the planning. Lewes knew that, despite her protests, money was not really a problem and, to mastermind work at their new home, engaged Owen Jones, an interior designer who had made his name decorating the Crystal Palace for the 1851 Exhibition. Apart from more mundane matters, Jones's brief was to design a drawing room which would be spacious and impressive enough for the sort of cultural gatherings Lewes envisaged. The result was a large reception area the width of the house created by the demolition of a wall. No expense was spared in decorating this room; the wallpaper was specially designed and printed; new carpets, drapes and furniture were bought to complete the effect. At that point Marian roused herself to object to the extravagance of purchasing new chairs and sofas when they already possessed perfectly good ones. Jones tactfully explained that to stint on these items would ruin the whole design, but second-hand furniture would be used in the new dining room. He kept his word: the dining chairs were antiques.

Once the stage set was organized, it was necessary to dress the principal character. Marian had shown no interest in her clothes ever since she had decided on Puritan outfits in her teenage years. Although she ceased to dress as austerely, she deliberately left an obsession with clothing to women of more limited intellect. When she was obliged to order new dresses she insisted they be of dark colour and plain design to enable her to blend into the background rather than draw attention to her strange countenance. For her first party in the new drawing room, Owen Jones was prevailed upon by Lewes to suggest some colours and fabrics Mrs Lewes might choose to complement the décor. Marian took the advice in good humour and reported to Sara Hennell: 'You would perhaps have been amused to see an affectionate but dowdy friend of yours, splendid in a grey moiré antique – the consequence of a severe lecture from Owen Jones on her general neglect of personal adornment.'[3]

In the event Marian's first reception was judged a success. Jones was as pleased to hear Mrs Lewes declare her pleasure in his drawing-room decoration as to receive the praise of other guests. The highlight of the evening was a violin recital by the elderly musician Leopold Jansa, who was accompanied by Marian on her grand piano, placed across the far end of the room. So much did Marian enjoy the occasion that she was quite willing for George to arrange other evenings of music-making or discussion.

What Lewes really had in mind was to make George Eliot the centrepiece of a salon. From reading and time spent on the Continent, he had become well-acquainted with the salons run by French blue-stockings like Madame de Staël and George Sand; these were Lewes's models. At The Priory he hoped to establish the sort of cultural interchange which Marian used to enjoy during soirées at 142 Strand or at dinner-parties with Joseph Parkes. At the same time Lewes believed he could regain for her the respectability she had lost in being associated with him. Now that she had achieved most of her other aims, he knew that rehabilitation into society was becoming increasingly important for Marian.

The idea of making The Priory a cultural centre in London might be of similar advantage to George, who sought his own recognition as an intellectual. The large sums of money generated by Marian's novels enabled him to reduce his dependence on the cut-throat world of journalism and settle to scientific studies. Although he continued to write articles, these were less lucrative as they were of a specialist physiological nature. He did, however, contrive to earn quite large sums of money from editorial consultancy work while spending most of his time chopping up frogs and looking down microscopes. Without doubt it was Marian's influence which made Lewes desire to go down in history as a man of science rather than as an actor, a journalist or even the man behind George Eliot. Despite lacking a good schooling and a university education, the knowledge he displayed in his publications and lectures to the British Association drew admiration from eminent scientists like Tyndall, Huxley and Darwin.

Marian also wanted to achieve lasting recognition for her work rather than just contemporary popularity. As Lewes occupied himself building up the image of the greatest contemporary writer in her salon, Marian set about justifying that notion in her writing, although she was still unsure as to how she should be proceeding. *Romola* had earned her a lot of money and received the praise of people she respected, but its sales in book form were disappointing and Smith & Elder lost heavily. Despite that, Marian believed *Romola* to be her best work so far because it involved the most creativity. She had not drawn on her own experiences but had researched extensively. She was proud that the authenticity of detail in the book was such that no one would ever be able to fault her on that score. She also assumed it must be her best work because it had been the hardest book to write and had caused her the greatest mental anguish. That it was not especially popular did not upset her; indeed she believed the general reading public were not yet ready for such a cerebral novel.

If Marian was to be remembered as a great writer, she thought it necessary to prove herself capable of greatness in all literary spheres. She had succeeded in publishing translations, non-fiction articles and a short story in addition to her novels. That left drama and poetry to conquer. One of her particular concerns was for recognition as a poet as she much admired Elizabeth Barret Browning's work. Robert Browning had been living in London since his wife's death and became a regular visitor to the Leweses. He took Marian and George to see some of Mrs Browning's personal possessions which, Marian said, being items associated with the dead were curiously inspiring.

She might have launched straight into poetry-writing had not George intervened in his eagerness for her to write a play. The talents of one particular actress had so excited him that he proposed that Marian write a play for her; a drama written by George Eliot specially for the popular Helen Faucit was bound to be a success. As always George's enthusiasm was irresistible, and since Miss Faucit had also expressed interest in the proposition, Marian consented. Before she had time to meditate further, Lewes presented her with a synopsis of the play which he had worked out one sleepless night.

With a detailed breakdown of the acts, a particular actress in mind and plenty of theatrical advice from Lewes, the writing of the play should have been straightforward. It was not. Having learned nothing from the experience of *Romola*, Lewes presented Marian with the same components that had caused her trouble last time – namely a plot which had not evolved from her own subconscious and an Italian setting; moreover a form which depended totally on dialogue was not the best medium for the transmission of her ideas.

She struggled on for a while, losing confidence in her ability. 'Horrible scepticism about all things – paralyzing my mind,' she confided in her diary. 'Shall I ever be good for anything again? Ever do anything again?'[4] At that point George had the sense to take the play away. Although that solved the immediate problem, Marian refused to be beaten. The idea for a drama stayed with her, but under the influence of Elizabeth Barrett Browning's work was transformed into a verse drama set in Spain rather than Italy. Once again it was the research which slowed her down and caused her to despair of ever completing the work. As had happened with *Romola*, the only way out of the impasse was to tackle an idea in the old familiar style. Previously it had been the novella *Silas Marner*; this time *Felix Holt, The Radical* was asking to be written.

For her fourth full-length novel, Marian returned to the Warwickshire of her childhood, choosing the year 1832 when she had been at home with her family for several months in the summer before starting at the Misses Franklin's school. The event which dominated that year was the first general election after the Great Reform Bill. As she recalled, nothing else was discussed at Griff House that summer, for her father was fully occupied campaigning for the Tory candidate. Even at school the election had been the chief topic of conversation among the girls and they had all rushed to the window to watch the riots on Greyfriars Green when polling started. Memories of the characters involved came flooding back to her. Experience had taught her not to rely on memory alone but to read contemporary accounts of the election to give greater realism. Another advantage of research was that it aided Marian's creativity, helping her to expand ideas beyond the actual events they were based on. Nevertheless, she put in much that had really happened in Nuneaton and Coventry, and those still living in the neighbourhood could identify portraits in the novel. Miss Rebecca Franklin recognized her late father as the Reverend Rufus Lyon, sketched in by Marian with indulgent humour. That she should have contrived to give the teetotal Baptist Minister the name of a public house, in slightly disguised form, showed that her old sense of fun had not deserted her.

For this novel, Marian's first impulse was to return to Blackwood's, at least so Lewes told them.[5] This was not true. Smith & Elder were originally offered the novel for £5,000 but, still smarting from the loss they had suffered over *Romola*, they declined, saying they did not believe they could make a profit from such a book at that price. Marian did have qualms of conscience about the failure of *Romola* and gave Smith & Elder the manuscript of her short story 'Brother Jacob' as a present. Although this was a piece of writing she did not rate highly, Smith & Elder had once been prepared to give her two hundred and fifty guineas for the story without even having read it. To actually give it away was a kind act on Marian's part, for in her eyes business was business and not normally open to acts of generosity.

The story was gratefully accepted and was the last of George Eliot's work to be published in *Cornhill*.

Blackwood's welcomed Marian back to their list with pleasure, agreeing to pay the £5,000 Lewes said *Felix Holt* would cost. Although less than the figure paid for *Romola*, this was still a large amount of money for a novel in 1866 and Blackwood's were also to make a loss on the deal. This they did not anticipate, bearing in mind that the book was in the same mould as George Eliot's previous big earners and that the subject was particularly topical. When it first appeared in June 1866, the country was buzzing with news of the Second Reform Bill currently going through Parliament.

Once the novel was published, Marian was emboldened to return to the verse drama. Her renewed confidence enabled her to complete *The Spanish Gypsy* and enjoy the experience. The stringency demanded by the form she had chosen suited her mood and inspired her to go on to write other shorter poems afterwards. Her poetry was written more for personal satisfaction than money,[6] and when Blackwood's said they could offer only three hundred pounds for a two-thousand print-run of her Spanish poem, she accepted without complaint. She knew her poetry was not for the average reader and was grateful to see it in print at all. However, the Americans were more sanguine about George Eliot's poetry and were ultimately to sell over eight thousand copies of *The Spanish Gypsy*.

What mattered most to Marian as time went on was that what she published had real literary merit. Compliments about the verse drama went a long way towards reassuring her. The need to prove her worth as a dramatist no longer mattered. What took its place was a desire to write a novel which would not only have popular appeal but ensure history would judge George Eliot as an equal to Jane Austen.

As Marian considered this new aim, Lewes continued working towards the establishment of Marian as a George Sand figure holding court over a salon at The Priory. He had early decided to make George Eliot exclusive. Since her unorthodox liaison made her disinclined to accept invitations to visit, he suggested she should let it be known that in London she never dined out, no matter who the host. When Cara sent a note to invite Marian to meet her in Sydenham during a forthcoming visit to London, she was shocked to be told: 'I find it more necessary than ever to keep rigidly to my rule of paying no visits in or near London, and to renounce seeing any friends unless they will kindly come to me.'[7] The terms on which they were permitted to visit Marian were also strictly laid down. Sunday afternoons between two o'clock and five o'clock were the usual hours when Mrs Lewes was available to receive visitors, although for old friends like Cara and Sara some exception could be made. They had invitations to lunch in the week but were not encouraged to consider extending their visit much into the afternoon and certainly not to stay overnight. Even though The Priory was a reasonably-sized house, Marian said she did not have a sufficiently comfortable bedroom to offer her old friends.[8]

Other old friends were encouraged to resume their visits within the set times. Spencer was back on the scene, very much his old self, full of delightful talk and with amiability in his eyes, Marian reported. She seemed unaware that the change was in her own attitude and not his. Chapman's philandering, however, had ceased to be a joke as far as Marian was concerned. The amorous doctor of medicine, who had qualified in 1857, had installed himself with his latest mistress in rooms in Somerset Street while housing his wife and family elsewhere. That he could behave with such promiscuity and still be received in society while Marian remained ostracized was more than she could bear. Dr John Chapman was never invited to The Priory.

Plenty of other notables were asked and came. During the Leweseses' early years in the house, it was quite common for eight or ten people to join them on a Sunday afternoon. The guests were rarely women, but that pleased Marian, who always preferred the company of men. Lewes was responsible for issuing the invitations and tried to select those he considered rising stars in various fields Marian would be interested in apart from writing. Naturally scientists loomed large, but so did artists like Frederic Burton and Burne-Jones, and university men like Edward Beesly, who was Professor of Latin at Bedford College, London.

When George Eliot held her salons, those who entered the Leweses' drawing room would find the great lady already seated to the left of the fireplace. Guests would be encouraged to draw their chairs close to hers and form a circle round the fire. The conversation was always spirited and ranged over all manner of subjects with Marian just as keen to participate as to hear others' views. Many felt there was an element of stage management in these receptions since Lewes only occasionally joined in the discussion. More often he hovered at the side ready to bring in the next guest or throw in a remark which would show his adored Marian in an even better light. Some thought Lewes's jokes about his mistress being 'a Mediaeval saint with a grand genius',[9] or the Madonna of the priory whom all came to worship, if not blasphemous, at least in poor taste.

As time passed, the numbers attending the Sunday salon increased and George Eliot was gradually set apart from the general hubbub, talking only to the people Lewes brought up to her, one at a time. The Priory came to look even more like a shrine to the great genius; the walls in the drawing room were hung with Frederick Leighton's illustrations for *Romola*; bound copies of her manuscripts along with various editions and translations of her books were always available for inspection and new worshippers were taken to admire Burton's flattering portrait of George Eliot, which was placed like a reredos in Lewes's study. To the unconverted it was all too introspective and self-congratulatory for comfort, but for the majority of visitors it merely heightened the experience of being in the presence of the great.

Paradoxically, while Marian enjoyed this adulation she had been seeking all her life, the more famous she became the more she shied away. At early parties at The Priory she took a leading part, playing the piano, singing, joining in the conversation and sometimes performing in the charades Lewes organized, but as time went on she adopted a more passive role. Someone else was paid to play an instrument or sing, for as numbers grew so did her insecurity, despite being on her own territory.

What she hoped celebrity would bring was respectability, that most essential of Evans virtues. As time passed it became increasingly apparent that those first thirty years Marian had spent within the family circle had inexorably shaped her personality. She was essentially Mary Ann Evans, no matter what name she called herself. 'George Eliot' became a convenient mask for her to hide behind because the androgynous author was rich, successful and, most important of all, lacked a past; Marian Evans Lewes by contrast was a woman scarred by her past. As a visiting American explained in a letter home in 1868, Mrs Lewes:

> is an object of great interest and great curiosity to society here. She is not received in general society, and the women who visit her are either so emancipée [sic] as not to mind what the world says about them, or have no social position to maintain. Lewes dines out a

good deal, and some of the men with whom he dines go without their wives to his house on Sundays. No one whom I have heard speak, speaks in other than terms of respect of Mrs Lewes, but the common feeling is that it will not do for society to condone so flagrant a breach as hers of a convention and a sentiment (to use no stronger terms) on which morality greatly relies for support. I suspect society is right in this . . . I do not believe that many people think that Mrs Lewes violated her own moral sense, or is other than a good woman in her present life, but they think her example pernicious, and that she cut herself off by her own act from the society of women who feel themselves responsible for the tone of social morals in England.[10]

This idea that she might infect others with evil angered Marian and made her all the more ultra-correct in her behaviour. She wanted to demonstrate that she was not immoral just because society had forced her to take an independent line. Many people then and since were disappointed that, like George Sand, George Eliot also moved away from the rebel stance to become a moralist. Was it that ultimately Marian Evans had her price and that wealth and distinction were powerful enough to lure her from her personal convictions? She would certainly have argued not. The Marian that was gradually emerging in the 1860s was the real Marian, the product of an Evans inheritance and upbringing, which had been temporarily overlaid by other experiences in middle life. As she matured, the bedrock of her personality became visible again. In essence Marian was as conservative as her father had been.

It showed in her religious views. Although George Lewes remained firmly agnostic, even to the point of refusing his sons permission to get confirmed at school, Marian yearned for the comfortable rituals she had enjoyed in her youth, even though intellectually she could not accept the doctrine. She achieved a compromise in the 1860s by limited attendance at Unitarian chapels with Barbara Bodichon and, on Christmas Day 1869, even succeeded in persuading the sceptical Lewes to accompany her. It was Bessie Parkes's conviction that Marian would have returned to the Church had Lewes not been so cynical.[11] Though Bessie, as a convert to Roman Catholicism, was keen to recruit new members, she had nevertheless identified the drift in Marian's thinking.

On her approach to her half-century, Marian was losing sympathy with most radical causes and wanted to dissociate herself from them. Those collecting for Mazzini, the Italian revolutionary she had known when she lived at Chapman's, now found her reluctant to donate. It was not that she was stingy, she said, but that she could not be sure how the money was going to be used.[12] Had Signor Mazzini himself approached her for money for his own needs, the case would have been different. Charles Bray would have been dubious about that. He asked Marian for a contribution to a fund for the ribbon weavers in Coventry, who were in dire straits following another recession. Marian always expressed concern about their plight and knew Bray was distributing food and clothing to them, so when he wrote asking if she could possibly spare a pound, he was hugely disappointed to find she took him at his word: just a pound arrived.[13]

The Women's Movement did not fare vastly better in gaining Mrs Lewes's support. Though an ardent adherent to the cause when she was a struggling journalist, as a wealthy novelist she appeared less enthusiastic. Had it not been for her friendship with Barbara Bodichon, Marian would have dropped the cause completely since it no longer accorded with her ambitions. Barbara kept her informed of its progress and also brought some of the pioneers, like Drs Elizabeth Blackwell and Elizabeth Garrett in medicine and Emily Davies and Elizabeth Malleson in the field of education, to meet her. These women assumed that the successful woman novelist would wish to spearhead the campaign for improved female educational opportunities, but their arrival was too late.

Marian would not be associated with anything which might jeopardize her steady progress towards acceptance into society. In the past she had agreed with feminists that women deserved a fairer deal in life and had written to urge Cara and Sara to put their signatures to the petition for the reform of the property laws, but in 1866, when the MP John Stuart Mill urged Parliament to extend the Second Reform Bill to give women the vote, Marian disagreed. Her earlier experience in the provinces had convinced her that women were interested only in ephemeral subjects and not likely to use their vote wisely. Since then she had seen nothing in the conduct of women in the metropolis to make her change her mind. The same sense of pettiness prevailed everywhere, she said, and women did not deserve the franchise.[14]

Barbara Bodichon, however, believed that her friend might support the campaign for further education for women, since Marian had gratefully attended classes at the Bedford Square College in 1851. Barbara donated £1,000 towards the fund to found a women's college at Cambridge University and went on to use her influence to glean money and support from others. Marian was not so easily won over to having her name linked with any cause or parting with her money. It took the combined efforts of Barbara and Emily Davies, later founder of Girton College, Cambridge, to woo Mrs Lewes. As always George Lewes was present during the interview and it was his enthusiasm for 'the great campaign' that finally persuaded Marian to part with £50.[15] That for her was a large donation, but less than Barbara and Miss Davies had hoped for, particularly as Lewes had been so enthusiastic on behalf of their enterprise. Speaking for Marian as well as himself, he said they thought it wise to aim for the full £30,000 to create the college from nothing, rather than waste time and effort collecting sundry smaller amounts. When Marian handed her donation over she was careful that the benefactor be listed as 'the author of *Romola*', so that neither her own name nor 'George Eliot's' would be tarnished if the project turned out a fiasco. Learning later that her donation was half most people's, Marian explained to Miss Davies that she did not wish to subscribe too large a sum to the Ladies' College lest it should prevent her from helping other worthy causes.[16]

This might have encouraged the founders of the College for Working Women in London's Queen's Square to anticipate a £50 donation when they approached her the following year, but they were sadly disappointed. After reading their prospectus, Marian said she had grave doubts about the whole undertaking: 'The instruction of working women on so high and difficult a scale seems to me unpracticable, nay, not desirable,' she told Mrs Elizabeth Malleson.[17] However, on grounds of friendship with Barbara Bodichon, Marian did pledge some money to the cause which Mrs Malleson, a principal teacher in one of Barbara's schools, espoused. Marian subscribed sixteen guineas, but spread over eight years so that the money could be stopped if the college appeared to be misusing its funds.

Feminists at the time and later have felt that Marian let them down. She would have been the best advertisement possible of a woman's intellect and triumph against the odds, yet she refused to help when it mattered. Her excuse was that the movement had changed and too many extremists had become involved, so that by 1869 she told a member of the Girton College committee: 'There is no subject on which I am more inclined to hold my peace and learn, than on the "Women Question".'[18] Her excuse has never satisfied anyone and is only part of the answer. What was playing a far more vital part was the innate conservatism of Marian Evans, which was gradually emerging. It could also be said that none of it accorded with her current ambition to be accepted into the highest echelons of a society which was not sympathetic to female suffrage, education or anything which might be construed as radical.

As Marian's views moved closer to her father's, the same strong sense of fatalism also reappeared, along with an awareness of her own mortality. Lewes's continual ill-health and a succession of deaths among people close to her made her own demise seem the more imminent. No permanent cure could be found for Lewes's headaches, nausea and gradual loss of weight. He sought periodic treatment at Malvern with the same water cure which had alleviated the symptoms in the past, but, never liking to be away from Marian for long, he would return to London before the cure had a chance to work its miracles, or at least so he persuaded himself. During their regular holidays in warmer climes, Lewes experienced better health than at home, but they never considered making mainland Europe their home as the Brownings had. George said he was concerned about the welfare of his elderly mother but he also knew that Marian was too quintessentially English ever to settle on the Continent.

Constant illness was reducing the vivacious Lewes to a shivering heap of skin and bone which terrified Marian. The intense love and happiness she had experienced with George would, she felt sure, ultimately have to be paid for in suffering. Though she herself was rarely free of headaches and general debility, she believed it would be her fate to inherit the same longevity as her father and drag out her days in sickness without George.[19] The fear of him dying before her became all the more real when Prince Albert died in 1859, leaving Queen Victoria a widow. Marian, the same age as the Queen, felt an empathy with the grieving woman whom she was sure had worshipped her husband. But other deaths nearer to home followed, which focused Marian's attention on her own mortality.

Her half-brother Robert Evans, a prosperous land agent and farmer in Derbyshire, died in 1864 at the age of sixty-two from cancer of the stomach. The letter of sympathy Marian impulsively penned to his widow Jane Evans produced the first correspondence from her family in years. In a kind reply, her sister-in-law related Robert's final moments when he requested a copy of *Adam Bede* to be brought so that Dinah's prayer and sermon could be read to him. He had then drifted away with the book clasped to him. Marian, who had not seen her half-brother since 1849, was deeply moved by this gesture of familial affection.

Then a few months later came word that Henry Houghton, Fanny's husband, had also died. With the deaths of two husbands in her family coming so close together, it was not surprising that she worried all the more about George's health.

In fact the deaths which followed were of three young people. The sequence of letters from Sara in 1864 and 1865 traced the steady decline of nineteen-year-old Nelly Bray, wasting away in Coventry with the much feared tuberculosis. Cara, who for years had found it hard to accept the illegitimate daughter that Charles had foisted on her, had grown very close to the girl by the end. It was she who nursed Nelly through the terrible final months and was devastated by the loss. Sara too was deeply affected by Nelly's death, for she had acted as foster-mother and governess to the girl from her earliest days at Rosehill.

Helpless to comfort her friends from a distance, Marian could only write of her belief that early death was an aspect of salvation, words she was to reiterate the following year when George's grandchild died at birth.[20] Charlie Lewes had married in February 1865, despite his father stating his grave reservations about the state of matrimony. Marian had welcomed the removal of Charlie from The Priory as a chance for herself and George to settle down together for the few years she believed were left to them. Charlie's wife Gertrude (sister of Octavia Hill, an ardent feminist friend of Barbara Bodichon) produced a healthy child in the year following the marriage. To everyone's horror, the infant strangled itself in the umbilical cord. Never having seen herself as a grandmotherly figure anyway, Marian was not deeply affected by the loss and could see no reason why Gertrude should not produce other children in the future.[21]

When faced by the death of George's son Thornie no philosophy could comfort her or George. This was a death which upset her as no other. Once his schooling was over, Thornie had returned home to his father and Mutter while his career was worked out. After an abortive attempt to push the boy into a conventional career in the Indian Civil Service, it was agreed that Thornie could go to South Africa. All the nineteen-year-old really wanted to do was fight, but his father refused to let him enlist and could only prevent him running off to join a mercenary army by offering him the bait of a pioneering life in Natal. Equipped with kit, guns and cash courtesy of Marian, he left in 1863 and was joined by his young brother Bertie three years later. Thornie soon found there was ample gratification of his desire to fight as he engaged in battles against the Basutos. Though he was successful at slaughtering Africans, he was less good at settling down to farm and was obliged to apply for more money to bail himself and Bertie out.

Early in January 1869 a letter arrived at The Priory from Thornie which caused great consternation. Money was again requested to settle debts and this time also to pay for Thornie's passage home. He said that he had become so ill he was wasting away, unable to work or even sit down. Every evening he suffered recurrent attacks that made him scream out aloud with the pain. Though he thought it likely he might be a cripple for the rest of his life, what mattered was to get back to England if there was to be any hope at all. George sent £250 immediately. In May an emaciated Thornie arrived at The Priory looking even worse than they had feared. As his letter had said, he could only bear to lie on the floor and even then was likely to roll around in agonizing convulsions when the pain was at its height.

For five months Marian tended Thornie, grateful for the opportunity to be of service to another human being. 'I never before felt so keenly the wealth one possesses in every being to whose mind and body it is possible to minister comfort through love and care,' she wrote to a friend.[22] The experience, however, was harrowing for herself and George. Thornie's real mother visited occasionally, finding it hard to recognize in the dying young man that child she had seen so infrequently since boyhood. Gratefully Agnes Lewes relinquished the nursing to Marian. Thornie was so ill he could find relief from the mysterious ailment only with heavy doses of morphia. Occasionally there seemed faint signs of improvement which gave Marian heart that the twenty-five-year-old might recover, but George was less optimistic. He never confided his worst fears in Marian but from his contact with leading doctors and scientists gradually came to believe the end was inevitable. No one at the time could diagnose the illness. It has since been identified as tuberculosis of the spine for which there would then have been no cure.

Tragically Thornie continued to decline. A severe attack in the summer paralysed him from the waist downwards, and in the middle of October Thornton Lewes died in the arms of his Mutter. This parting affected her more deeply than any other and Thornie's death marked a permanent change in herself and George. 'This death seems to me the beginning of our own,' she wrote simply in her journal on 19 October 1869.[23]

CHAPTER 15

Honour and Homage,
1870–1878

So successful was George Eliot's salon that by 1871 Lewes was talking of the need for a larger house to accommodate the rising tide of visitors and the dimensions of their persons. Against Marian's wishes, Lewes inspected some other properties in St John's Wood, but he was forced to agree that none was as secluded as The Priory and all would require major structural alterations to meet their purposes. The simplest solution by far was to extend their existing home. It was decided that the Leweses' splendid drawing room would have to be made even larger, and at the same time one or two other modern luxuries could be incorporated into the house, such as a bathroom. This was no extravagance, Marian insisted, merely a health aid for George's persistent lumbago.

As the decade progressed and the volume and importance of the guests grew even greater, Sunday afternoon at The Priory became less an intellectual salon and more a social event. 'Lords and Ladies, poets and cabinet minister, artists and men of science crowd upon us on Sundays – very delightful – but we as hosts have to pay for the pleasure – and they even flow into the week days,' George Lewes wrote with evident pride in 1872.[1] Though he regularly exaggerated for effect, he was in this instance absolutely truthful. By the mid-1870s attendance at The Priory was a must for anyone from home or abroad with cultural pretensions. Americans arriving in London tried hard to obtain a letter of introduction from somebody who could admit them into the presence of the great George Eliot; alarmed by the way she was becoming a public spectacle, Marian appealed to her friends and acquaintances not to write such letters.[2]

While Marian felt uncomfortable, Lewes was in his element. All his life he had been fascinated by high society and yearned for an entrée. Now to his delight, society was knocking on his door, albeit to crave an audience with George Eliot. He was never jealous of Marian's fame, just pleased that she was receiving her just desserts. He enjoyed her fame far more than she did; the more the crowds gathered, the more the leading lady shied away. As in the past, this led to accusations that Marian was haughty, though, as she was fond of saying, the wounded animal only wanted to hide in the quiet and darkness.[3] As people courted Lewes, eager to book an appointment for a brief word with the great George Eliot, Marian's few intimate friends withdrew. Their visits in fact took place on weekdays and encroached on her valuable working time.

Though Marian continued to hold the Sunday afternoon audiences on Lewes's advice, she insisted on escaping from public gaze on other occasions as much as possible. Continental holidays, which used to be her delight, were fast becoming a European version of the lionizing she was receiving at home. Their visit to Germany and Austria in 1870 finally turned Marian completely against foreign travel as it developed into a round of 'Princes, Professors, Ambassadors, and persons covered with stars and decorations'.[4] Lewes, however, enjoyed the whole thing and was delighted to discover he was known in his own right as Goethe's biographer and the author of many learned papers. His days were spent touring laboratories, lunatic asylums and hospitals, while Marian attempted to avoid the clutches of German socialites. It might be pleasant to have free use of the diplomatic box at the opera but it was not so enjoyable to find oneself surrounded by flocks of adoring women all eager to make an impression. They looked more like birds waiting to have a peck at her, she said cynically.[5] News of the famous couple's arrival in Berlin flashed round the city and soon a German duke was calling at their hotel for an introduction to the great George Eliot and pressing an invitation on the couple to attend his soirée. That was more than Marian could stand and she retreated into ill-health.

A few days later, when they travelled on to Vienna, a similar scenario awaited them because Lewes had advised the British Ambassador of their arrival beforehand. The Honourable Robert

Lytton was known to Lewes as a poet who had sought his assistance in having his work published. Never shy at cultivating contacts, Lewes had asked Lytton if suitable rooms could be found for them in the Austrian capital. This approach proved an expensive mistake since the aristocrat's idea of what was appropriate for international celebrities was not the same as the Leweses'. To entertain the couple, Lytton arranged a glittering programme of engagements at theatres, operas and galleries along with regular evening parties among royalty and the cream of Viennese society.

Marian was horrified when she realized what was in store for her. Within twenty-four hours she developed such a severe sore throat and cold that for most of her ten days in Vienna she could attend only selected functions. While sympathizing with Marian's suffering, Lewes was irritated that her illness prevented him from taking part in all the entertainments. 'This is the second chance we have missed of seeing the Empress,' he recorded with frustration in his diary.[6] But Marian never tried to keep him by her side. Indeed she encouraged him to attend dinners and soirées without her, much as he did in London. In practice it turned out that when the glitterati heard the great writer would not be in attendance, they did not bother to come either.

With their Continental holidays resembling a royal progress, Marian asked George to think in terms of spending the summer quietly in the English countryside. It was less strenuous than travelling all over Europe, she insisted, and the peace of the countryside would be most conducive to her writing. If the novel *Middlemarch* which she was struggling with was ever to see the light of day, a period of uninterrupted quiet was needed. What Marian would have liked was to leave London for good, take a house in the country far from the public gaze and settle contentedly with Lewes, her dog and her work. The older she grew the more she harked back nostalgically to her youth in the countryside round Griff. But it was impossible to persuade the town-bred Lewes to forsake the capital and the company he thrived on for a rural retreat. In the event a compromise was reached similar to that between Barbara Bodichon and her French husband. Lewes suggested they buy a country house and spend six months of the year there accepting only visits from their most intimate friends. In the winter season they could return to The Priory and receive people at Sunday afternoon receptions as before.

Though she agreed with Lewes, Marian anticipated that in time she would be able to win him round to living in the country permanently.

Selection of the Leweses' country property proved far more arduous than choosing the town house had been because Marian knew exactly what she wanted and would not settle for second best. Her house in the country would be an Eden where the serpent in the guise of the visitor would be forbidden. For the next five years they devoted their summers to sampling different locations and seeing what properties were available. After venturing into Kent, it was ultimately the part of Surrey around Haslemere, where they stayed in 1871 when Marian completed much of *Middlemarch*, that really appealed to them; but not until the end of 1876 did they succeed in finding a country house tucked away inside eight acres of gardens and woodland, which could be purchased for five thousand pounds. The Heights at Witley was certainly secluded; Marian made it clear that nobody was welcome unless they received a specific invitation, and that included Mr Alfred Tennyson, whose country house lay just over the hill.

It was hardly to be wondered at that Marian should have become so anti-social; she who had at one time been disdainfully ignored now found her every move reported in the newspapers. On one occasion when they were hiding away in Surrey, one newspaper confidently gave the name of a German spa town as their whereabouts and another one announced to Marian's annoyance that George Eliot's next book was to have an American setting.[7] She was clearly public property about which anything could be written, accurate or otherwise.

It was in the rural solitude of the hamlet at Shottermill near Haslemere during the summer of 1871 that Marian made huge strides with the novel which has been judged her greatest work. Like her other successful books, *Middlemarch* was set in the Midlands and contained elements from her past. Having been friendly with several medical men in her life, it was not surprising that Marian should have chosen to focus on the conflicts of a rural doctor. In her teens there had been ample opportunity to observe the work of her brother-in-law Dr Edward Clarke, a general practitioner and medical officer at the workhouse; in London, years later, John Chapman had always been keener on devoting his time to medical studies than to the *Westminster Review*, and sharing a life with Lewes had meant that his physiological investigations regularly took both of them into the company of England's leading physicians, several of whom had become their personal friends. It was, however, the sad career of Edward Clarke which provided her with the greatest inspiration. This well-born young man from outside the area, who had begun his career full of noble ambitions, had married her sister and was ultimately defeated by local prejudices and perpetual financial crises only to die prematurely, became the model for Dr Tertius Lydgate.

As always, her Midland books contained aspects of many people from her past, but as time went on they were not so much photographic portraits as the starting point for character development. Her father made one of his regular appearances as the honest respected land agent Caleb Garth in the book and there were also elements of herself, or at least the self she would like to have been, in the heroine Dorothea Brooke. Lewes recognized her: 'Surely Dorothea is the very cream of lovely womanhood? She is more like her creator than anyone else and more so than any other of her creations. Only those who know her (Dodo – or her creator) under all aspects can have any idea of her,' he told John Blackwood, who had recently received the manuscript to peruse.[8] In private and among friends Lewes adopted the habit of calling Marian 'Dorothea', or 'Dodo' as the heroine was affectionately known in the book. For himself he reserved the joke name 'Casaubon' after the staid academic Dorothea married, who made a great fuss about the learned tome he would write but never actually put pen to paper. Since Lewes himself was involved in writing and publishing his epic *Problems of Life and Mind*, which promised to run into several volumes, he thought the joke all the more appropriate. He was the antithesis of the humourless scholar in *Middlemarch*, but ironically like the character in the book, Lewes died before his *magnum opus* was finished. It was his dying wish that his Dorothea should complete the task for him.

In reality Lewes had more in common with the colourful cosmopolitan character Will Ladislaw in *Middlemarch*, who became Dorothea's second husband. But Ladislaw had a far closer similarity to another of Marian's former loves. The daring young man, who was neither understood nor accepted by the neighbourhood, played a controversial role in the Mechanics Institute, stirred up local politics, got himself involved in skirmishes between the local radical newspaper and its Tory counterpart and was not free to marry the woman he loved, bore a striking resemblance to Charles Bray.

Rooted in reality but developed creatively, *Middlemarch* was a brilliant piece of writing. Lewes said it was, but then he said that about everything Marian wrote. Blackwood's agreed; they had to because if they were not effusive about George Eliot's prose, they received a private ticking-off from Lewes. It was not always easy for John Blackwood to compose ever more laudatory comments about every section of the manuscript he received and continue to praise the work just as sincerely when he returned proofs of the same section for checking. Nevertheless he genuinely admired Marian's writing and did his best to supply all the fulsome remarks Lewes told him were essential if Marian were not to lose heart.

When it came to negotiating a contract for the new novel, Lewes once again proved what an excellent agent he was. He not only secured a lucrative deal but also initiated a better method of marketing George Eliot's work. Since this novel promised to be far longer than her earlier ones, running into four volumes, Lewes suggested it be issued in half-volumes at five shillings each. People who would not normally have bought a four-volume novel might then be persuaded to purchase the work in instalments. Blackwood's agreed and, in addition to serializing the book in the *Maga*, successfully employed this revolutionary method of publishing. Lewes had one or two other good ideas like printing the half-volumes on spongy paper to look better value for money and adding a few pages of advertisements at the end to bulk the volume out. These might not be the sort of ploys one associates with great works of literature, but Lewes was ahead of his time, demonstrating a very twentieth-century approach to the best-seller.

Once again his commercial genius combined with Marian's superb prose proved a winning combination. *Middlemarch* became the book of the moment, read and discussed by everybody, acclaimed by reviewers, in demand by translators and quickly netting over £9,000 for its author.

No sooner did *Middlemarch* have its umbilical cord severed than Marian was considering her next book. Always at the back of her mind was the awareness that time was running out: 'Physically I feel old and Death seems very near,' she said in 1871, yet there still remained much she wanted to write about.[9] One of the Continental holidays they had selected was in the fashionable German spa resort of Homburg on account of Lewes's continual ill-health. They were certainly not attracted by the casinos there, Marian told a friend. The gambling she witnessed was a revelation: 'Burglary is heroic compared with it,' she wrote in an impassioned letter. 'I am not fond of denouncing my fellow-sinners, but gambling being a vice I have no mind to, it stirs my disgust even more than my pity.'[10] The sight of an attractive twenty-six-year-old woman, so completely in the grasp of the 'mean, money-making demon' that she could lose £500 in one sitting, upset Marian. 'It made me cry to see her fresh young face among the hags and brutally stupid men around her.'[11]

This vision of hell and its occupants made such a profound impression on Marian that she conceived *Daniel Deronda*. This book, which was to be the last of her novels, has by far the most powerful message. Specific incidents from her youth played only a minor part this time; instead Marian chose to pen a forceful condemnation of so-called polite society. Men like Joseph Parkes, so concerned with keeping up a respectable appearance while indulging in adultery, were dealt with harshly. The lies and the misery implicit in contracting 'suitable' marriages for girls similarly received sharp condemnation. Though Marian would not give her name or money to the Women's Movement, in her writing she was their greatest asset. No reader was left in any doubt that George Eliot found much to criticize in the behaviour of a male-dominated society. By contrast the fact that the author should find a great deal to admire in the much-hated Jewish community made *Daniel Deronda* her most controversial book. The novel sold surprisingly well, but being published in instalments people did not know what there was to object to until they had read most of the book. George Eliot also had such a following that any new book she published was eagerly snapped up. However, as Blackwood's predicted, the early success of *Daniel Deronda* was not maintained. The book received heavy criticism for its sympathetic treatment of Jews. Although ostensibly shielded from opinions about her work, Marian heard that most of her readers would rather she had written about anything else but the Jews; she was disgusted by their prejudice and all the more pleased that she had chosen the theme.

In 1877, she was mulling over another book even further removed from her successful Midlands novels. *Theophrastus Such* was, like her poetry, Marian's idea of an indulgence, being a reflective piece of writing, hardly fiction, but not autobiography either as she suggested. Prosperity now meant she could retreat to the country and write exactly what she chose without an eye to the profit. Her wealth had also brought her that most prized of status symbols, the personal carriage. In itself not an expensive item, but requiring a horse, tack, a coachman and housing for man and beast, this was a luxury confined to the rich. The carriage and the country house were the only outward signs of Marian's affluence. Her annual income from shares regularly exceeded her literary earnings.

The wealthier Marian became, the greater the demands upon her. Although reluctant to part with cash, she was nevertheless generous to members of the family. Victorian society forced women to be dependants and thus the relatives who looked to her for assistance were all female. From the beginning of her life with Lewes there had always been his wife and her children to support, which meant two hundred and fifty pounds a year paid to Agnes Lewes for the rest of her life. When George Lewes's brother Edward Lewes died leaving a wife and young son, there was no one else to support them. Once again a regular allowance was paid and George assumed complete responsibility for the welfare of his sister-in-law and nephew. Marian made herself responsible for her niece Emily after the death of Chrissey Clarke, but since Emily could support herself by teaching music, the annuity was commensurate with that.

In 1875 the list of dependants increased again when word came that George's son Bertie had died leaving a wife and two little children, the younger barely a month old. The letters which arrived at The Priory detailing Bertie's last days were tragic and all too reminiscent of Thornie's demise. However, for six months previously Bertie's letters had contained reports of his deteriorating health, so Marian and George had prepared for the worst. If Bertie had remained in England the outcome would probably have been the same, Marian told George; he must not blame himself for sending his sons to their death in the colonies.[12] Urgent help for the young widow Eliza and her family was what was required. She was destitute; they had never lived above subsistence level and her husband's illness and death had run up debts she could not pay. Their farm had gone to rack and ruin when Bertie could not work. Once again Marian supported this family for the rest of her life and beyond.

Despite so many dependants, Marian was now more prepared to give to sundry charities. Hearing that Maria Lewis, the Evangelical teacher who had been kind to her when she had lived at Griff, was almost blind and living in poverty, Marian sent her £10, which figure she despatched annually. The much larger sum of £200 was made over to a trust set up to support Octavia Hill, sister of Charlie's wife Gertrude, because Marian strongly approved of the practical measures Octavia was taking to improve slum housing. Barbara Bodichon's pet cause, Girton College, Cambridge, also gained Marian's admiration. Despite initial reservations about the enterprise, Marian was forced to admit that the college had been most successful and the students, whom Barbara took good care to introduce to Marian, were intelligent, well-mannered young women. However, when it came to a further donation for the College, Marian regretted that other demands on her generosity prevented her from giving the £100 she would like.[13] Instead she preferred to donate £10 each to several students Barbara recommended who had places and were struggling to accumulate the fees; this had the added advantage that Marian knew exactly how her money was being spent.

During the 1870s, Marian felt a greater empathy with Cara Bray than at any time previously. The visits and correspondence of Charles Bray had gradually petered out mainly because Lewes had little sympathy with Bray and thought him a patent idiot. Marian still cherished fond memories of the man she had once loved, but Bray's regular applications for cash soon cooled her affections. As Marian lost sympathy with Charles, she felt it for Cara, the passive victim of her husband's excesses. Marian could not help but admire the way Cara had remained loyal to her husband while at the same time trying to create a life for herself. As the least intellectual and forceful of the Rosehill trio, Cara had taken up a humbler form of writing than the others; paradoxically her books had a wider readership than their philosophical treatises. Experience as a teacher in her husband's infant school stood Cara in good stead to write her books of instruction for use at home and in schools. One such volume encouraged a better awareness of hygiene, another informed children about the British Empire and several promoted kindness towards animals. In all Mrs Bray published six books for children but, unlike Marian, received nothing for them. With no one interested in her humble literary offerings, Cara was left to negotiate her own publishing contracts and she accepted half-profit agreements. As Marian well knew from her days at Chapman's, that meant in practice no income because the publishers always produced figures to demonstrate that the book had cost more to produce than it had earned.

When Cara eventually approached Marian for advice about getting back the copyright of one of her books, the professional writer regretted she had not helped her friend in the past. Thereafter, Marian tried to assist Cara in placing her next book and, to appease her own conscience, to persuade Cara to let her advance money against the new book's possible earnings.[14] But Cara was not one to accept charity; only when Marian insisted that the money was a donation for the Coventry Society for the Prevention of Cruelty to Animals which Cara had founded was the cheque cashed. Guessing at the financial hardships which had descended on Cara following Charles's ill-considered enterprises, Marian urged her friend not to be too proud to ask if there was some little comfort she required but could not afford. Mrs Bray, though grateful, had the same fierce pride as Marian and would never have entertained such an idea.

While it pleased Marian to receive news of old friends in Warwickshire from Cara, she was not so pleased to receive deputations from her relations in the area. Younger generations of Evanses were baffled by the fact that, though the novels of George Eliot were read avidly by everybody in the family, communication with their famous relative had ceased. Isaac's daughter Edith wrote asking if she and her new clergyman husband might call on Mrs Lewes in London. The wish was granted. Marian received them politely but coolly, making it clear that she had no desire to reopen any old wounds by making overtures to her brother. When a letter from her nephew Robert Evans III arrived at The Priory soon after, requesting Marian to write to her half-sister Fanny, now widowed and living with his mother, Marian replied that, as she recalled, it was Fanny who had chosen to terminate the correspondence by failing to answer the last letter twenty years previously.[15]

Stubbornness and pride were not restricted to Marian. Isaac had no wish to communicate with his sister and had no knowledge of his daughter's overtures. When he received a letter from Chrissey's son, who was on a visit from Australia to see his sister Emily, he refused a request for him to spend Christmas with his uncle at Griff. Marian, however, welcomed contact with her nephew and admired the way he had displayed true Evans grit in creating a successful life for himself 'down under'.

Having no children of her own, Marian valued her relationship with Chrissey's children and with George's remaining son Charlie. During the 1870s she also developed an attachment to another family whom she liked to think of as relatives. George introduced her to the Crosses, a banking family and friends of Herbert Spencer. Mrs Anna Cross, six years older than Marian, had been left a widow with ten children ranging in age from thirteen to thirty-four. She was a well-read and warm-hearted woman to whom Marian was drawn straightaway. Invitations to stay with the family at their impressive residence in Weybridge, Surrey, were readily accepted. There was plenty of stimulating conversation for Marian and boisterous good humour to suit George. After the artificial sanctity of Sunday afternoons at The Priory it was like a breath of fresh air to visit the Crosses, where no one stood on ceremony or made any fuss about the celebrities: they just welcomed Marian and George as two of the family. Weybridge rapidly became the Leweses' favourite weekend retreat. An invitation to join the Crosses for Christmas festivities was also accepted. Then there was much music-making, card-playing, charades and high-jinks which Lewes thrived on. Marian enjoyed such revelries in small doses but after a couple of days usually felt the onset of a bad cold which necessitated their return to London.

Large noisy gatherings never suited Marian, so it was not surprising that among the Cross children she should have been drawn to the quietest member. Predictably her favourite Cross child was a male: John Cross was a tall young man in his early thirties with reddish hair and a beard. A product of Rugby School, Cross had then gone to work for the transatlantic branch of the family bank, Dennistoun, Cross and Company, in New York. By the time he was thirty he decided he was sufficiently affluent to return to England and retire to the life of a gentleman dabbling in a little financial consultancy work to relieve any boredom. To Marian, John Cross was the ideal son for he combined the skill of the commercial world she admired with wide reading and culture. In his personality he displayed the same warmth and affection as his mother. It was not long before Marian suggested to George that Johnnie, as she liked to call him, should manage their financial affairs. He was soon a regular visitor at The Priory, calling on business and frequently staying on to discuss European literature with Marian or to play the piano. At Sunday afternoon receptions at The Priory he and some of his sisters were also to be seen among the rich and the titled. The more the young man called, the more he became one of the family, and both George and Marian referred to him affectionately as 'dear nephew'.[16] For his part, Johnnie Cross was just as eager to be accepted as one of the Lewes family, for he adored Mrs Lewes. As he confided to Herbert Spencer, she was his ideal woman.[17] Cross's visits became more numerous than Charlie Lewes's and he usually brought flowers or some other small gift for his heroine. It was a relationship all three were happy in.

Presents constantly arrived for Marian, and not just from Johnnie Cross, for a new breed of sycophant arrived in the 1870s whom Marian found difficult to accept. George's invitation to all and sundry to come and worship the Madonna encouraged other young men from Cross's generation, also unmarried and seeking a safe unattainable female on whom to focus their affections. Oscar Browning was one, a school teacher at Eton who lived with his mother and got into difficulties with the headmaster on account of his over-familiarity with the pupils. He corresponded with the Leweses and attended some of the salons.

Another was Alexander Main, a bachelor of thirty-one, who lived with his mother and sisters in Arbroath. He wrote to Marian in 1871 enquiring about the pronunciation of Romola and at the same time told the authoress how much her novels had changed his life.[18] Marian was always pleased to hear her writing had had some effect on people and replied that his words heartened her. The result of her encouragement was a profuse outpouring of praise, which Lewes thought wonderful and told him so. John Blackwood, who saw some of the correspondence, found it nauseating and privately remarked that 'the Gusher' was a rather peculiar young man who was tied to his mother's apron strings.[19] When Main approached Blackwood with the idea of publishing a tribute to his idol in the form of an anthology, Blackwood dreaded the result. Lewes, however, was enthusiastic and quick to point out that any public homage to George Eliot would be good for book sales.

Wise, Witty and Tender Sayings in Prose and Verse selected from the works of George Eliot by Alexander Main, was published by Blackwood's in 1872; Lewes thought it an enchanting little volume and distributed copies among the other worshippers who sent Marian presents. The preface to the book made Marian cringe, and the dedication, which referred to George Eliot having 'a morality as pure as it is impassioned' was, as John Blackwood privately remarked, unfortunate to say the least.[20] The hallowed manner in which Main served up the material further elevated George Eliot to pseudo-religious status and caused one worshipper at least to copy passages from the *Wise and Witty Sayings* into the front of her New Testament.[21] Blackwood could only raise his eyebrows.

In 1877, Main proposed another adulatory volume: a Birthday Book with an appropriate George Eliot saying for each day of the year. Lewes once again applauded the idea, though Marian was wary: 'I hate puffing, gaudy, claptrapping forms of publication, superfluous to all *good* ends,' she told Blackwood when they sought her opinion.[22] However, Lewes was persuasive and a highly decorated book, which Marian supposed was well 'adapted to the mind of the idiots who buy birthday books', appeared on the scene.[23] With sales exceeding nine thousand copies, there were clearly plenty of idiots around prepared to part with their cash. It is tempting to speculate that, born a hundred years later, Lewes would have had a field-day marketing a range of George Eliot duvet-covers and biscuit tins.

Adoring young men Marian could cope with, but women who prostrated themselves at her feet were another matter. In 1872, a young Scottish widow living in France sent a present to the great writer via Blackwood's and told George Eliot what an inspiration her writings were. With Mrs Elma Stuart living at a distance and prepared to correspond through Lewes, who said he had 'a stomach for any amount of eulogy' about his wife, Marian tolerated the growing correspondence.[24] Though the letters became ever more ardent with photographs enclosed and requesting similar mementoes in return, Lewes coped admirably. He fended off Mrs Stuart's entreaty as he had other worshippers'.

Nobody could claim that Marian had a photogenic face. The two photographs she had sat for in London, one when she was living at Chapman's and one after the publication of *Adam Bede*, were kept hidden. She regretted the impulse that had caused her to send copies to her Coventry friends and she asked them to remove the offending objects from their drawing room. When Cara wrote mentioning the existence of an even earlier and highly unflattering profile of Marian, there was consternation. Marian had forgotten about the daguerreotype taken in the 1840s, which Cara proposed to have rephotographed since it was fading. An immediate plea to let the glass image fade away altogether was despatched to Coventry, but to no avail.[25]

The daguerreotype was copied on to a negative and at the same time a brush was applied to the old glass image to restore the vanishing outlines. What have survived to the present day are two versions; a daguerreotype with Marian's nose cosmetically 'improved' by an artist and a copy photograph displaying the true object of her concern.

The official story was that no photographs of George Eliot existed, and Marian hoped such a categorical denial would discourage any researches. By contrast Lewes, considered by most people to be no better-looking than his consort, loved sitting for his portrait. Numerous photographs were taken and sold as postcards in book-shops. Marian's half-sister Fanny bought one in Nottingham: 'Apropos of M.A.,' she wrote to Isaac, not daring to mention the offending person by name, 'I have gratified my curiosity as to the sort of person she has chosen for husband. Among a host of literary celebrities I saw the other day a photograph of G. H. Lewes. Accordingly I straightway purchased it but never in my life have beheld a presentment of the human face with so *very* little *human* beauty in it.' She also added the gratuitous though quite superfluous advice that if Isaac was curious he too could possess a likeness, for they were to be had at any booksellers.[26]

Most George Eliot worshippers who applied for some memento had to content themselves with a copy of the *Wise and Witty Sayings*, along with a photograph of Lewes and possibly an autograph of the great lady. Elma Stuart, who believed herself absolutely in love with Mrs Lewes, was not to be palmed off with trifles and to Marian's consternation arrived at The Priory to view the object of her affection in person. The meeting was not as bad as Marian feared; indeed Elma turned out to be an interesting woman whose hobby was wood-carving. For Marian, whose own father had been a skilful carver in his younger days, it was fascinating to hear of the activity from a woman. Not surprisingly, Marian's interest in Elma's work ensured that carved tables, walking sticks, book slides and writing boards arrived at The Priory for years to come.

Although Marian froze at the woman's tendency to fawn over her, she nevertheless enjoyed the little feminine attentions Elma wanted to lavish on her. It was a novelty for Marian to discuss domestic issues with a woman; such mundane problems as poor circulation and cold feet or suitable clothing to keep the small of the back warm were poured into the waiting ears of Mrs Stuart. After her departure the lady began sending more personal gifts of underwear and warm shawls to her idol. In return, Mrs Stuart asked for a lock of her beloved's hair. After the younger woman's overwhelming kindness Marian felt obliged to accede to such a small request, but determined to put their intimacy on a safer footing. It was with 'maternal' love to Elma that the lock was sent and she was urged to think of herself as Mrs Lewes's 'spiritual daughter'.[27] This was not the ideal relationship in Elma's eyes but when Lewes told her she belonged to their 'inner circle' of friends and would be invited on occasions to their country house, she was reconciled.[28] Elma Stuart's lesbian devotion to Marian never troubled Lewes in the slightest. When she wrote to tell him that she treasured the handkerchief which she had used to wipe away a tear from her beloved's eye during the last visit, he applauded.[29]

The attentions of Miss Edith Simcox were altogether more irksome to Marian because the young woman lived in London and was wont to appear at The Priory on the slightest pretext. Fifteen years younger than Marian, a good linguist, possessed of a strong will and a passionate nature, Edith Simcox had much in common with the object of her devotion. Miss Simcox was largely self-taught, a moderately successful journalist and motivated by a strong socialist philosophy. With her friend Mary Hamilton she ran a shirt-making co-operative in Soho to provide employment for women in good working conditions, and together they travelled the country advocating trade union membership for women.

Edith entered Marian's life in 1872 and rapidly established herself as a regular visitor at The Priory for the remaining eight years of Marian's life. According to Edith, Marian was the 'love-passion' of her life, and Miss Simcox's diary, which came to light in the 1950s, charts the progress of this unrequited love-affair.[30] Marian tried hard to channel Edith's feelings into a safe mother–daughter relationship, but without success. Edith was fired by Lewes's talk of worshipping the Madonna and wanted to sit at Marian's feet. Though never wanting that sort of subjugation from anyone, Marian could nevertheless tolerate it if it made the younger woman happy. However Edith's insistence on literally kissing Marian's feet was not acceptable to the novelist. Even Edith noticed that Marian thereafter took care to move her feet out of reach.[31] It was an extremely difficult relationship for Marian to handle. Having been hurt herself by people harshly rejecting her affection in the past, Marian was unwilling to do the same to another. Lewes pointed out that Edith's attachment was harmless and if her visits could be made to coincide with those of others, her passionate displays might be avoided.

There followed a silent campaign. Edith's contrivance to call at The Priory on business (for her firm supplied George Lewes with shirts) at times when she thought she might catch her beloved alone was matched by Marian's moves to avoid being the object of passionate outbursts of kissing.

Edith was not the only one who visited on the slightest pretext: Johnnie Cross did as well. Edith hated him, but interestingly, being hypersensitive to every nuance of Marian's moods or feelings, she early identified Cross as the main object of Marian's affections after Lewes. Elma Stuart did not present a problem to Edith because she was in Dinant for most of the year, but Johnnie Cross was a different matter. He was always in town either at his club or at The Priory; Marian's eyes lit up when he came into the room and though he never attempted to kiss Mrs Lewes, Edith could see that he was besotted with her. Cross was more successful in gaining access than Edith, whose visits were restricted to the Leweses' London home, whereas he was also privy to their country address. Jealousy sometimes got the better of Edith and, in one passionate outburst, she told Marian that she had a mind one day to poison the shirts she made for Mr Cross. To this Marian could only gently say she hoped not, because he saved them a great deal of trouble about money affairs, 'being the best of sons and brothers'.[32]

Treading a difficult path between aristocrats who wanted to fête her and worshippers who wanted to kiss her, Marian tried to hurt no one yet still maintain her privacy. The summer of 1878 should have been perfect. She and Lewes spent it in their own country house at Witley, selected for them by Johnnie Cross and refitted and furnished to their taste. There in the delightful Surrey countryside, Marian and George enjoyed each other's company for the last time. The only shadow on the horizon was George's continuing ill-health, which he shrugged off as one of the penalties of being over sixty. His reading and visits to medical friends suggest that he too suspected his weight loss, nausea and agonizing spasms were caused by more than the under-cooked peas he had eaten at dinner, though Marian was prepared to accept this explanation.[33] She was so preoccupied with her own suffering caused by a kidney stone that she did not notice her lover's decline.

Blackwood did. Not having seen George for some months, he was horrified at how haggard and drawn the man looked and only prayed he was not as bad as he appeared.

To the end George put Marian first. For as long as possible he hid the severity of his own disease from her. When the discomfort was such that he could not keep still, he took himself for long walks round the Surrey countryside leaving Marian asleep in bed. As the frequency of his attacks increased he attempted to keep up the image of the funny man, telling his usual hilarious anecdotes or getting Marian to accompany his singing on the piano. Johnnie Cross was not taken in by the grim charade. He noticed the sick man could barely summon up enough voice to be heard.[34] Marian on the other hand seemed determined to shut out the reality.

When the Leweses returned to The Priory early in November it was no longer possible for either to pretend that George was simply having a recurrence of his old trouble. By Marian's fifty-ninth birthday, George was in bed and sinking fast. Though attended by the best doctors in London, he knew the end was inevitable and did his best to prepare Marian. How she would survive without him he had no idea, but he asked his son Charlie and their dear friend Johnnie Cross to take care of her. Remembering that work had been the one thing which had pulled her through difficult times in the past, he made her promise to complete his volumes of *Problems of Life and Mind*. Conscious until the last, he went on to arrange with his son the disposal of various personal possessions to friends. Then at six o'clock on the evening of 30 November 1878, George Henry Lewes died.

CHAPTER 16

I Am Now Determined to Live as Bravely as I Can, 1878–1880

G eorge's death stunned Marian. It was what she had dreaded far more than her own death, but she had tried to convince herself that she was the frailer of the two and therefore never likely to have to face life alone. In fact over the years Marian's preoccupation with her own poor health verged on hypochondria; her correspondents were regularly assailed with information about some ailment she was recovering from. For her vivacious, ebullient George to die so suddenly from a commonplace gastric upset was unbelievable. Sir James Paget's post-mortem revealed that though the immediate cause of death was a form of enteritis, Lewes had had a cancer which would have brought him to a far more painful end within six months. Marian had to take comfort from the knowledge of his early release from pain and the belief that George never realized he was dying.

For the first week she shut herself away in the room where he had died, refusing to see anyone beyond those strictly necessary. Blankly she stared at his photographs and letters in an effort to come to terms with reality. Charles Lewes was a daily visitor at The Priory but Marian refused his offer to stay with her. She had ample servants to look after her bodily needs, she insisted, and wanted to be alone. Indeed Charles was hurt to find that, now his father had died, Marian deliberately distanced herself from him. As she confided to a friend later, she had been prepared to give the schoolboy Charlie a home when he had needed one, but, at thirty-six, he had his own family to consider. Also the longer she knew Charles, the more she realized how little of his father there was about him. Kind though he was,

Charles Lewes had none of the mental agility of George. There was also at the back of her mind the fear that she might be a burden to the younger generation; the perpetual mourner who was wearisome to everybody, she said.[1]

She was, however, grateful that he offered to take over his father's funeral arrangements. Marian stated simply that she would not attend, which came as a relief to those most closely involved. It was difficult to know what position George Lewes's mistress should have in the official mourning party, when there was Mrs Agnes Lewes to consider as well. But Marian wanted no part in the burial process because she knew George had no belief in an after-life and would have rejected any form of religious service which preceded his interment. Since no agnostic rites existed, Charles settled for a Unitarian service in the chapel at Highgate Cemetery as the next best thing.

In the month following George's death, Marian attempted to come to terms with her loss and to reorganize her life. The promise George had extracted from her on his death-bed to see his psychology book through to publication helped to supply Marian with the necessary impetus to survive. It was vital she pay some attention to her own health in order to finish the task, or his years of study would be wasted. She laboured through piles of books and notes, forcing herself to consider the next stage. It was not easy to focus on complex philosophical issues when memories of him kept returning to fill her eyes with tears, but, setting herself a strict timetable for the completion of the work, she struggled on. The idea of a deadline seemed cruelly appropriate to Marian, certain as she was that her own life was drawing to a close. With a phenomenal amount of work to get through if all the volumes were to be published in a year, Marian could not afford to linger. If she failed to complete the task, who else could?

Those closest to Marian did not expect her to survive her lover long either. She had been perpetually ailing and so completely dependent on him that it seemed unlikely she would ever be able to do anything for herself. Few could remember her going outside the house without him by her side, and she freely admitted that she had never needed to carry a purse on her person for years because Lewes had handled most of the domestic as well as business arrangements. He had also acted as her personal secretary, perusing all the letters arriving at the house, answering the majority himself and only obliging her to read the minimum. His protective instincts had reached such a pitch that when she received her copy of *The Times* and the *Athenaeum* there was often a hole cut in a page where he had removed some reference to her work which he did not think beneficial for her to see.[2] How someone as shielded from reality as Marian was would cope with exposure to real life, no one could imagine. But those close to her in 1878 knew nothing of the old determination and willpower which had taken Mary Ann Evans from the obscurity of Griff to the literary pinnacle.

While Marian grieved deeply for her dead partner, she reasoned herself into a state of survival. That neither believed in an after-life proved a curious consolation. She knew that George had had sixty-one years of greater happiness than most people, achieving all he had set out to do. He had died without suffering the indignity of senility. With no existence beyond the grave, he would not be plagued by an eternity of regrets nor be made miserable by looking helplessly down on the activities of a loved one left behind. The only means of immortality for George and Marian was through their writings; this made her all the more determined to devote her remaining energies to George's work.

Another idea she conceived to perpetuate her lover's name was to establish some lasting academic memorial. In consultation with some of those university dons he used to visit at Cambridge, Marian established the George Henry Lewes Studentship in Physiology with a donation of five thousand pounds. Impressed by the new women students at Girton, introduced to her by Barbara Bodichon, Marian stipulated that the scholarship was to be open to the most able and impecunious student, whether male or female.[3] The correspondence and meetings which the establishment of this scholarship necessitated aided Marian's rehabilitation into society. As she had once wisely remarked to a friend, what the bereaved person was most in need of was distraction, not sympathy.[4]

As Lewes had been well known and well liked in many walks of life, letters of condolence arrived by the sackful, but Marian left Charles to deal with them. It was many weeks before she could bring herself to read these communications. When she did, there was one letter which touched her more deeply than most: it came from Griff House. It was written not by Isaac, but by his wife Sarah who expressed her personal sorrow at Marian's loss and assured her sister-in-law that she always thought of her with love and sympathy.[5]

As Marian gradually emerged from her cocoon of grief, she

contemplated seeing a few of her closest friends again. From her housemaid she knew there were many who enquired after her welfare at the gate, but she did not feel strong enough to face them yet. Her first thoughts went to Johnnie Cross, whom she felt sure must be just as lonely and bewildered following the death of his mother a week after Lewes. In January 1879, Marian wrote to reassure him that she had not forgotten him and would see him as soon as she could, 'perhaps sooner than anyone else', she told him.[6] His instant reply and plea for her to name a date convinced Marian of his devotion to her. But it was still early days and Johnnie had to content himself with her assurance that she still needed his affection: 'Every sign of care for me from the beings I respect and love is a help to me,' she wrote to him.[7] Two weeks later she felt strong enough to send word that his presence was greatly desired.

In addition to providing the kind of companionship Marian craved, Johnnie was able to advise her on the administration of George's will and her investments. The will had been drawn up in 1859 and, apart from leaving the copyright of his books to his sons, left the whole of his estate to Mary Ann Evans, spinster. The estate was worth far more than might be expected because Blackwood's had continued to pay 'George Eliot's' literary earnings into the account of 'his friend Mr Lewes'. The Priory and the house in Surrey were also in George Lewes's name, so in theory the person calling herself Marian Lewes possessed nothing.

Publication of Lewes's will in the newspapers reminded people that the celebrated George Eliot was actually Miss Mary Ann Evans. It was widely believed that the relationship between George Lewes and his mistress had in some way been regularized. Some thought the first wife dead and others that a divorce and remarriage had taken place on the Continent. Whatever the technicalities of the union, it was understood to have become socially acceptable since the Leweses had been received by three of Queen Victoria's daughters and many other high-ranking people. Back in Warwickshire there was anger at the publication of Lewes's will because it advertised the immorality of one member of the Evans family. Writing to her brother Isaac, Fanny said that she had been unable to sleep for thinking of the shame which this brought on them all.[8]

Marian had never worried about names, having adopted a variety during her life, so it was as Mary Ann Evans, sole executrix, that she administered George Henry Lewes's estate. Then, with her name officially changed to Marian Evans Lewes by deed poll in 1879, she signed the papers to set up the scholarship.

Under the guidance of Charles Lewes and Johnnie Cross, Marian eased herself back into reality. One of the early visitors to The Priory was Edith Simcox, who had suffered greatly on her beloved's behalf and was keen to offer solace in person. Grateful for affection from any quarter, Marian welcomed this disciple back with more warmth than usual. Unfortunately Edith took this as an indication that she had moved up one rung in Marian's esteem – above Elma Stuart and below Johnnie Cross was her calculation. This conviction encouraged her to be ever more demonstrative in her affections. For a while Marian tolerated the homage which George had always permitted, but then her own feelings got the better of her. Edith was asked to refrain from calling her 'Mother', for Marian had no maternal love for her, and anyway respected and admired her young friend too much to want any sort of pretence.[9] Instead of taking Marian's words as a hint to cool her passions, Edith understood the opposite. Faced with such a powerful affection Marian had to be even blunter, telling Edith that, while she liked women and sympathized with them, the friendship and intimacy of men would always mean more to her. As Edith correctly surmised, it was 'the ardour of the single-minded youth' that Marian actually wanted.[10]

By April 1879 Marian was back in the world, though in a much more restrained way than before. Gone were the grand receptions which Lewes had thrived on. Her attentions were focused completely on George's book, which gave purpose to her life. Though the subject matter was alien to her usual sort of writing, Marian had worked sufficiently closely with George in the past to be able to take over the reins without too much difficulty. Blackwood's were also corresponding with her again, not about Lewes's book, which did not fit their list, but about her own book, *Impressions of Theophrastus Such*. She thought her work insignificant compared with George's and was reluctant to consider it. But, as John Blackwood gently pointed out, it had been one of Mr Lewes's last acts to despatch the manuscript to Edinburgh and it was his wish that the essays be published.[11]

Proofs of the book were prepared and checked by Marian, but she insisted they remain in the cupboard until after a suitable period of mourning lest people think her so heartless as to carry on writing when the joy of her life had been buried. It was odd how Marian, who had always despised other people's obsession with appearances, should have begun to be swayed by them. With admirable tact, John Blackwood guided Marian towards publication some time in 1879, and then more concretely towards a date in May when the first part of Lewes's book would also be printed. *Theophrastus Such* was finally published with a brief note from the publishers to the effect that the manuscript had been delivered to them some time previously, but that publication had been delayed at the author's request. Marian was satisfied. Her book was well received by reviewers, though posterity has judged it to be the least worthy creation of its author. Without Lewes to act as censor, Marian read the reviews for herself and was sufficiently heartened to tell Blackwood's she was considering a sequel.[12] There is little evidence to support claims by biographers that Marian was so dependent on her lover that after his death she could not write. She had been a writer before meeting Lewes and would have carried on afterwards if death had not overtaken her.

As of old, hard work proved an excellent panacea for Marian. Six months after George's death she was telling her dear friend Barbara Bodichon of her determination to go on living as bravely as she could.[13] To that end she closed The Priory and set out for The Heights at Witley to spend the summer according to custom. It says much for Marian's courage that she was prepared to return to a place so full of memories of George, but she loved the countryside and wanted to enjoy it to the full in the time left to her. Although she continued to suffer discomfort from a kidney stone, her letters spoke optimistically about her health for the first time.

One reason why Marian felt able to cope at Witley was that Johnnie Cross had also left London for his Surrey home and was a daily visitor. While publicly Marian appeared to demonstrate her independence, privately she was becoming emotionally dependent on her young friend. He was flattered by Marian's attention and responded to her overtures by suggesting she might help him study Italian literature. Cross could imagine nothing more delightful than sitting at his idol's feet and learning, but Marian wanted him beside her, not at her feet. During the summer of 1879 in the seclusion of the Surrey countryside, a new relationship developed between Marian and Johnnie. The 'nephew' and 'aunt' names were dropped and various affectionate nicknames from Italian literature substituted. It never troubled

Marian to see Johnnie occupying George's chair, using his pen or taking the same walks with her; the memory of George existed in her heart, not in the inanimate objects round her. Life must move on, Marian maintained, for 'the realm of silence is large enough beyond the grave. This is the world of light and speech.'[14]

It was Cross's comparative youth, for he was twenty years her junior, which helped Marian to look forward, but what Cross never foresaw was that Marian's plans included him. Only one of the passionate letters she wrote to him has survived. Dated 16 October 1879, less than a year after her bereavement, and addressed to 'Best loved and loving one', it contains quite clear references to the love that she felt for Cross.[15] She signed it Beatrice, taking the name of Dante's love from the literature they were studying together so that Johnnie should be in no doubt as to her meaning. While welcoming the affection of the one he worshipped, Cross never dreamed that marriage was in her mind.

Soon after the year of mourning ended, Marian proposed to Johnnie Cross. Precise dates and details are vague, having been purposely obscured by Cross in an effort to protect Marian's posthumous image and his own self-respect. However, it appears that he avoided giving Marian a direct answer, but instead took refuge in excuses that marriage might harm her health, or tarnish her name and cause people to say that he had married her for money. Then, producing what he believed was his trump card, Cross expressed his great concern that marriage to him might harm her literary reputation. Never one to be easily put off in matters of the heart, Marian gradually circumvented each of the obstacles. When the much respected Sir James Paget, physician to the Queen and a friend of Lewes's for many years, pronounced her medically fit and wished her well, the marriage was decided – at least so Marian wrote in her journal.[16] Johnnie did not feel able to object. Though stories were later put about that Cross had proposed to her, and three times at that before she would accept, his family thought otherwise. They knew that Johnnie would never presume to propose marriage to someone so obviously his senior in all ways; rather he was too kind and gentlemanly to refuse her. They also believed that his attachment to Marian was a reaction to the death of his dominating mother, who was known to have prevented one of her other sons from ever marrying. Fond though the Crosses were of Marian, they thought it unlikely the wedding would go ahead.

It did, and at a speed which left no time for any second thoughts. A month elapsed between Marian noting the decision to marry and the actual event. The impending nuptials were to be kept a secret, Marian insisted, with only Johnnie's family and Charles Lewes being informed, and Charles to be told by Johnnie as late as possible. Cross was only too pleased to comply with the secrecy, but dreaded telling Charlie, much the same age as himself, that he would effectively be his stepfather. In the event, Charles Lewes, though completely taken aback, received the news calmly, wished them both well and agreed to give Marian away in church.

The search for a suitable house to bring his bride home to after the honeymoon provided the highly strung Johnnie Cross with some distraction from the dread of Marian's transmogrification from idol into wife. As Marian flourished, feeling better than she had for years, Johnnie looked ill. He lost so much weight by the day of his wedding that even Marian had to admit his clothes hung loosely on his long frame.[17]

The strange wedding between the grey-haired sixty-year-old and the gaunt-looking forty-year-old took place quietly on the morning of 6 May 1880 at fashionable St George's in Hanover Square. Marian's choice of the marriage rites of the Church of England, when she could have selected a Unitarian ceremony or even a civil one at this time, marked the beginning of Mary Ann Evans's respectability. That she also decided to revert to her old christian name and ask to be called Mary Ann Cross shows how strong a hold her Evans background had over her.

Immediately after the wedding, they signed their wills and then travelled to Dover. The itinerary of their honeymoon might well have been arranged by Lewes, for it took them to the same places Mary Ann had enjoyed with him, even to the extent of staying in the same hotels on occasions. To observers the couple must have looked remarkably like a mother showing her favourite son round Europe. Mary Ann did not notice, as she was too busy concentrating on the expressions on her husband's face while she took him to see ever more splendid sights.[18]

Cross noticed people's reactions and felt increasingly uncomfortable as the honeymoon progressed. He was struggling with the oedipal problem of a sexual relationship with someone he had always revered as a mother-figure. This was not helped by Marian presuming to exercise that sort of domination over him. Though he had been used to the freedom to come and go as he wished, Mary Ann wanted him by her side all the time. As she wrote to her new sister-in-law: 'We live in deep retirement'; they spoke to no one and, when not out sightseeing, were closeted together in their suite of rooms not even taking meals with the other guests.[19] Though quite natural behaviour for many honeymoon couples, this was far too claustrophobic for Cross. When they arrived in Venice on the second stage of their tour he became so agitated and hysterical that Mary Ann sent for a doctor, explaining that there was madness in the Cross family and she feared for her husband's sanity. During her interview with the doctor, Johnnie threw himself from the balcony of their room into the Grand Canal below. To make matters worse he fought against two gondoliers who tried to rescue him, and pleaded that he should be allowed to drown.[20]

He was ignominiously fished out and sedated; William Cross was urgently summoned from England on the electric telegraph. When he arrived two days later he found both husband and wife under varying degrees of sedation. Nevertheless Mary Ann's main concern was to stop any rumour of her husband's suicide attempt getting into the papers. Large sums of money were distributed in an effort to bribe those with any knowledge of the incident into silence.[21] So successful was this strategy that almost eighty years elapsed before the truth came out. The story given out at the time was that bad air emanating from the canals had caused Mr Cross to become very ill, and typhoid was feared.[22] The honeymoon was most certainly over. When the Venetian doctor pronounced Mr Cross well enough to travel, they began the trek back home in easy stages, escorted most of the way by William Cross. Mary Ann asked him to leave them to arrive in England alone and follow on later so as not to excite suspicion.

Only with Mary Ann in the sanitized role of nurse, gently wiping his brow and reading to him, did Johnnie feel comfortable. It was in his own interest to maintain the role of invalid as long as possible. There was no doubt in the minds of his brother and sisters that 'Johnnie's little upset', as they euphemistically called it, had indeed been an attempt at suicide. He was not the first nor the last in their family to resort to such a measure: two of his immediate family had already taken their own lives. Barbara Bodichon, not one given to gossip, said that this was not John Cross's first attempt either and that he had a history of mental depression.[23] Certainly the impartial advice given to a young suitor interested in Johnnie's sister Eleanor was to keep well clear of the Cross family because they were 'as mad as hatters'.

It was the end of July 1880 before Mr and Mrs John Cross arrived back in England and then they headed for The Heights at Witley, away from wagging tongues but conveniently close to the Cross family in case further assistance was needed. In the tranquillity of the Surrey countryside, Mary Ann hoped they could rebuild their marriage, but always at the back of her mind was the fear that Johnnie might try to kill himself again.

At Witley, however, Cross recovered his composure and began working off his energy in physical pursuits. Although Mary Ann employed a gardener, John bought himself an axe to hack at the dark conifers which hemmed the house in. More light and space were needed, he felt. He also paid regular visits to his sister's house at Weybridge for vigorous games of tennis. The preparation of their London home at 4 Cheyne Walk was, however, something Cross insisted required his personal attention if the house was ever to be ready for their occupation before winter. Reluctantly Mary Ann agreed to his visits to London, but wanted him to return home every evening. She even drove to the station in the carriage to meet her husband off the train.

Cross was to write later that his wife was in excellent health on her honeymoon, 'never ill – never even unwell', but the moment she returned to Witley, he suggested, there was a change. That was not true. Marian was depressed by the failure of her marriage and the continual need for vigilance, but her bodily health remained good throughout the summer. She played tennis or, when the weather was inclement, 'in-door battledore and shuttlecock' in the drawing room, believing it warmed her up and exercised her muscles more effectively than walking.[24] Towards the end of September she was taken ill with what she described as a bilious attack which in turn caused a renal spasm, though it was very mild, she insisted. None of this was sufficient to prevent her going to Brighton with Cross to visit her niece Emily Clarke at the beginning of October.

With the house in Chelsea nowhere near ready, the Crosses returned to Witley. In the damp autumn weather, Mary Ann had twinges of lumbago and felt generally out of sorts but never considered cancelling the planned weekend visit of Charles Lewes and his wife in the middle of October. The following weekend she complained of a pain in her side caused by a kidney stone, she believed, and, taking some opiates she kept ready, retired to bed to be nursed by Johnnie. Despite her personal discomfort, Mary Ann enjoyed the attentions he lavished on her and told Mrs Stuart: 'It takes a strong man to be perfectly tender – a strong man who has known what it is to suffer.'[25] He was quite happy to appease his guilt by nursing her completely himself and rejecting the need to fetch Dr Andrew Clark down from London for several days.

By the beginning of November, she was up and about: 'I am apparently getting better,' she wrote to a friend, 'but am still feeble.'[26] Despite Johnnie's assurances that she had only had one of her usual renal attacks, Mary Ann remained unconvinced, 'for though I appear to be quite cured of my main ailment, half my bodily self has vanished,' she noticed.[27] Johnnie maintained that the damp and chill air in Surrey, which she never usually experienced as late in the year as this, impeded her progress. Once they returned to London she would be restored to full health. Accordingly he spent more time in the capital packing up The Priory and arranging her books and possessions in the Cheyne Walk house. Mary Ann, advised to avoid all draughts and fatigue, was obliged to sit around 'passive and useless' in Surrey as her sixty-first birthday came round. In response to the 'many happy returns' of her birthday from Charles Lewes, Mary Ann responded that there was indeed every prospect that she would enjoy both thanks to the devoted tenderness of one who watched over her.

At the end of November, writing to her old friends in Coventry, Mary Ann remarked that seventy need no longer be considered the normal life-span since Mr Gladstone, their Prime Minister, was eighty-three. She was gathering her strength and Mr Cross too: 'He is exceedingly strong and well now, and cuts down a thickish tree in half an hour,' she reported proudly.[28]

Because the Chelsea house was not ready by 1 December as promised, but was close to completion, the Crosses moved back to London and stayed in a hotel for a few days. Mary Ann found London warmer than Surrey and once in her new home was soon writing to old friends inviting them to call. She was also planning visits to the concert and theatre when Johnnie caused her concern. He became very disturbed and feverish during the second week in December, which

worried Mary Ann enormously in case another 'upset' was precipitated, but medical opinion assured her it was just a bilious attack. Since
he seemed to be on the mend and herself 'quite flourishing again', she
asked Bessie Parkes (who was now Mrs Belloc and mother of Hilaire)
to lunch with them on the following Monday.

With Johnnie pronounced fit again, the Crosses attended a concert
on the Saturday evening at St James's Hall. The following day Mary
Ann complained of a sore throat and Dr Clark was consulted on the
Monday. Since nothing serious was suspected and he was busy, one of
his former pupils who lived close by was sent round. Dr Mackenzie
agreed that Mrs Cross had laryngitis, but her pulse and temperature
gave no anxiety; it was a common cold and after three days she could
expect to be better. Her progress seemed to follow his forecast
because, on the Tuesday, Mary Ann felt better in herself and when Dr
Mackenzie saw her that evening he agreed she was recovering well.
Though she slept well that night, towards morning she had a relapse,
'her pulse much faster and strength wonderfully reduced', Cross
noticed.[29] Dr Mackenzie called during the morning and agreed she
was weaker but apart from continuing with the beaten eggs in brandy
and cold beef tea, thought sleep the best medicine. At two o'clock in
the afternoon, Mackenzie called again and found Mrs Cross worse,
with pains in the kidney region, but remained optimistic about her
recovery. A visit from Dr Andrew Clark, who had returned to town
and sent word he would call at six that evening, completely changed
the prognosis. He examined Mrs Cross, who then lost consciousness,
and declared there was no hope. 'The cold had travelled down to the
pericardium and complete loss of power of the heart supervened' was
the official reason for her death at ten o'clock on the evening of 22
December 1880.[30]

Epilogue

George Eliot died at the height of her powers; since Dickens's death in 1870, she had been accepted as the leading novelist in the country. Indeed some would maintain that her popularity had exceeded Dickens's from the time *Adam Bede* was published. What had pleased Marian particularly was that she was recognized as a *great* novelist, not simply a great *woman* novelist. Like Charlotte Brontë before her, Marian asked to be judged solely on the basis of her work with no more consideration of her sex than of her hair colour. The ploy of using a man's name from the beginning had successfully forestalled both prejudice and patronizing praise.

As in Lewes's case, death came suddenly and unexpectedly. Though it is arguable that Lewes might have suspected he was dying, Marian most certainly did not. Marriage to a younger man had revitalized her and she felt better than she had for a decade. She thought she had taken a severe cold from which she would recover. Her suffering was minimal and her last words, whispered to her husband, asked him to explain to the doctor that she could feel some pain in her left side. She then slipped into a coma and died. For her there were no traditional death-bed farewells such as she had contrived for Millie Barton in her first short story.

It is impossible to overlook the timeliness of her demise from Johnnie Cross's point of view. Even Edith Simcox saw there was a change in Cross in the days before Marian's death: 'I noticed his countenance was transfigured, a calm look of pure *beatitude* had succeeded the ordinary good nature,' she recorded in her diary.[1] Cross knew that marriage to Marian had been a terrible mistake from which there could only be one escape – his death or hers. Had events in Venice turned out as he had intended the problem would have been solved, but his failure to end his life had brought him even further under Marian's domination than ever. She did not let him out of her sight lest he attempt suicide again. How could he face a future in which he was not permitted to move without his wife's permission? The sexual problems in the Crosses' marriage had not been resolved since the nightmarish honeymoon. The illness of one partner, followed by the illness of the other had temporarily shelved the issue, but Cross knew that that could not go on indefinitely. He had no idea how he was going to bring himself to accept a long-term intimate relationship with the great George Eliot. It would be wrong to presume Cross had homosexual tendencies, for there is no evidence to suggest that; indeed he is known to have had female friends when he lived in New York. But it is understandable that a forty-year-old bachelor might well be repelled by a sexual relationship with a sixty-year-old woman whose recent bereavement and renal illness left her looking gaunt and aged.

Quite apart from the problem of conjugal relations, Cross found it hard to adjust to being in the shadow of a famous wife. Until his marriage he had had a recognized life of his own with business associates in the city, at his club and in his own circle of friends. Although marriage traditionally entailed the wife taking on the husband's surname and identity, and Marian had been extremely eager to become Mrs John Cross, in practice Cross found himself referred to as 'the man who had married George Eliot'. His own identity had become submerged.

The ghost of Lewes was everywhere; George Lewes had so shaped Marian's life that everything she was interested in or talked about was influenced by him. Cross was haunted by his predecessor. The purchase of a new house in the smart area of Chelsea down by the Thames had been John's attempt to stamp his personality on their relationship, but the fact that Marian spent only two weeks there symbolized how little he succeeded. Without doubt John Cross found marriage to Marian far grimmer than anything he had imagined, and their relationship could never have survived for long. Her death seven months after the wedding was the perfect solution.

Paradoxically marriage to John Cross brought Marian that which she most desired – respectability, that vital Evans virtue which had eluded her since 1843 when she had renounced her faith. Although she had written sardonically in *The Mill on the Floss*, 'we don't ask what a woman does – we ask whom she belongs to', Marian really thought that ownership mattered. She had always defined herself in male terms.[2] First she had been Robert Evans's daughter, then John Chapman's assistant, then George Lewes's 'wife'. After his death she reverted to anonymity and needed some man to 'own' her officially. Significantly the influence of her first thirty years in the provinces had been so strong that even the powerful unconventionality of George Lewes only temporarily overlaid it.

To Marian's intense pleasure her brother Isaac deemed her respectable after her marriage and, when he had received official confirmation of his sister's status through the family solicitors, wrote to congratulate her.[3] Ultimately it was marriage, not literary fame, which made the Evanses respect their relative and welcome her back into the family fold. Though Marian always claimed she did not care about her brother, her tearful reception of his letter proved otherwise. Cross was pleased to have had the opportunity to give his wife this small though vital recompense and he sought to cement the relationship with the Evans family by meeting Marian's brother in person. The planned meeting between John Cross and Isaac Evans did take place, but not until Marian's burial.

Because of the proximity of Christmas, Marian's funeral had to be delayed until 29 December, but the impressiveness of the event exceeded even Sunday afternoons at The Priory. Everyone wanted to attend this funeral of the decade, and the list of mourners makes impressive reading. It was a social event Lewes would not have liked to miss. Cross knew Marian would most want to be buried in Poet's Corner, Westminster Abbey, along with other great literary figures, so a personal application was made to Dean Stanley, a one-time attender of some of the Leweses' Sunday afternoons, but even he was not prepared to break the rules so blatantly. No matter how great his own liking for Marian or the undoubted merit of her work, the fact that she was known to be agnostic rendered this request out of the question.

It was certainly in keeping with John Cross's subsequent behaviour that he should have made enormous efforts to obtain for Marian the respectability of a grave in Westminster Abbey rather than a plot near

Lewes in the Dissenters' part of Highgate Cemetery. Although he had found life with her unbearable, as George Eliot's widower, or 'widow' as some unkindly dubbed him, Cross coped with his memories well. Marian was put back where he liked her to be, on a pedestal. Then it was easy to take the part of the grieving husband, who spoke of his wife in suitably hallowed terms. Talk in various quarters about the need for a biography of his famous wife disturbed him. There was much about his own relationship with her he wanted hidden and other aspects of her life which he knew she would not want revealed. Cross cared deeply about the image of George Eliot and wanted nothing published which might spoil his idol.

When he heard that Edith Simcox was going round London interviewing people for her biography of Marian, he felt the time had come for him to write the official story which would impress his view of her life on posterity. By declaring the biography to be George Eliot's autobiography because it was constructed out of extracts from her letters and journals, Cross cleverly gave the work the stamp of authenticity. It was a brilliant ploy and had the desired effect. While the book was almost entirely in Marian's words, the editing was masterly. In the true tradition of Victorian biography any unseemly references were expurgated, as were remarks which might indicate that she possessed any human failings like sarcasm, avaraciousness or sensuality. If whole sentences could not be omitted because of the sense, then words were changed to maintain the sacredness of the picture.

Equally skilfully, Cross made many people and events completely vanish from his wife's life. Charles Bray was eclipsed by Cara, and John Chapman, alive and well in 1885 but living bigamously in Paris, never featured at all. To avoid damaging anyone's reputation, Cross sought advice from those he proposed to include in his book. Contact was made with Isaac Evans for information about Marian's childhood, and Cross travelled to Griff to see for himself the house where his wife had spent the first twenty-one years of her life. Isaac was then sixty-six, a prosperous retired land agent and very much a pillar of the establishment. He had four children and was particularly proud of his eldest Frederic, who was an ordained minister and later became a canon of the Church.

Cross found the Evanses reluctant to assist in any biography of Marian. As Fanny remarked privately: 'I *trust* he [Cross] will not carry out his intention for many reasons – I should not desire an *unreal* one

226

and rather shrink from a *real* one.'[4] John Cross was too gentlemanly and too much in awe of the formidable Mr Evans to push his case, so he departed intent on extracting information about Marian's early life from her novels. Not long after Cross's visit, there were other callers at Griff House wanting to see where the great novelist had spent her childhood and asking questions in the village. That changed Isaac's mind. It was clear that, no matter what he thought, biographies would be written about his famous sister, so it would be wise to co-operate with Mr Cross and ensure that an acceptable version was published.

Isaac was no writer and found it arduous to cast his mind back so far for details of his sister's activities. He therefore agreed that if Cross wrote the story the family would check it through. And this was what happened. Using *The Mill on the Floss* and the poem 'Brother and Sister' in conjunction with some information from the Reverend Frederic Evans, Cross wrote the first chapter and submitted it for approval. The three pages of alterations which Isaac insisted on have survived and bear witness to the fact that he was more concerned about the way the family were portrayed than about the accuracy of the account. Suggestions that Griff House had been a cultural desert for the young Mary Ann had to be altered, and Evans objected strongly to Cross's expression about 'the slavery of being a girl'. 'I suppose you would not like to say that her nephew is now Rector through the presentation of Lord Aylesford, as a useful antidote to the impression which certainly prevails that her family is altogether unworthy of and beneath her,' was Isaac's helpful suggestion.[5] With his eye on the main chance, Evans also thought a credit for the constant friendship and support of Colonel Newdigate might be a good idea. The resultant picture of Mary Ann Evans's early life was a romantic fiction.

The publication of George Eliot's obituaries brought further tourists to Griff, and Isaac delegated his son to deal with them. Frederic Evans gave the visitors a guided tour of the gardens at Griff House, taking care to point out the particular places and arbours which featured in his aunt's novels. He also had his prepared talk to 'correct a lot of misconceptions about the childhood and youth of my Aunt'.[6] The text of this talk, copied into an exercise book, survives and shows once again how concerned the family were about their good name. Reference was made to the embarrassment everyone had suffered from the way in which George Eliot continually parodied people in the locality.

The Brays, whose influence on Marian had been enormous, had limited contact with Cross. He had read sufficient of his wife's old letters to know that censorship was called for in this area. The Brays were just as concerned to limit public knowledge of their friendship and volunteered nothing. Cara had already destroyed many old letters with Marian's approval several years previously.[7] Hardly any of the large number of letters which passed between Charles and Marian from 1841 to 1880 survived: they too were destroyed by Cara after her husband's death. Despite the coolness of their friendship during Lewes's lifetime, Cara and Marian grew closer in the last years. Marian was most concerned about Cara's financial future, knowing how cavalier Bray was when it came to money, and an annuity of £100 was left her in Marian's will. For the rest of her days, Mrs Bray was careful never to say anything about 'dear Marian': everything anyone needed to know was in Cross's *Life*, she said. Her final years were spent as a kindly old lady who assisted animal charities until her death in 1905 at the age of ninety. As the last survivor of the trio, Cara took care to put everyone's papers in order and leave nothing which might harm anyone's reputation.

Sara Hennell was not likely to elaborate much on Marian's life either. She was sixty-eight at the time of Marian's death and had not seen her friend for years. Correspondence had dwindled to an annual birthday letter which conveyed little more than greetings, for their paths had diverged widely. Sara's time was spent planning ever more esoteric theological treatises, but she suffered increasingly from mental instability and was nursed with sisterly devotion by Cara until her death in 1899.

Charles Bray was one of the few people alive at the time of Marian's death who could have provided a different view of her from the one Cross published, but he had no wish to. Time had mellowed him. He still cherished an affection for Marian, though they rarely met in later life. In his study he kept various mementoes from the earlier days of their friendship, like her photograph, letters and the cast of her head taken at Deville's in the 1840s. In later life he acquired a very portly figure and suffered a number of asthmatic attacks. Though seen less in public, he still continued writing and published his pseudo-scientific manuals on psychology and anthropology which contained masses of 'Brayisms' but few facts. His autobiography, *Phases of Opinion and Experience During a Long Life*, published shortly before his death in

1884, was less revealing than might have been expected, for Bray had had a great many experiences best not written down. His relationship with George Eliot was handled with a discretion worthy of Cross.

When the three volumes of *George Eliot's Life as Related in Her Letters and Journals, Arranged and Edited by Her Husband, J. W. Cross* were published by Blackwood's in 1885, there were some sighs of relief at the innocuous nature of the contents, mingled with a few expressions of disbelief. One man whom Marian had worked with on the *Westminster Review* said that he could not reconcile the character in the book with the person he had known. Cross would have been well pleased if he had heard that comment, for he had worked hard to create an idealized picture. He skilfully managed to include George Lewes in the story, while avoiding any specific details of this 'first marriage'.

Once the work was completed, Cross was content. The myth had been created, the distasteful memories obliterated and George Eliot immortalized in the way he wanted. The house in Cheyne Walk was sold, Cross being unable to face life there. Instead he shared his time between the houses of his sisters, hotels in the south of France and his club in London. Like most who had known her well, he could rarely be persuaded to speak about Marian and, in deference to his wishes, his sisters never mentioned the subject either. It was many years before his nieces and nephews realized that kindly Uncle Johnnie had been married at all. He lived on until 1924 without recurrence of his 'little upset' and with only the barest reference to 'Her' or 'Your Aunt George'. Significantly he could never bring himself to call his wife by her christian name or any name which suggested a personal relationship to him.

So retiring did John Cross become that people forgot he existed. That suited him admirably, for he had certainly never married George Eliot to share in her reflected glory. When the centenary of her birth came round in 1919 celebrations were planned in Nuneaton and Coventry. Cross was hurt that the organizers never considered extending an invitation to him.

George Eliot's literary reputation suffered a decline after her death, and by the end of the century her work had become too *démodé* to be read. It was seen as the product of the stuffy Victorian matron that Cross had drawn, with no relevance to the excitement and spirit of the *fin de siècle*. It took the interest first of Virginia Woolf and later of F. R. Leavis to revitalize George Eliot's position in English literature and recognize that her novels ranked among the greatest in the language. By the middle of this century George Eliot was accorded the recognition and immortality she had always sought.

Equally what would have flattered and probably amused Marian is the unusual influence she has continued to exert over men even from beyond the grave. Her most ardent supporters have been male, notably the eminent American scholar the late Professor Gordon Haight, whose life's work was to edit the nine volumes of letters of George Eliot and to write the standard biography. Like many before him, Haight too was interested in perpetuating the sacred image of a great Victorian novelist and genius. His reliance on Cross's *Life* as the ostensible truth meant that the mask of George Eliot has continued to obscure the real Marian Evans for almost a hundred years. Behind the mask was a living breathing woman who made mistakes, distorted the truth, enjoyed sex and was everything a Victorian female was not supposed to be. How much more engaging an individual she was because of that.

Appendix I

A recently discovered manuscript for
an episode in *The Mill on the Floss*,
which George Eliot wrote but discarded.

LEGEND OF ST OGG
The blessed Saint Ogg did from his youth follow the calling of a
wood-carver, but was of light esteem among his fellows for as much
as he was not fair of countenance & of a somewhat slow & heavy wit,
neither was his carving held of any great account. Now at that time the
country was oppressed & spoiled greatly by the heathen folk, & they
entered into the house of God, & hewed in pieces the image of the
Blessed Mother, & used it for fuel. And by reason of this destruction
of the sacred image, the faith of the people had begun to wither so that
the great poverty wherein they were left by the marauders made them
to grovel in despair & dejection, instead of finding themselves up &
resting on the help of the Most High.

Now while they were in this condition, it came to pass that one
morning there was found in the house of God a new image of the
Blessed Mother of exceeding beauty, so that they who came to
worship were touched with a new spirit & went away & spoke thereof
to their friends, saying, there is an image come down from heaven &
virtue goes forth from it. Then all the dwellers in the town flocked to
look at the image, & truly a virtue went forth from it, & the hands that
hung down were held up & the feeble knees were strengthened. And
all said, 'The image came down from heaven: it is the gift of God.'
Then came one who bore witness & said, 'The image was planted here
by Ogg, the wood-carver, I marked him carrying it in the morning
twilight.' And the folk gathered together about Ogg's dwelling and

The opening of a recently discovered piece of manuscript in George Eliot's handwriting. The subject, 'Legend of St Ogg', appears in The Mill on the Floss, but this would seem to be a draft of the legend which George Eliot abandoned. In October 1869 she gave it to Rosalind Howard, Ninth Countess of Carlisle, who pasted it in her album. The whole of the legend is now in Castle Howard Archives and appears in this book by kind permission of the Honourable Simon Howard and Mr Jonathan Ouvry.

said 'Is it so, that thou didn't find this image descended from heaven, & didn't raise it up & carry it & set it in its place?' And he answered, 'Nay, but I carved the image, after a vision that I saw, wherein the Blessed Mother came down with the Divine Child, & the eyes of both beamed on me, so that a new spirit entered within me, & I wrought so as I had not done before.' Then the crowd grew furious, & said, 'he is a blasphemer bring him out & cast him into the river, that we may see whether God will save or punish him.' And they carried him to the brink of the river & threw him in, & he swam not, but clinging to a floating plank was carried by the ebbing tide down the river and was seen no more.

But it came [to] pass after the generation that killed Ogg was dead, & when many wonders of healing had been done by the sight of the image, one looking more narrowly saw within the folds of the garment these words 'This is the work of Ogg the son of Beorl.' And he reported thereof to Theowulf the priest, & he said, 'Surely a great spirit was given to this Ogg the son of Beorl, but knoweth any man aught of him?' Then came one & said, 'My father's father saw him cast into the river, for that the people were angry a man should blaspheme & say, he had brought the image which had been sent from heaven to do wonders.' And Theowulf answered. 'Then was Ogg a blessed martyr, for it was the people who blasphemed inasmuch as they rejected the vessel God had chosen, & denied the manner of the divine working, setting up their own will instead.' And thereafter the Holy Church declared Ogg to be a saint & martyr.

Written 1859   George Eliot

Appendix 2

George Eliot's Published Works
(apart from her journalism)

1846   *The Life of Jesus, critically examined by D. F. Strauss* (translation).

1854   *The Essence of Christianity* by L. Feuerbach, translated by Marian Evans.

1858   *Scenes of Clerical Life*, 2 vols.

1859   *Adam Bede*, 3 vols.

1859   'The Lifted Veil' (short story in *Blackwood's Magazine*).

1860   *The Mill on the Floss*.

1861   *Silas Marner: the Weaver of Raveloe*.

1863   *Romola*, 3 vols.

1864   'Brother Jacob' (short story in *Cornhill Magazine*).

1856   *Felix Holt, The Radical*, 3 vols.

1868   *The Spanish Gypsy* (poem).

1868   *Address to Working Men*, by Felix Holt (in *Blackwood's Magazine*).

1871–2   *Middlemarch, A Study of Provincial Life*.

1874   *The Legend of Jubal and other Poems*.

1876   *Daniel Deronda*, 4 vols.

1879   *Impressions of Theophrastus Such*.

Notes and References

Chapter 1: A Proud Race

1 Canon F. Evans' Notebook (Evans Papers, Mrs S. Womersley).
2 Mary Ann's School Book is in the Beinecke Library, Yale.
3 G.E. to Charles Bray, 30/9/59, vol. 3, p. 168. All references to letters are from G. S. Haight (ed.), *The George Eliot Letters* (Yale University Press; vols 1–7, 1954–6; vols 8–9, 1978), unless otherwise stated.
4 'Memorandum Book of the Occurrences at Nuneaton 1810', Nuneaton Public Library, (G.N. 400), is a valuable contemporary account of life in the first half of the nineteenth century in the town.
5 *Impressions of Theophrastus Such*, p. 45.
6 *Felix Holt the Radical*, p. 79 (Penguin).
7 Isaac Evans's notes for John Cross (Evans Papers, Mrs S. Womersley).
8 *Impressions of Theophrastus Such*, p. 39.

Chapter 2: The Long Sad Years of Youth, 1819–1836

1 Robert Evans to Colonel Newdigate, 7/12/34, Warwick Record Office (WRO B 3806).
2 A series of weekly articles in the Nuneaton Chronicle during August 1950 sheds much light on the business activities of Robert Evans.
3 Robert Evans to Colonel Newdigate, 31/7/37 (WRO B 3961).
4 Robert Evans to Colonel Newdigate, 17/1/37 (WRO B 3811).
5 *Nuneaton Observer*, 31/12/80, contains the reminiscences of one of George Eliot's contemporaries at school.
6 The gift is noted in Robert Evans' diary and mentioned in a letter from Katherine Lee to Barbara Bodichon, 21/5/80, Coventry Library.
7 Canon F. Evans' Notebook.
8 J. W. Cross, *George Eliot's Life as Related in Her Letters and Journals*, 3 vols (Blackwood's, 1885), p. 395.
9 Occurrences at Nuneaton.
10 Robert Evans to Colonel Newdigate, 12/4/35 (WRO B 3814).

Chapter 3: Neither Use Nor Ornament, 1836–1841

1 Robert Evans's Diary, 2/3/36 (Mr Robin Evans).
2 G.E. to Maria Lewis, 11/3/41, vol. 1, p. 84.
3 Robert Evans to Colonel Newdigate, September, 1836, (WRO. B3820)
4 G.E. to Maria Lewis, 20/7/40, vol. 1, p. 59.
5 G.E. to Martha Jackson, 6/4/40, vol. 1, p. 48.
6 G.E. to Martha Jackson, 4/9/38, vol. 1, p. 8.
7 G.E. to Maria Lewis, 28/5/40, vol. 1, p. 51.
8 Canon F. Evans' Notebook.
9 G.E. to Elizabeth Evans, 5/3/39, vol. 1, p. 19.
10 G.E. to Maria Lewis, 16/3/39, vol. 1, p. 23.
11 G.E. to Martha Jackson, 16/12/41, vol. 1, p. 123.
12 Ibid.
13 Canon F. Evans' Notebook.
14 G.E. to Maria Lewis, 28/5/40, vol. 1, p. 51.
15 G.E. to Maria Lewis, 13/3/40, vol. 1, p. 41.
16 G.E. to Maria Lewis, 23/6/40, vol. 1, p. 54.
17 G.E. to Maria Lewis, 4/6/41, vol. 1, p. 95.
18 G.E. to Maria Lewis, 28/5/40, vol. 1, p. 51.
19 G.E. to Martha Jackson, March 1841, vol. 1, p. 86.

Chapter 4: You Excommunicate Me, 1841–1843

1 G.E. to Maria Lewis, 27/10/40, vol. 1, p. 70.
2 Undated newspaper extract, 'George Eliot's Classical Tutor', from the *Disciple, a Magazine for Unitarians*, Nuneaton Library.
3 G.E. to Maria Lewis, 16/10/41, vol. 1, p. 15.
4 G.E. to Maria Lewis, 21/12/40, vol. 1, p. 76.
5 G.E. to Maria Lewis, 20/5/41, vol. 1, p. 90.
6 Charles Bray, *Phases of Opinion and Experience During a Long Life* (Longman, 1884), p. 53.
7 G.E. to Maria Lewis, 8/12/41, vol. 1, p. 122.
8 G.E. to Maria Lewis, 8/12/41, vol. 1, p. 122.
9 G.E. to Maria Lewis, 13/11/41, vol. 1, p. 121.
10 G.E. to Robert Evans, 28/2/41, Vol. 1, p. 129.
11 K. A. McKenzie, *Edith Simcox and George Eliot* (Greenwood Press, 1978), p. 129.
12 Caroline Bray to Sara Hennell, 22/2/43, vol. 1, p. 157.
13 G.E. to Robert Evans, 28/2/42, vol. 1, p. 129.
14 G.E. to Maria Lewis, 18/2/42, vol. 1, p. 127.
15 G.E. to Caroline Bray, 12/3/42, vol. 1, p. 131.
16 Caroline Bray to Mary Hennell, 17/3/42, vol. 1, p. 132.

Chapter 5: Rosehill and the Inhabitants of that Paradise, 1842–1849

1 G.E. to Maria Lewis, 12/8/41, vol. 1, p. 102.
2 G.E. to Sara Hennell, 3/11/42, vol. 1, p. 150.
3 Bray, *Phases of Opinion*, p. 70.
4 Sara S. Hennell, *A Memoir of Charles Christian Hennell* (private publication, 1899).

5　Coventry *Herald*, 1884.

6　Caroline Bray to Rufa Hennell, 28/7/44, vol. 1, p. 180.

7　Bray, *Phases of Opinion*, p. 22.

8　J. De Ville, *Manual of Phrenology, as an accompaniment to the phrenological bust* (1835).

9　Bray, *Phases of Opinion*, p. 74–5.

10　Cross, *George Eliot's Life*, p. 409.

11　Hennell, *Memoir of Charles Christian Hennell.*

12　G. S. Haight, *George Eliot and John Chapman* (Yale Univ. Press, 1941), p. 155.

13　G.E. to Sara Hennell, March 1846, vol. 1, p. 210.

14　G.E. to Sara Hennell, 16/9/47, vol. 1, p. 238.

15　Coventry *Herald*, 10/3/99, Obituary of Sara Hennell.

16　Cross, *George Eliot's Life*, p. 408 (Appendix by Mary Cash).

17　Bray, *Phases of Opinion*, p. 122.

18　Caroline Bray's Commonplace Book, Coventry City Library.

19　Haight, *George Eliot and John Chapman*, p. 175.

20　Caroline Bray to Sara Hennell, 22/2/43, vol. 1, p. 146.

21　Caroline Bray to Sara Hennell, 9/10/43, vol. 1, p. 162.

22　Kathleen Adams first discovered this and published it in her book, *Those of Us Who Loved Her* (The George Eliot Fellowship, 1980).

23　Haight, *George Eliot and John Chapman*, p. 185.

24　Cross, *George Eliot's Life*, p. 409.

Chapter 6: His Inspiration has So Quickened My Faculties, 1842–1849

1　Bray, *Phases of Opinion*, p. 71.

2　*Cornhill*, February 1906, p. 235.

3　Susan Lowndes (ed.), *Diaries & Letters Of Marie Belloc Lowndes* (Chatto & Windus, 1971).

4　In *George Eliot: a Centenary Tribute*, essay by Gordon Haight; 'George Eliot's Bastards' (Macmillan, 1982).

5　G.E. to Sara Hennell, 16/9/43, vol. 1, p. 161.

6　Bray, *Phases of Opinion*, p. 70.

7　*Letters of George Eliot*, vol. 1, p. 172–3.

8　Cross, *George Eliot's Life*, pp. 406–9.

9　G.E. to J. Sibree, 8/3/48, vol. 1, pp. 252–5.

10　G.E. to Francis Watts, December 1842, vol. 1, p. 154.

11　G.E. to Sara Hennell, April 1844, vol. 1, p. 176.

12　R. K. Webb, *Harriet Martineau: A Radical Victorian*, (Heinemann, 1960), p. 4.

13　G.E. to Martha Jackson, 21/4/45, vol. 1, p. 189.

14　Caroline Bray to Sara Hennell, 19/4/45, vol. 1, p. 188.

15　McKenzie, *Edith Simcox and George Eliot*, p. 131.

16　Caroline Bray to Sara Hennell, 30/3/45, vol. 1, p. 183.

17　More details of this romance are given by Caroline Bray to Herbert Spencer, 27/1/86, Reserve 49, BM.

18　Patricia Thomson, *George Sand and the Victorians*, (Macmillan, 1977), p. 22.

19　G.E. to Charles Bray, 11/6/48, vol. 1, p. 268.

20 Margot Peters, *Charlotte Brontë: The Unquiet Soul* (Hodder & Stoughton, 1975), p. 274.
21 Ibid., p. 289.
22 G.E. to Charles Bray, May 1849, vol. 1, p. 284.
23 Caroline Bray to Sara Hennell, 11/9/48, vol. 1, p. 272.
24 G.E. to Sara Hennell, 4/6/48, vol. 1, p. 264.

Chapter 7: Metamorphosis, 1849–1850

1   Robert Evans's Will, Public Record Office.
2   G.E. to J. Sibree, 14/5/48, vol. 1, p. 261.
3   G.E. to Mr and Mrs Bray, 27/7/49, vol. 1, pp. 290–1.
4   G.E. to Mr and Mrs Bray, 27/7/49, vol. 1, p. 209–10, and 5/8/49, vol. 1, p. 292.
5   G.E. to Mr and Mrs Bray, 20/9/49, vol. 1, p. 309.
6   G.E. to Mr and Mrs Bray, 20/8/49, vol. 1, p. 298.
7   G.E. to Mr and Mrs Bray, 28/1/50, vol. 1, p. 326.
8   G.E. to Mr and Mrs Bray, 13/9/49, vol. 1, p. 307.
9   G.E. to Fanny Houghton, 6/9/49, vol. 1, p. 303.
10 G.E. to Fanny Houghton, 4/2/50, vol. 1, p. 327.
11 'The Lifted Veil', p. 20 (Virago edition).
12 G.E. to Mr and Mrs Bray, 4/12/49, vol. 1, p. 321.
13 G.E. to Mr and Mrs Bray, 24/10/49, vol. 1, p. 317.
14 G.E. to Charles Bray, 1/3/50, vol. 1, p. 331.
15 Under the terms of the will of her aunt, Mrs John Everard, who died in 1844 Marian received an eighth of her estate in trust, which yielded an annual income of around £120.
16 G.E. to Sara Hennell, 11/5/50, vol. 1, p. 335.
17 G.E. to Caroline Bray, 1/5/50, vol. 1, p. 336.

Chapter 8: The Wicked *Westminster*, 1851

1   Manuscript of the reminiscences of Beatrice Chapman, daughter of John (Chapman Papers).
2   *Letters*, vol. 1, p. 335.
3   G.E. to George Combe, 22/1/53, vol. 1, p. 69, and 13/11/52, vol. 8, p. 66.
4   Haight, *George Eliot and John Chapman*, p. 130.
5   John Chapman to George Combe, 26/11/51, vol. 8, p. 31.
6   Beatrice Chapman manuscript.
7   Ibid.
8   G.E. to Mr and Mrs Bray, 28/1/51, vol. 1, p. 342.
9   Haight, *George Eliot and John Chapman*, pp. 135–6.
10 Ibid., pp. 140–2.
11 Ibid., p. 129.
12 G.E. to Mr and Mrs Bray, 15/2/51, vol. 1, p. 346.
13 Beatrice Chapman manuscript.
14 G.E. to Mr and Mrs Bray, 28/1/51, vol. 1, p. 342.
15 Beatrice Chapman manuscript.
16 G.E. to John Chapman, 4/4/51, vol. 1, p. 348.

17 Haight, *George Eliot and John Chapman*, p. 182.
18 *Letters*, vol. 8, p. 29, prospectus for the *Westminster Review*, 10/10/51.
19 Haight, *George Eliot and John Chapman*, p. 171.
20 G.E. to John Chapman, 15/6/51, vol. 1, p. 352.
21 Haight, *George Eliot and John Chapman*, p. 176.
22 Letters from John Chapman to Barbara Leigh Smith, Beinecke Library, Yale.
23 Haight, *George Eliot and John Chapman*, p. 175.
24 Ibid., p. 176.
25 G.E. to Caroline Bray, 3/10/51, vol. 1, p. 363.
26 G.E. to John Chapman, 18/8/51, vol. 1, p. 361.
27 George Combe's Journal in *Letters*, vol. 8, pp. 27–8, 28/8/51; Lucretia Coffin Mott (1793–1880) was an American abolitionist and feminist.
28 G.E. to John Chapman, 7/12/51, vol. 8, p. 33.

Chapter 9: The Man Question, 1852–1853

1 G.E. to Charles Bray, 6/9/51, vol. 1, p. 365.
2 Bessie Parkes to Mrs Eliza Parkes, 16/10/51, Girton (BRP II 3).
3 Eliza Lynn Linton, *My Literary Life*, (Hodder & Stoughton, 1899), p. 96.
4 Bessie Parkes Papers, Girton (BRP I 12).
5 Ibid. (BRP I 12/2).
6 Ibid. (BRP I 12/1).
7 G.E. to Bessie Parkes, 21/1/54, vol. 2, p. 138.
8 G.E. to Clementia Taylor, 27/3/52, vol. 2, p. 15.
9 G.E. to Sara Hennell, 21/1/51, vol. 2, p. 5.
10 G.E. to Clementia Taylor, 30/5/67, vol. 4, p. 366.
11 G.E. to Mr and Mrs Bray, 5/6/52, vol. 2, p. 83.
12 William Hale White, *Athenaeum*, 28/11/85, p. 702.
13 Haight, *George Eliot and John Chapman*, p. 213.
14 Beatrice Chapman manuscript.
15 Herbert Spencer, *An Autobiography* (William & Norgate, 1904), vol. 1, p. 394.
16 G.E. to Caroline Bray, 27/5/52, vol. 2, p. 29.
17 G.E. to Caroline Bray, 25/5/52, vol. 2, p. 29.
18 Spencer, *Autobiography*, p. 394.
19 G.E. to Mr and Mrs Bray, 14/6/52, vol. 2, p. 35.
20 G.E. to Herbert Spencer, 8/7/52, vol. 8, pp. 50–1.
21 G.E. to Herbert Spencer, 8/7/52, vol. 8, pp. 50–1.
22 G.E. to Herbert Spencer, 16/7/51, vol. 8, p. 56.
23 G.E. to Caroline Bray, 19/8/52, vol. 2, p. 51.
24 G.E. to Mr and Mrs Bray, 31/12/52, vol. 2, p. 75.

Chapter 10: I Am a Heathen and an Outlaw, 1853–1854

1 G.E. to Bessie Parkes, 29/6/53, vol. 2, p. 107.
2 G.E. to Mr and Mrs Bray, 19/2/53, vol. 2, p. 88.
3 G.E. to Charles Bray, 17/1/53, vol. 2, p. 81.
4 Linton, *My Literary Life*, p. 10.
5 Jane Welsh Carlyle, *Letters to Her Family* (1942), p. 329.

6 My thanks to Robert Burchfield (*Sunday Times Books*) for drawing my attention to this under-used word as the counterbalance to misogynistic.

7 G.E. to Charles Bray, 9/9/51, vol. 1, p. 367.

8 G.E. to Sara Hennell, 2/9/52, vol. 2, p. 54.

9 G.E. to Sara Hennell, 2/9/52, vol. 2, p. 54.

10 G.E. to Caroline Bray, 16/4/53, vol. 2, p. 98.

11 G.E. to Mr and Mrs Bray, 19/9/53, vol. 2, p. 117.

12 Joseph Parkes to Bessie Parkes, 1/10/54, (BRP II 53) and 14/10/54 (BRP II 54).

13 G.E. to Sara Hennell, 22/11/53, vol. 2, p. 127.

14 G.E. to Charles Bray, 5/11/53, vol. 2, p. 123.

15 G.E. to Sara Hennell, 8/11/53, vol. 2, p. 124.

16 G.E. to Caroline Bray, 14/4/54, vol. 2, p. 149.

17 G.E. to John Chapman, 2/12/53, vol. 2, p. 130.

18 G.E. to John Chapman, 2/12/53, vol. 2, p. 130.

Chapter 11: An Infamous Seduction, 1854–1855

1 Joseph Parkes to Bessie Parkes, 14/10/54, (BRP II 54).

2 Joseph Parkes to Bessie Parkes, 14/10/54, (BRP II 54).

3 Joseph Parkes to Bessie Parkes, 1/10/54 (BRP II 53).

4 Bessie Parkes Papers, Girton (BRP I 12).

5 Thomas Carlyle to John Carlyle, 2/11/54 (National Library of Scotland: 516.86).

6 Charles Bray to George Combe, 8/10/54, vol. 8, p. 122.

7 G.E. to Charles Bray, 16/8/54, vol. 2, p. 170.

8 G.E. Journal in *Letters*, vol. 2, p. 170.

9 G.E. to John Chapman, 30/8/54, vol. 2, p. 173.

10 T. Pinney (ed.), *Essays of George Eliot* (Routledge & Kegan Paul, 1963), p. 56.

11 G.E. to Charles Bray, 23/10/54, vol. 2, p. 179.

12 Caroline Bray to Mrs Combe, 23/9/54, vol. 8, p. 119.

13 G.E. to Sara Hennell, 31/10/54, vol. 2, p. 102.

14 Sara Hennell to G.E., 15/11/54, vol. 2, p. 186.

Chapter 12: A New Era of My Life, 1855–1857

1 George Combe to Charles Bray, 15/11/54, vol. 8, p. 129.

2 G.E. to Charles Bray, 17/6/55, vol. 2, p. 202.

3 G.E. to Fanny Houghton, 28/12/55, vol. 2, p. 223.

4 G.E. to Charles Bray, 1/1/56, vol. 2, p. 224.

5 Letters of Henry Bohn to G. H. Lewes in June 1856, vol. 8, pp. 156–60.

6 G.E. to Charles Bray, 15/10/55, vol. 2, p. 218.

7 These are in Nuneaton Museum and Art Gallery.

8 G. H. Lewes to John Blackwood, 22/11/56, vol. 2, p. 276.

9 G. H. Lewes to John Blackwood, 22/11/56, vol. 2, p. 276.

10 I am grateful to Mr A. A. Phillips for drawing my attention to this on Hewitt's map of Chilvers Coton (1687–9).

11 G.E. to William Blackwood, 4/12/57, vol. 2, p. 292.

12 G.E. to Charles Bray, January, 1857, vol. 2, p. 287.

13 G.E. to William Blackwood, 4/1/57, vol. 2, p. 288.

14 Joseph Langford to John Blackwood, 16/2/57, vol. 2, p. 298.

15 William Jones to Messrs Blackwood, 12/8/57, vol. 2, p. 375.

16 G.E. to Fanny Houghton, 2/6/57, vol. 2, p. 337.

17 There are lists to be found in the Bray papers at Nuneaton Museum and amongst the Evans papers of Mrs S. Womersley.

18 G.E. to John Blackwood, 18/8/57, vol. 2, p. 375.

19 G.E. to Isaac Evans, 26/5/57, vol. 2, p. 331.

20 Vincent Holbeche to G.E., 9/6/57, vol. 2, p. 346.

21 G.E. to Vincent Holbeche, 13/6/57, vol. 2, p. 349.

22 G.E. to Sara Hennell, 14/7/57, vol. 2, p. 364.

23 G.E. to John Blackwood, 15/12/57, vol. 2, p. 414.

Chapter 13: I Certainly Care a Good Deal for the Money, 1858–1863

1 G.E. to John Blackwood, 13/9/59, vol. 3, p. 151.

2 William Blackwood to John Blackwood, 5/10/89, vol. 3, p. 172.
John Blackwood to William Blackwood, 30/10/59, vol. 3, p. 192.

3 G.E. to John Blackwood, 16/8/59, vol. 3, p. 132.

4 G. Simpson to Joseph Langford, 3/11/59, vol. 3, p. 194.

5 G.E. to Charles Bray, 9/9/59, vol. 3, p. 155.

6 Fanny Houghton to Isaac Evans, 13/6/66 (Mrs K. Adams).

7 G.E. to Sara Hennell, 19/2/59, vol. 3, p. 16.

8 G.E. Journal in *Letters*, vol. 2, p. 505.

9 Ibid., vol. 3, p. 90.

10 Sara Hennell to G.E., 26/6/59, vol. 3, p. 95.

11 Sara Hennell to G.E., 26/6/59, vol. 3, p. 95.

12 Footnote to G. E. to Charles Bray, 23/7/59, vol. 3, p. 120.

13 G.E. to Charles Bray, 18/7/60, vol. 3, p. 325.

14 G. H. Lewes to Barbara Bodichon, 30/6/59, vol. 3, p. 106.

15 G.E. to Sara Hennell, 26/2/59, vol. 3, p. 26.

16 G.E. to Caroline Bray, 24/2/59, vol. 3, p. 24.

17 G.H. Lewes Journal in *Letters*, vol. 3, p. 24.

18 G.E. to Sara Hennell, 21/3/59, vol. 3, p. 38.

19 G.E. to Sara Hennell, 5/12/59, vol. 3, p. 229.

20 G. H. Lewes Journal in *Letters* vol. 3, p. 116.

21 G. H. Lewes Journal, 26/6/60, vol. 3, p. 309.

22 G.E. to John Blackwood, 1/1/61, vol. 3, p. 369.

23 G. H. Lewes Journal, 27/2/62, vol. 4, p. 17.

24 John Blackwood to William Blackwood, May 1862, vol. 4, p. 38.

Chapter 14: Changing the Image, 1863–1869

1 Barbara Bodichon to G.E., 28/6/59, vol. 3, p. 103.

2 G.E. to Barbara Bodichon, 5/1/69, vol. 4, p. 3.

3 G.E. to Sara Hennell, 28/11/63, vol. 4, p. 116.

4 G.E. Journal, 17/7/64, *Letters*, vol. 4, p. 158.

5 John Blackwood to G. H. Lewes, 20/4/66, vol. 4, p. 240 and footnote.

6 G.E. to François D'Albert Durade, 12/1/65, vol. 4, p. 176.

7 G.E. to Caroline Bray, 11/10/68, vol. 4, p. 477.
8 G.E. to Caroline Bray, 6/4/67, vol. 4, p. 356.
9 G. H. Lewes to Richard Horn, 12/6/66, vol. 8, p. 365.
10 C. H. Norton to G. W. Curtis, 26/1/89 (Harvard).
11 Bessie Parkes Papers, Girton (BRP I 12).
12 G.E. to Clementia Taylor, 1/8/65, vol. 4, p. 199.
13 G.E. to Charles Bray, 15/12/64, vol. 4, p. 169.
14 G.E. to Sara Hennell, 12/10/67, vol. 4, p. 390.
15 B. Stephen, Emily Davies and Girton College (Constable, 1927), p. 193.
16 G.E. to Emily Davies, 4/3/68, vol. 8, p. 414.
17 G.E. to Elizabeth Malleson, 20/7/69, vol. 8, p. 460.
18 G.E. to Mrs Jane Senior, 4/10/69, vol. 5, p. 58.
19 Emily Davies to Jane Crow, 21/8/69, vol. 8, p. 465.
20 G.E. to Maria Congreve, 18/3/65, vol. 4, p. 183.
21 G.E. to Francois D'Albert Durade, 21/9/66, vol. 4, p. 311.
22 G.E. to Harriet Beecher Stowe, 10/12/69, vol. 5, p. 71.
23 G.E. Journal 19/10/69, Letters, vol. 5, p. 60.

Chapter 15: Honour and Homage, 1870–1878

1 G. H. Lewes to Alexander Main, 31/5/72, vol. 5, p. 275.
2 G. H. Lewes to Mrs Lankester, April 1878, vol. 9, p. 222.
3 G.E. to Maria Congreve, 3/4/70, vol. 5, p. 86.
4 G. H. Lewes to Mrs Willim, 28/3/70, vol. 5, p. 83.
5 G. H. Lewes to Mrs Willim, 28/3/70, vol. 5, p. 83.
6 G. H. Lewes Journal, 13/5/70, vol. 5, p. 90.
7 Athenaeum, 18/9/75, p. 373.
8 G. H. Lewes to John Blackwood, 10/9/72, vol. 5, p. 308.
9 G.E. to Francois D'Albert Durade, 27/1/71, vol. 5, p. 135.
10 G.E. to Mrs William Cross, 25/9/72, vol. 5, p. 311.
11 G.E. to John Blackwood, 4/10/72, vol. 5, p. 314.
12 McKenzie, Edith Simcox and George Eliot, p. 90.
13 G.E. to Barbara Bodichon, 13/8/75, vol. 6, p. 161 and G.E. to Barbara Bodichon, 15/5/77, vol. 6, p. 369.
14 G.E. to Caroline Bray, 29/5/74, vol. 6, p. 52.
15 G.E. to Robert Evans, 26/9/74, vol. 9, p. 134.
16 G. H. Lewes to Mrs Anna Cross, 29/12/72, vol. 5, p. 352.
17 Spencer Papers, Reserve 49, BM
18 G.E. to Alexander Main, 3/8/71, vol. 5, p. 174.
19 John Blackwood to William Blackwood, 24/10/71, vol. 5, p. 205.
20 John Blackwood to William Blackwood, 2/11/71, vol. 5, p. 212.
21 G. H. Lewes to Alexander Main, 31/5/72, vol. 5, p. 276.
22 G.E. to John Blackwood, 22/11/77, vol. 6, p. 423.
23 G.E. to William Blackwood, 19/7/78, vol. 7, p. 44.
24 G. H. Lewes to Elma Stuart, 1/2/72, vol. 5, p. 244.
25 G.E. to Caroline Bray, 21/12/76, vol. 6, p. 321.
26 Fanny Houghton to Isaac Pearson Evans, 11/12/66 (Mrs K. Adams).
27 G.E. to Elma Stuart, 10/1/75, vol. 6, p. 113.

28 G. H. Lewes to Elma Stuart, 2/2/75, vol. 6, p. 121.
29 G. H. Lewes's Journal, 18/2/75, *Letters*, vol. 6, p. 121.
30 McKenzie, *Edith Simcox and George Eliot*, p. 87.
31 Ibid., p. 93.
32 Ibid, p. 90.
33 G.E. to John Blackwood, 27/6/78, vol. 7, p. 33.
34 Cross, *Life of George Eliot*, p. 333.

Chapter 16: I Am Now Determined to Live as Bravely as I Can, 1878–1880
1   G.E. to John Cross, 7/2/79, vol. 7, p. 102.
2   G.E. to Elma Stuart, 3/3/76, vol. 6, p. 230.
3   Cross, *Life of George Eliot*, p. 379.
4   Robert Lytton to G.E., 22/2/80, vol. 9, p. 296.
5   G.E. to Sara Evans, 20/2/79, vol. 7, p. 105.
6   G.E. to John Cross, 22/1/79, vol. 7, p. 97.
7   G.E. to John Cross, 7/2/29, vol. 7, p. 101.
8   Fanny Houghton to Isaac Pearson Evans, 28/11/81 (Mrs K. Adams).
9   Edith Simcox, *Autobiography*, 26/12/79, *Letters*, vol. 9, p. 283.
10 Ibid., 1/2/80, *Letters*, vol. 9, p. 293.
11 John Blackwood, 1/4/79, vol. 7, p. 125.
12 G. E. to John Blackwood, 5/4/79, vol. 7, p. 126.
13 G.E. to Barbara Bodichon, 29/4/79, vol. 7, p. 144.
14 G.E. to Georgiana Burne-Jones, 11/5/75, vol. 6, p. 142.
15 G.E. to John Cross, 16/10/75, vol. 7, p. 211.
16 G.E. Journal, 9/4/80, vol. 7, p. 259.
17 G.E. to Richard Cross, 6/6/80, vol. 7, p. 292.
18 G.E. to Eleanor Cross, 9/5/80, vol. 7, p. 272.
19 G.E. to the Misses Cross, 13/6/80, vol. 7, p. 293.
20 Footnote in *Letters*, vol. 7, p. 301, in vol. 9, p. 311.
21 Ibid., and information from Mrs J. Osiakovski.
22 Cross, *Life of George Eliot*, p. 407.
23 Edith Simcox, *Autobiography*, 5/2/82.
24 G.E. to Charles Lewes, 19/9/80, vol. 7, p. 325.
25 G.E. to Elma Stuart, 13/10/80, vol. 7, p. 330.
26 G.E. to Clementia Taylor, 30/10/80, vol. 7, p. 330.
27 G.E. to Maria Congreve, 3/11/80, vol. 7, p. 332.
28 G.E. to Caroline Bray, 26/11/80, vol. 7, p. 340.
29 J. Cross to Elma Stuart, 23/12/80, vol. 7, p. 357.
30 J. Cross to Isaac Evans, 22/12/80, vol. 9, p. 322.

Epilogue
1   Edith Simcox, *Autobiography*, 23/12/80, *Letters*, vol. 9, p. 321.
2   *The Mill on the Floss*, vol. 3, book 6, chapter 8.
3   Isaac Evans to G.E., 17/5/80, vol. 7, p. 280.
4   Fanny Houghton to Isaac Pearson Evans, 28/1/81, (Mrs K. Adams).
5   Isaac Evans notes for John Cross (Mrs S. Womersley).
6   Canon F. Evans' Notebook.
7   G.E. to Caroline Bray, 28/11/70, vol. 7, p. 340.

Select Bibliography

Published Sources
Adams, Kathleen, *Those of Us Who Loved Her: The Men in George Eliot's Life*
  The George Eliot Fellowship, 1980).
Banks, Olive and J.A., *Feminism and Family Planning in Victorian England*
  (Liverpool University Press, 1964).
Belloc, Bessie Rayner, *In a Walled Garden* (Ward & Downey, 1896).
Blind, Mathilde, *George Eliot* (W. H. Allen, 1883).
Bray, Caroline, *Physiology for Schools in 27 Easy Lessons* (1860).
Bray, Caroline, *The British Empire* (Longman, 1863).
Bray, Caroline, *Elements of Morality*, (1883).
Bray, Charles, *The Philosophy of Necessity* (1841).
Bray, Charles, *The Education of the Feelings* (Longman, 1849).
Bray, Charles, *Phases of Opinion and Experience During a Long Life*
  (Longman, 1884).
Burton, Hester, *Barbara Bodichon, 1827–1891* (John Murray, 1949).
By Two *Home Life with Herbert Spencer* (J. W. Arrowsmith, 1906).
Cartwright, Julia (ed.), *The Journals of Lady Knightley of Fawsley* (John
  Murray, 1915).
Combe, George, *A System of Phrenology*, 2 vols (Maclachlan & Stewart,
  1843).
Cross, J. W., *George Eliot's Life as Related in Her Letters and Journals*, 3 vols
  (Blackwood's, 1885). (Revised edition in one vol. 1887)
Elliott, Hugh, *Herbert Spencer* (Constable, 1917).
Haight, Gordon S., *George Eliot: A Biography* (Oxford University Press,
  1968).
Haight, Gordon S., *George Eliot and John Chapman* (Yale University Press,
  1941; Archon Books, 1969).
Haight, Gordon S., and Vanarsdel, Rosemary T., *George Eliot: A Centenary
  Tribute* (Macmillan, 1982).

Hennell, Michael, *Sons of the Prophets: Evangelical Leaders of the Victorian Church* (SPCK, 1979).

Hennell, Sara S., *A Memoir of Charles Christian Hennell* (private publication, 1899).

Herstein, Sheila, *A Mid-Victorian Feminist: Barbara Leigh Smith Bodichon* (Yale University Press, 1985).

Hollis, Patricia (ed.), *Women in Public 1850–1900: Documents of the Victorian Women's Movement* (Allen & Unwin, 1979).

Lacey, Candida Ann (ed.), *Barbara Leigh Smith Bodichon and the Langham Place Group* (Routledge & Kegan Paul, 1986).

Linton, Mrs Eliza Lynn, *My Literary Life* (Hodder & Stoughton, 1899).

Lowndes, Marie Belloc, *I Too have Lived in Arcadia* (Macmillan, 1941).

McKenzie K.A., 'Edith Simcox & George Eliot' (Greenwood Press, 1978)

Milburn, Dennis, *Nuneaton: The Growth of a Town* (Nuneaton Corporation, 1963).

Parkinson, S., *Scenes from the George Eliot Country* (R. Jackson Leeds, 1888).

Pinney T. (ed) 'Essays of George Eliot' (Routledge & Kegan Paul, 1963).

Rendall, Jane, *The Origins of Modern Feminism: Women in France, Britain and the United States, 1780–1860* (Macmillan, 1985).

Rose, Phyllis, *Parallel Lives: Five Victorian Marriages* (Chatto & Windus, 1984).

Shuttleworth, Sally, *George Eliot and Nineteenth-Century Science* (Cambridge University Press, 1984).

Spencer, Herbert, *An Autobiography* (Williams & Norgate, 1904).

Stephen, Barbara, *Emily Davies and Girton College* (Constable, 1927).

Thomson, Patricia, *George Sand and the Victorians* (Macmillan, 1977).

Trevedy, F., *The House of Blackwood 1804–1954* (William Blackwood, 1954).

Vincinus, Martha (ed.), *Suffer and Be Still: Women in the Victorian Age* (Indiana University Press, 1972).

Webb, R. K., *Harriet Martineau: A Radical Victorian* (Heinemann, 1960).

Williams, David, *Mr George Eliot: A Biography of G. H. Lewes* (Hodder & Stoughton, 1983).

Periodicals

Cornhill, 'George Eliot's Coventry Friends', February 1906.

Country Life, 'Arbury Hall', 13 April 1907.

James Bryce Memorial Lecture, Somerville College, Oxford, 'Barbara Bodichon, George Eliot and the Limits of Feminism', Muriel Bradbrook, 1975.

Journal of the History of Medicine, 'John Chapman: Publisher, Physician and Medical Reformer', F. N. L. Poynter, Winter 1950.

Nineteeth-Century Fiction, 'A Russian View of George Eliot', Raymond Chapman and Eleanor Gottlieb, 1978, pp. 348–65; 'The Greening of Sister George', Elaine Showalter, 1980, pp. 292–311; 'Pseudoscience and George Eliot's "The Lifted Veil" ', B. M. Gray, 1981, pp. 407–23.

Notes and Queries, 'John Chapman', Sidney Race, 26 April 1941, pp. 293–5; C. Evans, 17 May 1941, pp. 347–9.

Henry Lewes and His "Physiology of Common Life" ', R. E. Smith, FRCP.

The Victorian Periodical Press, 'The Financing of Radical Opinion: John Chapman and the *Westminster Review*', Sheila Rosenberg, 21 April 1983.

Westminster Review, 'The Lady Novelists', G. H. Lewes, 9 June 1852, pp. 129–41; 'Illusion and Delusion in the Writings of Charles Bray', pp. 488–506.

Women's Studies, vol. 7, 1980, pp. 97–108, 'George Eliot's Rebels: Portraits of the Artist as a Woman', Marcia S. Midler.

Unpublished Sources in Public Collections

Beinecke Rare Books and Manuscripts Library, Yale University: George Eliot papers, Bray and Hennell papers, John Chapman letters.

British Library: Herbert Spencer papers.

Coventry City Library: Bray and Hennell papers, Cara Bray Commonplace Book, George Eliot letters, much local studies material.

Girton College Archives, Cambridge: Barbara Bodichon and Bessie Parkes papers.

Lichfield Joint Record Office: Mary Everard's will, 1844.

New York Public Library, Berg Collection: Diary of G. H. Lewes, George Eliot letters.

Nuneaton Library: George Eliot papers, Memorandum Book of the Occurrences at Nuneaton 1810, much local studies material.

Nuneaton Museum and Art Gallery: Bray and Hennell papers, Robert Evans's diary.

Public Record Office: Robert Evans's will.

Warwick Record Office: Newdigate Papers – an extensive collection containing letters of Robert Evans and Isaac Evans to Colonel Francis Newdigate, and Mrs Newdigate's Charity Book.

Unpublished Sources in Private Collections

Castle Howard Archives: Letters of George Eliot and George Henry Lewes, 'Legend of St Ogg', J23/491.

Mr John Wallis Chapman: Reminiscences of Dr John Chapman's daughter Beatrice.

Mr Robin Evans: Papers and diaries of Robert Evans.

Canon Michael Hennell: Papers of Dr Robert Brabant and Charles Christian Hennell.

Mr Robert Nuttall: Papers of George Henry Lewes.

Mrs Susan Womersley: Papers of the Evans family.

Those interested in the life and work of George Eliot might like to know of the existence of the George Eliot Fellowship. The secretary is Mrs Kathleen Adams, 71 Stepping Stones Road, Coventry CV5 8JT.

Index

Dr Robert Brabant, 46–7,
64, 140–1; Caroline Bray,
41, 44, 52–9, 64–5, 68, 72, 99,
114, 129, 133; Charles Bray, 37,
39, 41, 46–64, 67, 74, 83, 85–6,
97, 108, 112, 114, 119–20, 123,
125, 129, 132, 144–6; John
Chapman, 80, 83–100, 104, 108,
110, 114–15, 119, 123, 128–31,
143–4, 150–1, 166–7, 185, 197;
Rufa Brabant Hennell, 151;
Hennell family, 40–1, 47, 53–4,
80, 151, 155; Sara Hennell, 55,
64–5, 68, 89, 133, 144–6, 151,
158, 168–9, 171, 180, 185, 228;
Thornton Hunt, 95; Maria
Lewis, 18–19, 26, 28–31, 42–5,
67–8, 210; Eliza Lynn, 85, 103–
4; Bessie Parkes, 102–5, 118,
125–6, 129, 134, 137–8, 171,
187, 222; Herbert Spencer,
109–15, 120, 125, 136, 167–8,
185; scientific interests, 49–51,
66, 89, 154–5, 179, 185, 213;
interest in art, 55, 185;
Westminster Review, 61, 66, 91,
93–4, 96–8, 104, 106–8, 119–20,
123, 128–32, 136, 143–4, 150,
154–5, 161, 167; Feminism, xiii,
101–2, 106, 116, 126, 129, 138–
9, 143, 187–9, 190–200; Girton
College, Cambridge, 188–9,
202, 213; first meets George
Lewes, 117, 120, 123–5; Queen
Victoria, 170, 190;
responsibility for Emily Clarke,
172–3, 201, 203, 220;
sycophants, 205–9, 215; Priory,
177–81, 184–5, 194, 204;
Heights at Witley, 197–209,
216–17, 220; John Cross, 59, 96,
204–5, 209, 214–17; marriage
to, 217–18; honeymoon with,
218–20, 224; final illness, 220–2;
death, 222–3; funeral 225;

biographies of, xi–xiii, 52, 59,
96, 226–30
Emerson, Ralph Waldo, 61, 87
Engels, Friedrich, 63
English Woman's Journal, 171
Evangelical Movement, 14, 16, 24,
28, 35, 63, 159
Evans, Mrs Christiana Pearson, 6–7,
10–11, 16–18, 22–5, 74
Evans, Edith, (Mrs Griffiths), 203
Evans, Canon Frederic, 226–7
Evans, George, 2–3, 198
Evans, Mrs Harriet Poynton, 3–7
Evans, Isaac Pearson, 1, 7, 10, 17, 20,
27, 31, 33–4, 42–3, 57, 71, 73,
81, 99, 106, 116, 118, 132, 147–
8, 152, 159, 161–2, 166–8, 171,
178, 203, 207, 213–14, 225–7
Evans, Mrs Jane, 190
Evans, Mary Ann, 'Marian', *see*
George Eliot
Evans I, Robert, 2–7, 9–11, 13–16,
20, 22–5, 28, 30, 32–5, 42–3, 45,
64, 69, 71–5, 117, 119, 143, 160,
166, 177–8, 198, 225
Evans II, Robert, 6, 11, 73, 152,
190–1
Evans III, Robert, 203
Evans, Mrs Samuel, 27–8, 167
Evans, Mrs Sarah Rawlings, 32, 34,
213
Evans, Samuel, 14, 27
Evans, Sir Thomas, 2
Evans, Thomas, 3
Evans, William, 2–3
Everard, Mrs Mary, legacies of, 80,
116, 238

Faraday, Michael, 89
Faucit, Helen, 182
Felix Holt, The Radical, 6, 13, 25,
138, 183–4
Feminism, xiii, 101–2, 111, 126, 129,
188–90, 200